C-2765   CAREER EXAMINATION SERIES

*This is your
PASSBOOK for...*

Support Investigator

*Test Preparation Study Guide
Questions & Answers*

NATIONAL LEARNING CORPORATION®

COPYRIGHT NOTICE

This book is SOLELY intended for, is sold ONLY to, and its use is RESTRICTED to individual, bona fide applicants or candidates who qualify by virtue of having seriously filed applications for appropriate license, certificate, professional and/or promotional advancement, higher school matriculation, scholarship, or other legitimate requirements of education and/or governmental authorities.

This book is NOT intended for use, class instruction, tutoring, training, duplication, copying, reprinting, excerption, or adaptation, etc., by:

1) Other publishers
2) Proprietors and/or Instructors of "Coaching" and/or Preparatory Courses
3) Personnel and/or Training Divisions of commercial, industrial, and governmental organizations
4) Schools, colleges, or universities and/or their departments and staffs, including teachers and other personnel
5) Testing Agencies or Bureaus
6) Study groups which seek by the purchase of a single volume to copy and/or duplicate and/or adapt this material for use by the group as a whole without having purchased individual volumes for each of the members of the group
7) Et al.

Such persons would be in violation of appropriate Federal and State statutes.

PROVISION OF LICENSING AGREEMENTS – Recognized educational, commercial, industrial, and governmental institutions and organizations, and others legitimately engaged in educational pursuits, including training, testing, and measurement activities, may address request for a licensing agreement to the copyright owners, who will determine whether, and under what conditions, including fees and charges, the materials in this book may be used them. In other words, a licensing facility exists for the legitimate use of the material in this book on other than an individual basis. However, it is asseverated and affirmed here that the material in this book CANNOT be used without the receipt of the express permission of such a licensing agreement from the Publishers. Inquiries re licensing should be addressed to the company, attention rights and permissions department.

All rights reserved, including the right of reproduction in whole or in part, in any form or by any means, electronic or mechanical, including photocopying, recording, or by any information storage and retrieval system, without permission in writing from the Publisher.

Copyright © 2024 by
National Learning Corporation

212 Michael Drive, Syosset, NY 11791
(516) 921-8888 • www.passbooks.com
E-mail: info@passbooks.com

PUBLISHED IN THE UNITED STATES OF AMERICA

PASSBOOK® SERIES

THE *PASSBOOK® SERIES* has been created to prepare applicants and candidates for the ultimate academic battlefield – the examination room.

At some time in our lives, each and every one of us may be required to take an examination – for validation, matriculation, admission, qualification, registration, certification, or licensure.

Based on the assumption that every applicant or candidate has met the basic formal educational standards, has taken the required number of courses, and read the necessary texts, the *PASSBOOK® SERIES* furnishes the one special preparation which may assure passing with confidence, instead of failing with insecurity. Examination questions – together with answers – are furnished as the basic vehicle for study so that the mysteries of the examination and its compounding difficulties may be eliminated or diminished by a sure method.

This book is meant to help you pass your examination provided that you qualify and are serious in your objective.

The entire field is reviewed through the huge store of content information which is succinctly presented through a provocative and challenging approach – the question-and-answer method.

A climate of success is established by furnishing the correct answers at the end of each test.

You soon learn to recognize types of questions, forms of questions, and patterns of questioning. You may even begin to anticipate expected outcomes.

You perceive that many questions are repeated or adapted so that you can gain acute insights, which may enable you to score many sure points.

You learn how to confront new questions, or types of questions, and to attack them confidently and work out the correct answers.

You note objectives and emphases, and recognize pitfalls and dangers, so that you may make positive educational adjustments.

Moreover, you are kept fully informed in relation to new concepts, methods, practices, and directions in the field.

You discover that you are actually taking the examination all the time: you are preparing for the examination by "taking" an examination, not by reading extraneous and/or supererogatory textbooks.

In short, this PASSBOOK®, used directedly, should be an important factor in helping you to pass your test.

SUPPORT INVESTIGATOR

DUTIES

Conducts investigations to assist in determining the location and financial status of individuals legally responsible for the support of recipients; contacts friends, relatives, informers, neighbors, associates, and various governmental agencies in an effort to locate an individual who is legally responsible for support. Trains new staff in the unit functions and familiarizes them with departmental procedures and investigative techniques. Determines the financial resources of persons responsible for the support of others by contacting banks, insurance companies, credit agencies, and employers; performs related duties as required.

SCOPE OF EXAMINATION

Written test will cover knowledge, skills, and/or abilities in such areas as:
1. Interviewing;
2. Investigating and evaluating financial resources;
3. Arithmetic reasoning related to child support;
4. Preparing written material; and
5. Understanding written material based upon Social Services law.

HOW TO TAKE A TEST

I. YOU MUST PASS AN EXAMINATION

A. *WHAT EVERY CANDIDATE SHOULD KNOW*

Examination applicants often ask us for help in preparing for the written test. What can I study in advance? What kinds of questions will be asked? How will the test be given? How will the papers be graded?

As an applicant for a civil service examination, you may be wondering about some of these things. Our purpose here is to suggest effective methods of advance study and to describe civil service examinations.

Your chances for success on this examination can be increased if you know how to prepare. Those "pre-examination jitters" can be reduced if you know what to expect. You can even experience an adventure in good citizenship if you know why civil service exams are given.

B. *WHY ARE CIVIL SERVICE EXAMINATIONS GIVEN?*

Civil service examinations are important to you in two ways. As a citizen, you want public jobs filled by employees who know how to do their work. As a job seeker, you want a fair chance to compete for that job on an equal footing with other candidates. The best-known means of accomplishing this two-fold goal is the competitive examination.

Exams are widely publicized throughout the nation. They may be administered for jobs in federal, state, city, municipal, town or village governments or agencies.

Any citizen may apply, with some limitations, such as the age or residence of applicants. Your experience and education may be reviewed to see whether you meet the requirements for the particular examination. When these requirements exist, they are reasonable and applied consistently to all applicants. Thus, a competitive examination may cause you some uneasiness now, but it is your privilege and safeguard.

C. *HOW ARE CIVIL SERVICE EXAMS DEVELOPED?*

Examinations are carefully written by trained technicians who are specialists in the field known as "psychological measurement," in consultation with recognized authorities in the field of work that the test will cover. These experts recommend the subject matter areas or skills to be tested; only those knowledges or skills important to your success on the job are included. The most reliable books and source materials available are used as references. Together, the experts and technicians judge the difficulty level of the questions.

Test technicians know how to phrase questions so that the problem is clearly stated. Their ethics do not permit "trick" or "catch" questions. Questions may have been tried out on sample groups, or subjected to statistical analysis, to determine their usefulness.

Written tests are often used in combination with performance tests, ratings of training and experience, and oral interviews. All of these measures combine to form the best-known means of finding the right person for the right job.

II. HOW TO PASS THE WRITTEN TEST

A. NATURE OF THE EXAMINATION

To prepare intelligently for civil service examinations, you should know how they differ from school examinations you have taken. In school you were assigned certain definite pages to read or subjects to cover. The examination questions were quite detailed and usually emphasized memory. Civil service exams, on the other hand, try to discover your present ability to perform the duties of a position, plus your potentiality to learn these duties. In other words, a civil service exam attempts to predict how successful you will be. Questions cover such a broad area that they cannot be as minute and detailed as school exam questions.

In the public service similar kinds of work, or positions, are grouped together in one "class." This process is known as *position-classification*. All the positions in a class are paid according to the salary range for that class. One class title covers all of these positions, and they are all tested by the same examination.

B. FOUR BASIC STEPS

1) Study the announcement

How, then, can you know what subjects to study? Our best answer is: "Learn as much as possible about the class of positions for which you've applied." The exam will test the knowledge, skills and abilities needed to do the work.

Your most valuable source of information about the position you want is the official exam announcement. This announcement lists the training and experience qualifications. Check these standards and apply only if you come reasonably close to meeting them.

The brief description of the position in the examination announcement offers some clues to the subjects which will be tested. Think about the job itself. Review the duties in your mind. Can you perform them, or are there some in which you are rusty? Fill in the blank spots in your preparation.

Many jurisdictions preview the written test in the exam announcement by including a section called "Knowledge and Abilities Required," "Scope of the Examination," or some similar heading. Here you will find out specifically what fields will be tested.

2) Review your own background

Once you learn in general what the position is all about, and what you need to know to do the work, ask yourself which subjects you already know fairly well and which need improvement. You may wonder whether to concentrate on improving your strong areas or on building some background in your fields of weakness. When the announcement has specified "some knowledge" or "considerable knowledge," or has used adjectives like "beginning principles of…" or "advanced … methods," you can get a clue as to the number and difficulty of questions to be asked in any given field. More questions, and hence broader coverage, would be included for those subjects which are more important in the work. Now weigh your strengths and weaknesses against the job requirements and prepare accordingly.

3) Determine the level of the position

Another way to tell how intensively you should prepare is to understand the level of the job for which you are applying. Is it the entering level? In other words, is this the position in which beginners in a field of work are hired? Or is it an intermediate or advanced level? Sometimes this is indicated by such words as "Junior" or "Senior" in the class title. Other jurisdictions use Roman numerals to designate the level – Clerk I, Clerk II, for example. The word "Supervisor" sometimes appears in the title. If the level is not indicated by the title, check the description of duties. Will you be working under very close supervision, or will you have responsibility for independent decisions in this work?

4) Choose appropriate study materials

Now that you know the subjects to be examined and the relative amount of each subject to be covered, you can choose suitable study materials. For beginning level jobs, or even advanced ones, if you have a pronounced weakness in some aspect of your training, read a modern, standard textbook in that field. Be sure it is up to date and has general coverage. Such books are normally available at your library, and the librarian will be glad to help you locate one. For entry-level positions, questions of appropriate difficulty are chosen – neither highly advanced questions, nor those too simple. Such questions require careful thought but not advanced training.

If the position for which you are applying is technical or advanced, you will read more advanced, specialized material. If you are already familiar with the basic principles of your field, elementary textbooks would waste your time. Concentrate on advanced textbooks and technical periodicals. Think through the concepts and review difficult problems in your field.

These are all general sources. You can get more ideas on your own initiative, following these leads. For example, training manuals and publications of the government agency which employs workers in your field can be useful, particularly for technical and professional positions. A letter or visit to the government department involved may result in more specific study suggestions, and certainly will provide you with a more definite idea of the exact nature of the position you are seeking.

III. KINDS OF TESTS

Tests are used for purposes other than measuring knowledge and ability to perform specified duties. For some positions, it is equally important to test ability to make adjustments to new situations or to profit from training. In others, basic mental abilities not dependent on information are essential. Questions which test these things may not appear as pertinent to the duties of the position as those which test for knowledge and information. Yet they are often highly important parts of a fair examination. For very general questions, it is almost impossible to help you direct your study efforts. What we can do is to point out some of the more common of these general abilities needed in public service positions and describe some typical questions.

1) General information

Broad, general information has been found useful for predicting job success in some kinds of work. This is tested in a variety of ways, from vocabulary lists to questions about current events. Basic background in some field of work, such as sociology or economics, may be sampled in a group of questions. Often these are principles which have become familiar to most persons through exposure rather than through formal training. It is difficult to advise you how to study for these questions; being alert to the world around you is our best suggestion.

2) Verbal ability

An example of an ability needed in many positions is verbal or language ability. Verbal ability is, in brief, the ability to use and understand words. Vocabulary and grammar tests are typical measures of this ability. Reading comprehension or paragraph interpretation questions are common in many kinds of civil service tests. You are given a paragraph of written material and asked to find its central meaning.

3) Numerical ability

Number skills can be tested by the familiar arithmetic problem, by checking paired lists of numbers to see which are alike and which are different, or by interpreting charts and graphs. In the latter test, a graph may be printed in the test booklet which you are asked to use as the basis for answering questions.

4) Observation

A popular test for law-enforcement positions is the observation test. A picture is shown to you for several minutes, then taken away. Questions about the picture test your ability to observe both details and larger elements.

5) Following directions

In many positions in the public service, the employee must be able to carry out written instructions dependably and accurately. You may be given a chart with several columns, each column listing a variety of information. The questions require you to carry out directions involving the information given in the chart.

6) Skills and aptitudes

Performance tests effectively measure some manual skills and aptitudes. When the skill is one in which you are trained, such as typing or shorthand, you can practice. These tests are often very much like those given in business school or high school courses. For many of the other skills and aptitudes, however, no short-time preparation can be made. Skills and abilities natural to you or that you have developed throughout your lifetime are being tested.

Many of the general questions just described provide all the data needed to answer the questions and ask you to use your reasoning ability to find the answers. Your best preparation for these tests, as well as for tests of facts and ideas, is to be at your physical and mental best. You, no doubt, have your own methods of getting into an exam-taking mood and keeping "in shape." The next section lists some ideas on this subject.

IV. KINDS OF QUESTIONS

Only rarely is the "essay" question, which you answer in narrative form, used in civil service tests. Civil service tests are usually of the short-answer type. Full instructions for answering these questions will be given to you at the examination. But in case this is your first experience with short-answer questions and separate answer sheets, here is what you need to know:

1) Multiple-choice Questions

Most popular of the short-answer questions is the "multiple choice" or "best answer" question. It can be used, for example, to test for factual knowledge, ability to solve problems or judgment in meeting situations found at work.

A multiple-choice question is normally one of three types—
- It can begin with an incomplete statement followed by several possible endings. You are to find the one ending which *best* completes the statement, although some of the others may not be entirely wrong.
- It can also be a complete statement in the form of a question which is answered by choosing one of the statements listed.

- It can be in the form of a problem – again you select the best answer.

Here is an example of a multiple-choice question with a discussion which should give you some clues as to the method for choosing the right answer:

When an employee has a complaint about his assignment, the action which will *best* help him overcome his difficulty is to
- A. discuss his difficulty with his coworkers
- B. take the problem to the head of the organization
- C. take the problem to the person who gave him the assignment
- D. say nothing to anyone about his complaint

In answering this question, you should study each of the choices to find which is best. Consider choice "A" – Certainly an employee may discuss his complaint with fellow employees, but no change or improvement can result, and the complaint remains unresolved. Choice "B" is a poor choice since the head of the organization probably does not know what assignment you have been given, and taking your problem to him is known as "going over the head" of the supervisor. The supervisor, or person who made the assignment, is the person who can clarify it or correct any injustice. Choice "C" is, therefore, correct. To say nothing, as in choice "D," is unwise. Supervisors have and interest in knowing the problems employees are facing, and the employee is seeking a solution to his problem.

2) True/False Questions

The "true/false" or "right/wrong" form of question is sometimes used. Here a complete statement is given. Your job is to decide whether the statement is right or wrong.

SAMPLE: A roaming cell-phone call to a nearby city costs less than a non-roaming call to a distant city.

This statement is wrong, or false, since roaming calls are more expensive.

This is not a complete list of all possible question forms, although most of the others are variations of these common types. You will always get complete directions for answering questions. Be sure you understand *how* to mark your answers – ask questions until you do.

V. RECORDING YOUR ANSWERS

Computer terminals are used more and more today for many different kinds of exams.

For an examination with very few applicants, you may be told to record your answers in the test booklet itself. Separate answer sheets are much more common. If this separate answer sheet is to be scored by machine – and this is often the case – it is highly important that you mark your answers correctly in order to get credit.

An electronic scoring machine is often used in civil service offices because of the speed with which papers can be scored. Machine-scored answer sheets must be marked with a pencil, which will be given to you. This pencil has a high graphite content which responds to the electronic scoring machine. As a matter of fact, stray dots may register as answers, so do not let your pencil rest on the answer sheet while you are pondering the correct answer. Also, if your pencil lead breaks or is otherwise defective, ask for another.

Since the answer sheet will be dropped in a slot in the scoring machine, be careful not to bend the corners or get the paper crumpled.

The answer sheet normally has five vertical columns of numbers, with 30 numbers to a column. These numbers correspond to the question numbers in your test booklet. After each number, going across the page are four or five pairs of dotted lines. These short dotted lines have small letters or numbers above them. The first two pairs may also have a "T" or "F" above the letters. This indicates that the first two pairs only are to be used if the questions are of the true-false type. If the questions are multiple choice, disregard the "T" and "F" and pay attention only to the small letters or numbers.

Answer your questions in the manner of the sample that follows:

32. The largest city in the United States is
 A. Washington, D.C.
 B. New York City
 C. Chicago
 D. Detroit
 E. San Francisco

1) Choose the answer you think is best. (New York City is the largest, so "B" is correct.)
2) Find the row of dotted lines numbered the same as the question you are answering. (Find row number 32)
3) Find the pair of dotted lines corresponding to the answer. (Find the pair of lines under the mark "B.")
4) Make a solid black mark between the dotted lines.

VI. BEFORE THE TEST

Common sense will help you find procedures to follow to get ready for an examination. Too many of us, however, overlook these sensible measures. Indeed, nervousness and fatigue have been found to be the most serious reasons why applicants fail to do their best on civil service tests. Here is a list of reminders:

- Begin your preparation early – Don't wait until the last minute to go scurrying around for books and materials or to find out what the position is all about.
- Prepare continuously – An hour a night for a week is better than an all-night cram session. This has been definitely established. What is more, a night a week for a month will return better dividends than crowding your study into a shorter period of time.
- Locate the place of the exam – You have been sent a notice telling you when and where to report for the examination. If the location is in a different town or otherwise unfamiliar to you, it would be well to inquire the best route and learn something about the building.
- Relax the night before the test – Allow your mind to rest. Do not study at all that night. Plan some mild recreation or diversion; then go to bed early and get a good night's sleep.
- Get up early enough to make a leisurely trip to the place for the test – This way unforeseen events, traffic snarls, unfamiliar buildings, etc. will not upset you.
- Dress comfortably – A written test is not a fashion show. You will be known by number and not by name, so wear something comfortable.

- Leave excess paraphernalia at home – Shopping bags and odd bundles will get in your way. You need bring only the items mentioned in the official notice you received; usually everything you need is provided. Do not bring reference books to the exam. They will only confuse those last minutes and be taken away from you when in the test room.
- Arrive somewhat ahead of time – If because of transportation schedules you must get there very early, bring a newspaper or magazine to take your mind off yourself while waiting.
- Locate the examination room – When you have found the proper room, you will be directed to the seat or part of the room where you will sit. Sometimes you are given a sheet of instructions to read while you are waiting. Do not fill out any forms until you are told to do so; just read them and be prepared.
- Relax and prepare to listen to the instructions
- If you have any physical problem that may keep you from doing your best, be sure to tell the test administrator. If you are sick or in poor health, you really cannot do your best on the exam. You can come back and take the test some other time.

VII. AT THE TEST

The day of the test is here and you have the test booklet in your hand. The temptation to get going is very strong. Caution! There is more to success than knowing the right answers. You must know how to identify your papers and understand variations in the type of short-answer question used in this particular examination. Follow these suggestions for maximum results from your efforts:

1) Cooperate with the monitor

The test administrator has a duty to create a situation in which you can be as much at ease as possible. He will give instructions, tell you when to begin, check to see that you are marking your answer sheet correctly, and so on. He is not there to guard you, although he will see that your competitors do not take unfair advantage. He wants to help you do your best.

2) Listen to all instructions

Don't jump the gun! Wait until you understand all directions. In most civil service tests you get more time than you need to answer the questions. So don't be in a hurry. Read each word of instructions until you clearly understand the meaning. Study the examples, listen to all announcements and follow directions. Ask questions if you do not understand what to do.

3) Identify your papers

Civil service exams are usually identified by number only. You will be assigned a number; you must not put your name on your test papers. Be sure to copy your number correctly. Since more than one exam may be given, copy your exact examination title.

4) Plan your time

Unless you are told that a test is a "speed" or "rate of work" test, speed itself is usually not important. Time enough to answer all the questions will be provided, but this does not mean that you have all day. An overall time limit has been set. Divide the total time (in minutes) by the number of questions to determine the approximate time you have for each question.

5) Do not linger over difficult questions

If you come across a difficult question, mark it with a paper clip (useful to have along) and come back to it when you have been through the booklet. One caution if you do this – be sure to skip a number on your answer sheet as well. Check often to be sure that you have not lost your place and that you are marking in the row numbered the same as the question you are answering.

6) Read the questions

Be sure you know what the question asks! Many capable people are unsuccessful because they failed to *read* the questions correctly.

7) Answer all questions

Unless you have been instructed that a penalty will be deducted for incorrect answers, it is better to guess than to omit a question.

8) Speed tests

It is often better NOT to guess on speed tests. It has been found that on timed tests people are tempted to spend the last few seconds before time is called in marking answers at random – without even reading them – in the hope of picking up a few extra points. To discourage this practice, the instructions may warn you that your score will be "corrected" for guessing. That is, a penalty will be applied. The incorrect answers will be deducted from the correct ones, or some other penalty formula will be used.

9) Review your answers

If you finish before time is called, go back to the questions you guessed or omitted to give them further thought. Review other answers if you have time.

10) Return your test materials

If you are ready to leave before others have finished or time is called, take ALL your materials to the monitor and leave quietly. Never take any test material with you. The monitor can discover whose papers are not complete, and taking a test booklet may be grounds for disqualification.

VIII. EXAMINATION TECHNIQUES

1) Read the general instructions carefully. These are usually printed on the first page of the exam booklet. As a rule, these instructions refer to the timing of the examination; the fact that you should not start work until the signal and must stop work at a signal, etc. If there are any *special* instructions, such as a choice of questions to be answered, make sure that you note this instruction carefully.

2) When you are ready to start work on the examination, that is as soon as the signal has been given, read the instructions to each question booklet, underline any key words or phrases, such as *least, best, outline, describe* and the like. In this way you will tend to answer as requested rather than discover on reviewing your paper that you *listed without describing*, that you selected the *worst* choice rather than the *best* choice, etc.

3) If the examination is of the objective or multiple-choice type – that is, each question will also give a series of possible answers: A, B, C or D, and you are called upon to select the best answer and write the letter next to that answer on your answer paper – it is advisable to start answering each question in turn. There may be anywhere from 50 to 100 such questions in the three or four hours allotted and you can see how much time would be taken if you read through all the questions before beginning to answer any. Furthermore, if you come across a question or group of questions which you know would be difficult to answer, it would undoubtedly affect your handling of all the other questions.

4) If the examination is of the essay type and contains but a few questions, it is a moot point as to whether you should read all the questions before starting to answer any one. Of course, if you are given a choice – say five out of seven and the like – then it is essential to read all the questions so you can eliminate the two that are most difficult. If, however, you are asked to answer all the questions, there may be danger in trying to answer the easiest one first because you may find that you will spend too much time on it. The best technique is to answer the first question, then proceed to the second, etc.

5) Time your answers. Before the exam begins, write down the time it started, then add the time allowed for the examination and write down the time it must be completed, then divide the time available somewhat as follows:
   - If 3-1/2 hours are allowed, that would be 210 minutes. If you have 80 objective-type questions, that would be an average of 2-1/2 minutes per question. Allow yourself no more than 2 minutes per question, or a total of 160 minutes, which will permit about 50 minutes to review.
   - If for the time allotment of 210 minutes there are 7 essay questions to answer, that would average about 30 minutes a question. Give yourself only 25 minutes per question so that you have about 35 minutes to review.

6) The most important instruction is to *read each question* and make sure you know what is wanted. The second most important instruction is to *time yourself properly* so that you answer every question. The third most important instruction is to *answer every question*. Guess if you have to but include something for each question. Remember that you will receive no credit for a blank and will probably receive some credit if you write something in answer to an essay question. If you guess a letter – say "B" for a multiple-choice question – you may have guessed right. If you leave a blank as an answer to a multiple-choice question, the examiners may respect your feelings but it will not add a point to your score. Some exams may penalize you for wrong answers, so in such cases *only*, you may not want to guess unless you have some basis for your answer.

7) Suggestions
   a. Objective-type questions
      1. Examine the question booklet for proper sequence of pages and questions
      2. Read all instructions carefully
      3. Skip any question which seems too difficult; return to it after all other questions have been answered
      4. Apportion your time properly; do not spend too much time on any single question or group of questions

5. Note and underline key words – *all, most, fewest, least, best, worst, same, opposite,* etc.
6. Pay particular attention to negatives
7. Note unusual option, e.g., unduly long, short, complex, different or similar in content to the body of the question
8. Observe the use of "hedging" words – *probably, may, most likely,* etc.
9. Make sure that your answer is put next to the same number as the question
10. Do not second-guess unless you have good reason to believe the second answer is definitely more correct
11. Cross out original answer if you decide another answer is more accurate; do not erase until you are ready to hand your paper in
12. Answer all questions; guess unless instructed otherwise
13. Leave time for review

   b. Essay questions
     1. Read each question carefully
     2. Determine exactly what is wanted. Underline key words or phrases.
     3. Decide on outline or paragraph answer
     4. Include many different points and elements unless asked to develop any one or two points or elements
     5. Show impartiality by giving pros and cons unless directed to select one side only
     6. Make and write down any assumptions you find necessary to answer the questions
     7. Watch your English, grammar, punctuation and choice of words
     8. Time your answers; don't crowd material

8) Answering the essay question

Most essay questions can be answered by framing the specific response around several key words or ideas. Here are a few such key words or ideas:

M's: manpower, materials, methods, money, management
P's: purpose, program, policy, plan, procedure, practice, problems, pitfalls, personnel, public relations

   a. Six basic steps in handling problems:
     1. Preliminary plan and background development
     2. Collect information, data and facts
     3. Analyze and interpret information, data and facts
     4. Analyze and develop solutions as well as make recommendations
     5. Prepare report and sell recommendations
     6. Install recommendations and follow up effectiveness

   b. Pitfalls to avoid
     1. *Taking things for granted* – A statement of the situation does not necessarily imply that each of the elements is necessarily true; for example, a complaint may be invalid and biased so that all that can be taken for granted is that a complaint has been registered

2. *Considering only one side of a situation* – Wherever possible, indicate several alternatives and then point out the reasons you selected the best one
3. *Failing to indicate follow up* – Whenever your answer indicates action on your part, make certain that you will take proper follow-up action to see how successful your recommendations, procedures or actions turn out to be
4. *Taking too long in answering any single question* – Remember to time your answers properly

IX. AFTER THE TEST

Scoring procedures differ in detail among civil service jurisdictions although the general principles are the same. Whether the papers are hand-scored or graded by machine we have described, they are nearly always graded by number. That is, the person who marks the paper knows only the number – never the name – of the applicant. Not until all the papers have been graded will they be matched with names. If other tests, such as training and experience or oral interview ratings have been given, scores will be combined. Different parts of the examination usually have different weights. For example, the written test might count 60 percent of the final grade, and a rating of training and experience 40 percent. In many jurisdictions, veterans will have a certain number of points added to their grades.

After the final grade has been determined, the names are placed in grade order and an eligible list is established. There are various methods for resolving ties between those who get the same final grade – probably the most common is to place first the name of the person whose application was received first. Job offers are made from the eligible list in the order the names appear on it. You will be notified of your grade and your rank as soon as all these computations have been made. This will be done as rapidly as possible.

People who are found to meet the requirements in the announcement are called "eligibles." Their names are put on a list of eligible candidates. An eligible's chances of getting a job depend on how high he stands on this list and how fast agencies are filling jobs from the list.

When a job is to be filled from a list of eligibles, the agency asks for the names of people on the list of eligibles for that job. When the civil service commission receives this request, it sends to the agency the names of the three people highest on this list. Or, if the job to be filled has specialized requirements, the office sends the agency the names of the top three persons who meet these requirements from the general list.

The appointing officer makes a choice from among the three people whose names were sent to him. If the selected person accepts the appointment, the names of the others are put back on the list to be considered for future openings.

That is the rule in hiring from all kinds of eligible lists, whether they are for typist, carpenter, chemist, or something else. For every vacancy, the appointing officer has his choice of any one of the top three eligibles on the list. This explains why the person whose name is on top of the list sometimes does not get an appointment when some of the persons lower on the list do. If the appointing officer chooses the second or third eligible, the No. 1 eligible does not get a job at once, but stays on the list until he is appointed or the list is terminated.

X. HOW TO PASS THE INTERVIEW TEST

The examination for which you applied requires an oral interview test. You have already taken the written test and you are now being called for the interview test – the final part of the formal examination.

You may think that it is not possible to prepare for an interview test and that there are no procedures to follow during an interview. Our purpose is to point out some things you can do in advance that will help you and some good rules to follow and pitfalls to avoid while you are being interviewed.

What is an interview supposed to test?

The written examination is designed to test the technical knowledge and competence of the candidate; the oral is designed to evaluate intangible qualities, not readily measured otherwise, and to establish a list showing the relative fitness of each candidate – as measured against his competitors – for the position sought. Scoring is not on the basis of "right" and "wrong," but on a sliding scale of values ranging from "not passable" to "outstanding." As a matter of fact, it is possible to achieve a relatively low score without a single "incorrect" answer because of evident weakness in the qualities being measured.

Occasionally, an examination may consist entirely of an oral test – either an individual or a group oral. In such cases, information is sought concerning the technical knowledges and abilities of the candidate, since there has been no written examination for this purpose. More commonly, however, an oral test is used to supplement a written examination.

Who conducts interviews?

The composition of oral boards varies among different jurisdictions. In nearly all, a representative of the personnel department serves as chairman. One of the members of the board may be a representative of the department in which the candidate would work. In some cases, "outside experts" are used, and, frequently, a businessman or some other representative of the general public is asked to serve. Labor and management or other special groups may be represented. The aim is to secure the services of experts in the appropriate field.

However the board is composed, it is a good idea (and not at all improper or unethical) to ascertain in advance of the interview who the members are and what groups they represent. When you are introduced to them, you will have some idea of their backgrounds and interests, and at least you will not stutter and stammer over their names.

What should be done before the interview?

While knowledge about the board members is useful and takes some of the surprise element out of the interview, there is other preparation which is more substantive. It *is* possible to prepare for an oral interview – in several ways:

1) Keep a copy of your application and review it carefully before the interview

This may be the only document before the oral board, and the starting point of the interview. Know what education and experience you have listed there, and the sequence and dates of all of it. Sometimes the board will ask you to review the highlights of your experience for them; you should not have to hem and haw doing it.

2) Study the class specification and the examination announcement

Usually, the oral board has one or both of these to guide them. The qualities, characteristics or knowledges required by the position sought are stated in these documents. They offer valuable clues as to the nature of the oral interview. For example, if the job involves supervisory responsibilities, the announcement will usually indicate that knowledge of modern supervisory methods and the qualifications of the candidate as a supervisor will be tested. If so, you can expect such questions, frequently in the form of a hypothetical situation which you are expected to solve. NEVER go into an oral without knowledge of the duties and responsibilities of the job you seek.

3) Think through each qualification required

Try to visualize the kind of questions you would ask if you were a board member. How well could you answer them? Try especially to appraise your own knowledge and background in each area, *measured against the job sought*, and identify any areas in which you are weak. Be critical and realistic – do not flatter yourself.

4) Do some general reading in areas in which you feel you may be weak

For example, if the job involves supervision and your past experience has NOT, some general reading in supervisory methods and practices, particularly in the field of human relations, might be useful. Do NOT study agency procedures or detailed manuals. The oral board will be testing your understanding and capacity, not your memory.

5) Get a good night's sleep and watch your general health and mental attitude

You will want a clear head at the interview. Take care of a cold or any other minor ailment, and of course, no hangovers.

What should be done on the day of the interview?

Now comes the day of the interview itself. Give yourself plenty of time to get there. Plan to arrive somewhat ahead of the scheduled time, particularly if your appointment is in the fore part of the day. If a previous candidate fails to appear, the board might be ready for you a bit early. By early afternoon an oral board is almost invariably behind schedule if there are many candidates, and you may have to wait. Take along a book or magazine to read, or your application to review, but leave any extraneous material in the waiting room when you go in for your interview. In any event, relax and compose yourself.

The matter of dress is important. The board is forming impressions about you – from your experience, your manners, your attitude, and your appearance. Give your personal appearance careful attention. Dress your best, but not your flashiest. Choose conservative, appropriate clothing, and be sure it is immaculate. This is a business interview, and your appearance should indicate that you regard it as such. Besides, being well groomed and properly dressed will help boost your confidence.

Sooner or later, someone will call your name and escort you into the interview room. *This is it.* From here on you are on your own. It is too late for any more preparation. But remember, you asked for this opportunity to prove your fitness, and you are here because your request was granted.

What happens when you go in?

The usual sequence of events will be as follows: The clerk (who is often the board stenographer) will introduce you to the chairman of the oral board, who will introduce you to the other members of the board. Acknowledge the introductions before you sit down. Do not be surprised if you find a microphone facing you or a stenotypist sitting by. Oral interviews are usually recorded in the event of an appeal or other review.

Usually the chairman of the board will open the interview by reviewing the highlights of your education and work experience from your application – primarily for the benefit of the other members of the board, as well as to get the material into the record. Do not interrupt or comment unless there is an error or significant misinterpretation; if that is the case, do not hesitate. But do not quibble about insignificant matters. Also, he will usually ask you some question about your education, experience or your present job – partly to get you to start talking and to establish the interviewing "rapport." He may start the actual questioning, or turn it over to one of the other members. Frequently, each member undertakes the questioning on a particular area, one in which he is perhaps most competent, so you can expect each member to participate in the examination. Because time is limited, you may also expect some rather abrupt switches in the direction the questioning takes, so do not be upset by it. Normally, a board member will not pursue a single line of questioning unless he discovers a particular strength or weakness.

After each member has participated, the chairman will usually ask whether any member has any further questions, then will ask you if you have anything you wish to add. Unless you are expecting this question, it may floor you. Worse, it may start you off on an extended, extemporaneous speech. The board is not usually seeking more information. The question is principally to offer you a last opportunity to present further qualifications or to indicate that you have nothing to add. So, if you feel that a significant qualification or characteristic has been overlooked, it is proper to point it out in a sentence or so. Do not compliment the board on the thoroughness of their examination – they have been sketchy, and you know it. If you wish, merely say, "No thank you, I have nothing further to add." This is a point where you can "talk yourself out" of a good impression or fail to present an important bit of information. Remember, *you close the interview yourself*.

The chairman will then say, "That is all, Mr. _____, thank you." Do not be startled; the interview is over, and quicker than you think. Thank him, gather your belongings and take your leave. Save your sigh of relief for the other side of the door.

How to put your best foot forward

Throughout this entire process, you may feel that the board individually and collectively is trying to pierce your defenses, seek out your hidden weaknesses and embarrass and confuse you. Actually, this is not true. They are obliged to make an appraisal of your qualifications for the job you are seeking, and they want to see you in your best light. Remember, they must interview all candidates and a non-cooperative candidate may become a failure in spite of their best efforts to bring out his qualifications. Here are 15 suggestions that will help you:

1) Be natural – Keep your attitude confident, not cocky

If you are not confident that you can do the job, do not expect the board to be. Do not apologize for your weaknesses, try to bring out your strong points. The board is interested in a positive, not negative, presentation. Cockiness will antagonize any board member and make him wonder if you are covering up a weakness by a false show of strength.

2) Get comfortable, but don't lounge or sprawl

Sit erectly but not stiffly. A careless posture may lead the board to conclude that you are careless in other things, or at least that you are not impressed by the importance of the occasion. Either conclusion is natural, even if incorrect. Do not fuss with your clothing, a pencil or an ashtray. Your hands may occasionally be useful to emphasize a point; do not let them become a point of distraction.

3) Do not wisecrack or make small talk

This is a serious situation, and your attitude should show that you consider it as such. Further, the time of the board is limited – they do not want to waste it, and neither should you.

4) Do not exaggerate your experience or abilities
   In the first place, from information in the application or other interviews and sources, the board may know more about you than you think. Secondly, you probably will not get away with it. An experienced board is rather adept at spotting such a situation, so do not take the chance.

5) If you know a board member, do not make a point of it, yet do not hide it
   Certainly you are not fooling him, and probably not the other members of the board. Do not try to take advantage of your acquaintanceship – it will probably do you little good.

6) Do not dominate the interview
   Let the board do that. They will give you the clues – do not assume that you have to do all the talking. Realize that the board has a number of questions to ask you, and do not try to take up all the interview time by showing off your extensive knowledge of the answer to the first one.

7) Be attentive
   You only have 20 minutes or so, and you should keep your attention at its sharpest throughout. When a member is addressing a problem or question to you, give him your undivided attention. Address your reply principally to him, but do not exclude the other board members.

8) Do not interrupt
   A board member may be stating a problem for you to analyze. He will ask you a question when the time comes. Let him state the problem, and wait for the question.

9) Make sure you understand the question
   Do not try to answer until you are sure what the question is. If it is not clear, restate it in your own words or ask the board member to clarify it for you. However, do not haggle about minor elements.

10) Reply promptly but not hastily
   A common entry on oral board rating sheets is "candidate responded readily," or "candidate hesitated in replies." Respond as promptly and quickly as you can, but do not jump to a hasty, ill-considered answer.

11) Do not be peremptory in your answers
   A brief answer is proper – but do not fire your answer back. That is a losing game from your point of view. The board member can probably ask questions much faster than you can answer them.

12) Do not try to create the answer you think the board member wants
   He is interested in what kind of mind you have and how it works – not in playing games. Furthermore, he can usually spot this practice and will actually grade you down on it.

13) Do not switch sides in your reply merely to agree with a board member
   Frequently, a member will take a contrary position merely to draw you out and to see if you are willing and able to defend your point of view. Do not start a debate, yet do not surrender a good position. If a position is worth taking, it is worth defending.

14) Do not be afraid to admit an error in judgment if you are shown to be wrong

The board knows that you are forced to reply without any opportunity for careful consideration. Your answer may be demonstrably wrong. If so, admit it and get on with the interview.

15) Do not dwell at length on your present job

The opening question may relate to your present assignment. Answer the question but do not go into an extended discussion. You are being examined for a *new* job, not your present one. As a matter of fact, try to phrase ALL your answers in terms of the job for which you are being examined.

Basis of Rating

Probably you will forget most of these "do's" and "don'ts" when you walk into the oral interview room. Even remembering them all will not ensure you a passing grade. Perhaps you did not have the qualifications in the first place. But remembering them will help you to put your best foot forward, without treading on the toes of the board members.

Rumor and popular opinion to the contrary notwithstanding, an oral board wants you to make the best appearance possible. They know you are under pressure – but they also want to see how you respond to it as a guide to what your reaction would be under the pressures of the job you seek. They will be influenced by the degree of poise you display, the personal traits you show and the manner in which you respond.

ABOUT THIS BOOK

This book contains tests divided into Examination Sections. Go through each test, answering every question in the margin. We have also attached a sample answer sheet at the back of the book that can be removed and used. At the end of each test look at the answer key and check your answers. On the ones you got wrong, look at the right answer choice and learn. Do not fill in the answers first. Do not memorize the questions and answers, but understand the answer and principles involved. On your test, the questions will likely be different from the samples. Questions are changed and new ones added. If you understand these past questions you should have success with any changes that arise. Tests may consist of several types of questions. We have additional books on each subject should more study be advisable or necessary for you. Finally, the more you study, the better prepared you will be. This book is intended to be the last thing you study before you walk into the examination room. Prior study of relevant texts is also recommended. NLC publishes some of these in our Fundamental Series. Knowledge and good sense are important factors in passing your exam. Good luck also helps. So now study this Passbook, absorb the material contained within and take that knowledge into the examination. Then do your best to pass that exam.

EXAMINATION SECTION

INTERVIEWING
EXAMINATION SECTION
TEST 1

DIRECTIONS: Each question or incomplete statement is followed by several suggested answers or completions. Select the one that BEST answers the question or completes the statement. *PRINT THE LETTER OF THE CORRECT ANSWER IN THE SPACE AT THE RIGHT.*

1. Of the methods given below for obtaining desired information from applicants, the one considered the BEST interviewing method is to
   A. work from an outline, asking the questions in the order in which they appear and requiring the applicant to give specific answers
   B. let the applicant tell what he has to say in his own way first, the interviewer then taking responsibility for asking questions on points not covered
   C. tell the applicant all the facts that it is necessary to have, then letting him give the information in any way he chooses
   D. verify all such facts as birth date, income, and past employment before seeing the applicant, then asking the applicant to fill in the remaining gaps when he is interviewed

1._____

2. Suppose an applicant objects to answering a question regarding his recent employment and asks, "What business is it of yours, young man?"
   In conducting the interview, the MOST constructive course of action for you to take under the circumstances would be to
   A. tell the applicant you have no intention of prying into his personal affairs and go on to the next question
   B. refer the applicant to your supervisor
   C. rephrase the question so that only a "Yes" or "No" answer is required
   D. explain why the question is being asked

2._____

3. An interview is BEST conducted in private PRIMARILY because
   A. the person interviewed will tend to be less self-conscious
   B. the interviewer will be able to maintain his continuity of thought better
   C. it will insure that the interview is "off the record"
   D. people tend to "show off" before an audience

3._____

4. An interviewer will be better able to understand the person interviewed and his problems if he recognizes that much of the person's behavior is due to motives
   A. which are deliberate   B. of which he is unaware
   C. which are inexplicable   D. which are kept under control

4._____

5. When an applicant is repeatedly told that "everything will be all right," the effect that can USUALLY be expected is that he will
   A. develop overt negativistic reactions toward the agency
   B. become too closely identified with the interviewer
   C. doubt the interviewer's ability to understand and help with his problems
   D. have greater confidence in the interviewer

6. While interviewing a client, it is PREFERABLE that the interviewer
   A. take no notes in order to avoid disturbing the client
   B. focus primary attention on the client while the client is talking
   C. take no notes in order to impress upon the client the interviewer's ability to remember all the pertinent facts of his case
   D. record all the details in order to show the client that what he says is important

7. During an interview, a curious applicant asks several questions about the interviewer's private life.
   As the interviewer, you should
   A. refuse to answer such questions
   B. answer his questions fully
   C. explain that your primary concern is with his problems and that discussion of your personal affairs will not be helpful in meeting his needs
   D. explain that it is the responsibility of the interviewer to ask questions and not to answer them

8. An interviewer can BEST establish a good relationship with the person being interviewed by
   A. assuming casual interest in the statements made by the person being interviewed
   B. asking questions which enable the person to show pride in his knowledge
   C. taking the point of view of the person interviewed
   D. showing a genuine interest in the person

9. An interviewer's attention must be directed toward himself as well as toward the person interviewed.
   This statement means that the interviewer should
   A. keep in mind the extent to which his own prejudices may influence his judgment
   B. rationalize the statements made by the person interviewed
   C. gain the respect and confidence of the person interviewed
   D. avoid being too impersonal

10. More complete expression will be obtained from a person being interviewed if the interviewer can create the impression that
    A. the data secured will become part of a permanent record
    B. official information must be accurate in every detail
    C. it is the duty of the person interviewed to give accurate data
    D. the person interviewed is participating in a discussion of his own problems

11. The practice of asking leading questions should be avoided in an interview because the
    A. interviewer risks revealing his attitudes to the person being interviewed
    B. interviewer may be led to ignore the objective attitudes of the person interviewed
    C. answers may be unwarrantedly influenced
    D. person interviewed will resent the attempt to lead him and will be less cooperative

12. A good technique for the interviewer to use in an effort to secure reliable data and to reduce the possibility of misunderstanding is to
    A. use casual undirected conversation, enabling the person being interviewed to talk about himself, and thus secure the desired information
    B. adopt the procedure of using direct questions regularly
    C. extract the desired information from the person being interviewed by putting him on the defensive
    D. explain to the person being interviewed the information desired and the reason for needing it

13. In interviewing an applicant, your attitude toward his veracity should be that the information he has furnished you is
    A. *untruthful* until you have had an opportunity to check the information
    B. *truthful* only insofar as verifiable facts are concerned
    C. *untruthful* because clients tend to interpret everything in their own favor
    D. *truthful* until you have information to the contrary

14. When an agency assigns its most experienced interviewers to conduct initial interviews with applicants, the MOST important reason for its action is that
    A. experienced workers are always older and, therefore, command the respect of applicants
    B. the applicant may be given a complete understanding of the procedures to be followed and the time involved in obtaining assistance
    C. applicants with fraudulent intentions will be detected, and prevented from obtaining further services from the agency
    D. the applicant may be given an understanding of the purpose of the assistance program and of the bases for granting assistance, in addition to the routine information

15. In conducting the first interview with an applicant, you should
    A. ask questions requiring "Yes" or "No" answers in order to simplify the interview
    B. rephrase several of the key questions as a check on his previous statements
    C. let him tell his own story while keeping him to the relevant facts
    D. avoid showing any sympathy for the applicant while he is revealing his personal needs and problems

16. When an interview opens an interview by asking the client direct questions about his work, it is very likely that the client will feel
    A. that the interview is interested in him
    B. at ease if his work has been good
    C. free to discuss his attitudes toward his work
    D. that good reports are of great importance to the interviewer in his thinking

16.____

17. When an interviewer does NOT understand the meaning of a response that a client has made, the interviewer should
    A. proceed to another topic
    B. state that he does not understand and ask for clarification
    C. act as if he understands so that the client's confidence in him should not be shaken
    D. ask the client to rephrase his response

17.____

18. When an interviewer makes a response which brings on a high degree of resistance in the client, he should
    A. apologize and rephrase his remark in a less evocative manner
    B. accept the resistance on the part of the client
    C. ignore the client's resistance
    D. recognize that little more will be accomplished in the interview and suggest another appointment

18.____

19. Most definitions of interviewing would NOT include the following as a necessary aspect:
    A. The interviewer and client meet face-to-face and talk things out
    B. The client is experiencing considerable emotional disturbance
    C. A valuable learning opportunity is provided for the client
    D. The interviewer brings a special competence to the relationship

19.____

20. A powerful dynamic in the interviewing process and often the very *antonym* of its counterpart in the instructional process is
    A. encouraging accuracy
    B. emphasizing structure
    C. pointing up sequential and orderly thinking
    D. processing ambiguity and equivocation

20.____

21. Interviewing techniques are frequently useful in working with clients.
    A basic fundamental is an atmosphere which may BEST be described as
    A. non-threatening
    B. motivating for creativity
    C. highly charged to stimulate excitement
    D. fairly-well structured

21.____

22. In interviewing the disadvantaged client, the subtle technique of steering away from high-level educational and vocational plans must be *replaced* by
    A. a wait-and-see explanation to the client
    B. the use of prediction tables to determine possibilities and probabilities of overcoming this condition

22.____

C. avoidance in discussing controversial issues of deprivation
D. encouragement and concrete consideration for planning his future

23. The process of collecting, analyzing, synthesizing, and interpreting information about the client should be
    A. completed prior to interviewing
    B. completed early in the interviewing process
    C. limited to a type of interviewing which is primarily diagnostic in purpose
    D. continuously pursued throughout interviewing

24. Catharsis, the "emotional unloading" of the client's feelings, has a value in the early stages of interviewing because it accomplishes all BUT which one of the following goals?
    It
    A. relieves strong physiological tensions in the client
    B. increases the client's anxiety and aggrandizes his motivation to continue counseling
    C. provides a strong substitute for "acting out" the client's feelings
    D. releases emotional energy which the client has been using to bulwark his defenses

25. In the interviewing process, the interviewer should *usually* give information
    A. whenever it is needed
    B. at the end of the process
    C. in the introductory interview
    D. just before the client would ordinarily request it

KEY (CORRECT ANSWERS)

1.	B	11.	C
2.	D	12.	D
3.	A	13.	D
4.	B	14.	D
5.	C	15.	C
6.	B	16.	D
7.	C	17.	B
8.	D	18.	B
9.	A	19.	B
10.	D	20.	D

21.	A
22.	D
23.	D
24.	B
25.	A

TEST 2

DIRECTIONS: Each question or incomplete statement is followed by several suggested answers or completions. Select the one that BEST answers the question or completes the statement. *PRINT THE LETTER OF THE CORRECT ANSWER IN THE SPACE AT THE RIGHT.*

1. Of the following problems that might affect the conduct and outcome of an interview, the MOST troublesome and usually the MOST difficult for the interviewer to control is the
   A. tendency of the interviewee to anticipate the needs and preferences of the interviewer
   B. impulse to cut the interviewee off when he seems to have reached the end of an idea
   C. tendency of interviewee attitude to bias the results
   D. tendency of the interviewer to do most of the talking

1.____

2. The supervisor MOST likely to be a good interviewer is one who
   A. is adept at manipulating people and circumstances toward his objective
   B. is able to put himself in the position of the interviewee
   C. gets the more difficult questions out of the way at the beginning of the interview
   D. develops one style and technique that can be used in any type of interview

2.____

3. A good interviewer guards against the tendency to form an overall opinion about an interviewee on the basis of a single aspect of the interviewee's makeup.
   This statement refers to a well-known source of error in interviewing known as the
   A. assumption error   B. expectancy error
   C. extension effect   D. halo effect

3.____

4. In conducting an "exit interview" with an employee who is leaving voluntarily, the interview's MAIN objective should be to
   A. see that the employee leaves with a good opinion of the organization
   B. learn the true reasons for the employee's resignation
   C. find out if the employee would consider a transfer
   D. try to get the employee to remain on the job

4.____

5. During an interview, an interviewee unexpectedly discloses a relevant but embarrassing personal fact.
   It would be BEST for the interviewer to
   A. listen calmly, avoiding any gesture or facial expression that would suggest approval or disapproval of what is related
   B. change the subject, since further discussion in this area may reveal other embarrassing, but irrelevant, personal facts

5.____

C. apologize to the interviewee for having led him to reveal such a fact and promise not to do so again
D. bring the interview to a close as quickly as possible in order to avoid a discussion which may be distressing to the interviewee

6. Suppose that, while you are interviewing an applicant for a position in your office, you notice a contradiction in facts in two of his responses.
   For you to call the contradictions to his attention would be
   A. *inadvisable*, because it reduces the interviewee's level of participation
   B. *advisable*, because getting the facts is essential to a successful interview
   C. *inadvisable*, because the interviewer should use more subtle techniques to resolve any discrepancies
   D. *advisable*, because the interviewee should be impressed with the necessity for giving consistent answers

7. An interviewer should be aware that an undesirable result of including "leading questions" in an interview is to
   A. cause the interviewee to give a "yes" or "no" answers with qualification or explanation
   B. encourage the interviewee to discuss irrelevant topics
   C. encourage the interviewee to give more meaningful information
   D. reduce the validity of the information obtained from the interviewee

8. The kind of interview which is particularly helpful in getting an employee to tell about his complaints and grievances is one in which
   A. a pattern has been worked out involving a sequence of exact questions to be asked
   B. the interviewee is expected to support his statements with specific evidence
   C. the interviewee is not made to answer specific questions but is encouraged to talk freely
   D. the interviewer has specific items on which he wishes to get or give information

9. Suppose you are scheduled to interview an employee under your supervision concerning a health problem. You know that some of the questions you will be asking him will seem embarrassing to him, and that he may resist answering these questions.
   In general, to hold these questions for the last part of the interview would be
   A. *desirable*; the intervening time period gives the interviewer an opportunity to plan how to ask these sensitive questions.
   B. *undesirable*; the employee will probably feel that he has been tricked when he suddenly must answer embarrassing questions
   C. *desirable*; the employee will probably have increased confidence in the interviewer and be more willing to answer these questions
   D. *undesirable*; questions that are important should not be deferred until the end of the interview

10. In conducting an interview, the BEST types of questions with which to begin the interview are those which the person interviewed is
    A. willing and able to answer
    B. willing but unable to answer
    C. able but unwilling to answer
    D. unable and unwilling to answer

11. In order to determine accurately a child's age, it is BEST for an interviewer to rely on
    A. the child's grade in school
    B. what the mother says
    C. birth records
    D. a library card

12. In his first interview with a new employee, it would be LEAST appropriate for a unit supervisor to
    A. find out the employee's preference for the several types of jobs to which he is able to assign him
    B. determine whether the employee will make good promotion material
    C. inform the employee of what his basic job responsibilities will be
    D. inquire about the employee's education and previous employment

13. If an interviewer takes care to phrase his questions carefully and precisely, the result will MOST probably be that
    A. he will be able to determine whether the person interviewed is being truthful
    B. the free flow of the interview will be lost
    C. he will get the information he wants
    D. he will ask stereotyped questions and narrow the scope of the interview

14. When, during an interview, is the person interviewed LEAST likely to be cautious about what he tells the interviewer?
    A. Shortly after the beginning when the questions normally suggest pleasant associations to the person interviewed
    B. As long as the interviewer keeps his questions to the point
    C. At the point where the person interviewed gains a clear insight into the area being discussed
    D. When the interview appears formally ended and goodbyes are being said

15. In an interview held for the purpose of getting information from the person interviewed, it is sometimes desirable for the interviewer to repeat the answer he has received to a question.
    For the interviewer to rephrase such an answer in his own words is good practice MAINLY because it
    A. gives the interviewer time to make up his next question
    B. gives the person interviewed a chance to correct any possible misunderstanding
    C. gives the person interviewed the feeling that the interviewer considers his answer important
    D. prevents the person interviewed from changing his answer

16. There are several methods of formulating questions during an interview. The particular method used should be adapted to the interview problems presented by the person being questioned.
    Of the following methods of formulating questions during an interview, the ACCEPTABLE one is for the interviewer to ask questions which
    A. incorporate several items in order to allow a cooperative interviewee freedom to organize his statements
    B. are ambiguous in order to foil a distrustful interviewee
    C. suggest the correct answer in order to assist an interviewee who appears confused
    D. would help an otherwise unresponsive interviewee to become more responsive

17. For an interviewer to permit the person being interviewed to read the data the interviewer writes as he records the person's responses on a routine departmental form is
    A. *desirable*, because it serves to assure the person interviewed that his responses are being recorded accurately
    B. *undesirable*, because it prevents the interviewer from clarifying uncertain points by asking additional questions
    C. *desirable*, because it makes the time that the person interviewed must wait while the answer is written seem shorter
    D. *undesirable*, because it destroys the confidentiality of the interview

18. Of the following methods of conducting an interview, the BEST is to
    A. ask questions with "yes" or "no" answers
    B. listen carefully and ask only questions that are pertinent
    C. fire questions at the interviewee so that he must answer sincerely and briefly
    D. read standardized questions to the person being interviewed

KEY (CORRECT ANSWERS)

1.	A	11.	C
2.	B	12.	B
3.	D	13.	C
4.	B	14.	D
5.	A	15.	B
6.	B	16.	D
7.	D	17.	A
8.	C	18.	B
9.	C		
10.	A		

EXAMINATION SECTION
TEST 1

DIRECTIONS: Each question or incomplete statement is followed by several suggested answers or completions. Select the one that BEST answers the question or completes the statement. *PRINT THE LETTER OF THE CORRECT ANSWER IN THE SPACE AT THE RIGHT.*

1. In handling a case, an investigator should summarize the facts he has gathered and the observations he has made about the family and incorporate this material into a formal social study of the family.
   Of the following, the CHIEF advantage of such a practice is that it will provide a(n)

   A. picture of the family on the basis of which evaluations and plans can be made
   B. easily accessible listing of the factors pertaining to eligibility
   C. simple and uniform method of recording the family's social history
   D. opportunity for the investigator to record his evaluation of the family's situation

   1._____

2. An applicant for assistance tells the investigator that he has always supported himself by doing odd jobs.
   While attempting to verify the applicant's history of past maintenance, it is MOST important for the investigator to determine, in addition,

   A. how the applicant was able to obtain a sufficient number of odd jobs to support himself
   B. what skills the applicant had that enabled him to obtain these jobs
   C. why the applicant never sought or kept a steady job
   D. whether such jobs are still available as a source of income for the applicant

   2._____

3. For an investigator to make a collateral contact with a client's legally responsible relative when that relative is herself receiving assistance is

   A. *advisable,* mainly because the relative may be able to assist the client with needed services
   B. *inadvisable,* mainly because the relative is in receipt of assistance and cannot assist the client financially
   C. *advisable,* mainly because the worker may obtain information concerning the relative's eligibility for assistance
   D. *inadvisable,* because any information concerning the relative can be obtained from other sources

   3._____

4. An applicant for assistance tells the investigator that her bank savings are exhausted. While a bank clearance can verify her statement, it is still important for the investigator to see her bank book CHIEFLY in order to

   A. determine when the account was first opened and the amount of the initial deposit
   B. correlate withdrawals and deposits with the applicant's story of past management
   C. learn if the applicant had closed this account in order to open an account in another bank
   D. verify that the last withdrawal was made before the applicant applied for assistance

   4._____

5. It has been suggested that all investigators be kept currently informed about general departmental actions taken, changes in other departmental work units, and new developments of general interest in their department.
   For a department to put this suggestion into effect is, generally,

   A. *inadvisable;* investigators should perform the duties specifically assigned to them and not get involved in matters that do not concern them directly
   B. *advisable;* investigators may often need to know such information in order to coordinate their work properly with that of other work units
   C. *inadvisable;* changes in other work units have little effect on the work performed by investigators not assigned to these units
   D. *advisable;* broad knowledge of the activities in any agency tends to improve work skills

6. Although there is a normal distinction between the successive ranks of supervision in an agency, the greatest distinction and change in rank occurs, however, when an investigator becomes a supervisor.
   This is true CHIEFLY because the supervisor

   A. must be better informed than his investigators in all aspects
   B. must learn to assume new and more complex duties
   C. becomes responsible for the first time for the job performance of members of the investigation staff
   D. has greater responsibility and authority than the investigators under his supervision

7. When an experienced supervisory investigator does not agree personally with some of the procedurally correct objectives and directions of his supervisor, it would be MOST correct for him to

   A. continue to supervise his unit in accordance with the supervisor's directions
   B. direct his workers to follow the supervisor's directions, but indicate the weaknesses therein and be somewhat more lenient in the supervision of these duties
   C. seek to change the supervisor's directions through use of grievance procedures
   D. develop his own methods and apply them to the work of his unit on a trial basis

8. It has been said that the success or failure of the work of his unit rests on the supervisor. If the supervisor wants to stimulate growth among his investigators, it would generally be BEST for him to

   A. set an easy pace for his investigators so that they will not become confused because of having to learn too much too rapidly
   B. set the pace for his investigators so that the job is never too easy but is a constant challenge calling for more and better work
   C. spot check the investigators' records at irregular intervals in order to determine whether they are performing their duties properly
   D. see to it that the broad objectives and goals of the department are periodically communicated and interpreted to his investigators

9. The effectiveness of the work of a unit of investigators depends in a large measure on that unit's will to work.
   The BEST of the following methods for the supervisor to employ in order to increase the will of the members of the unit to work is for the unit supervisor to

A. allow each investigator to proceed at his own pace
B. be constantly on guard for any laxity among his investigators
C. provide comfortable working facilities for his investigators
D. clearly discuss with his investigators the functions and objectives of the agency

10. For a supervisor to encourage his investigators to think about the reasons for a policy is

    A. *advisable,* mainly because the investigators are then more likely to apply the policy appropriately
    B. *inadvisable,* mainly because the investigators may then apply the policy too flexibly
    C. *advisable,* mainly because the investigators then feel that they have participated in policy making
    D. *inadvisable,* mainly because the investigators may interpret the policy incorrectly if they misunderstand its meaning

11. A supervisor who plans his work properly and who has no difficulty in meeting deadlines insists that his new investigators pattern their activities after his in every detail.
    This method is

    A. *undesirable,* chiefly because such compliance can cause antagonism and hamper the investigators' growth
    B. *undesirable,* chiefly because this method cannot work as successfully for the new investigators
    C. *desirable,* chiefly because the supervisor's methods have proved successful and will eliminate waste
    D. *desirable,* chiefly because the untrained investigator needs guidelines to follow

12. Of the following, the MOST important reason for obtaining information in an initial investigation regarding financial maintenance of the applicant prior to the application for assistance is to

    A. comply with the provisions in the Social Welfare Law requiring that a record be made of the financial history of applicants for public assistance
    B. determine if the applicant may be expected to handle properly public assistance grants in the form of money
    C. determine the way in which the present situation differs from the past
    D. show the applicant that the department is interested in his past and present circumstances and may be expected to maintain this interest in the future

13. An applicant for assistance who has legally responsible relatives is informed by the investigator of the responsibility of such relatives to contribute to the applicant's support. The applicant requests permission to discuss the matter privately with these relatives prior to any contact by the department.
    In this case, it would be ADVISABLE for the investigator to

    A. *agree* to the request because the applicant is entitled to an opportunity to prepare the relatives for the coming official contact
    B. *agree* to the request because the applicant is in a better position than the investigator to uncover any concealment of assets by his relatives
    C. *refuse* the request because it might give the applicant and his relatives opportunity to devise means of avoiding or minimizing the existing responsibility
    D. *refuse* the request because the applicant is not likely to be able to give a proper interpretation to the relatives of their responsibility

14. The findings of a medical examination of a client who has claimed to be unemployable because of physical illness are that the client is employable. When told of these findings, the client reiterates that she is too ill to work.
In this case, the BEST of the following actions for the investigator to take FIRST is to

   A. discuss the situation with the client in an attempt to discover what reasons she may have for not wanting to accept employment
   B. make arrangements for a psychiatric examination of the client
   C. request that a second medical examination of the client be made by another doctor
   D. tell the client that the case will be closed unless she accepts employment

15. An investigator is told by a relative of a recipient that the recipient has won $6000 in a lottery and is soon to receive the prize money.
Of the following, the BEST action for the investigator to take FIRST is to

   A. close the case since the recipient did not notify the department of his winnings and since he now has enough money on which to live and pay his bills
   B. discuss the situation with the recipient, planning with him the future management of his funds
   C. let the recipient know that the use of relief money for gambling is illegal and that the police department must be notified of the facts in the case
   D. see that legal steps are taken to recover for services rendered to the client by the department.

16. When told at an interview with the investigator that he must agree to give to the department a lien on his real estate property, a client assumes a resistant attitude.
Of the following, it would usually be BEST for the investigator to

   A. discuss with the client the laws governing the giving of such liens and the purposes to be served by his giving the lien
   B. drop the matter, hoping to meet with less resistance at some future time
   C. tell the client that this is not a matter for discussion, that he must either agree to the lien or the case will be closed
   D. terminate the interview, telling the client that he may return when he is willing to discuss the means of providing the department with the lien

17. An investigator refers to his supervisor an applicant for assistance who has refused to supply certain information which is regularly asked of applicants. The applicant complains that he is being asked to supply private and personal information about himself that has nothing to do with his application for assistance and that the investigator has treated him with discourtesy.
The BEST of the following courses of action for the supervisor to take is to

   A. apologize for any appearance of discourtesy but insist that the applicant supply him with the information that had been sought
   B. apologize for any appearance of discourtesy, explain the need for the information that has been requested, and ask the applicant to supply it to the investigator
   C. explain that the investigator is doing a difficult job under difficult conditions and instruct the applicant to cooperate with him
   D. explain why the information is needed and state that no assistance will be forthcoming unless it is supplied

18. At an interview, in order to secure as efficiently as possible the information necessary to determine whether an applicant for assistance is eligible, investigators should generally be instructed to

    A. allow the applicant to explain his problem without interrupting him and then ask him to answer a previously prepared list of detailed questions covering necessary information
    B. confine the interview to a set of detailed questions prepared in advance by the investigator except that new questions may be added on the basis of leads provided by the answers to previous questions
    C. permit the applicant to explain his problems, using questions to keep the applicant from wandering from the subject and to bring out necessary information not covered by him in his narrative
    D. supply the applicant with a set of written questions immediately prior to the interview and confine the interview to a discussion of these questions

19. Assume that a client believes that his case has been unfairly closed, in spite of the fact that the investigator has explained the pertinent rules to him.
    It would be MOST proper, at this point, for the investigator to refer this client to

    A. an assistant to the commissioner at the central office
    B. an official of the state
    C. the supervisor in charge
    D. the supervisor in charge of the unit

20. An investigator is told by a client who is a resident of a nursing home that he is being neglected and not receiving proper care in the home.
    The investigator should

    A. discuss the situation with the proprietor of the nursing home
    B. investigate the situation on subsequent visits to determine the validity of the complaint
    C. report the matter to the medical social worker upon return to his center
    D. write a memorandum to the central nursing home service reporting the situation

21. Modern thinking and research on the efficient conduct of business has developed concepts of democratic supervision and human relations.
    Proper application of these concepts in dealing with investigators USUALLY results in

    A. a reduction in the use of formal discipline
    B. an increase in the use of formal discipline
    C. discarding discipline imposed from without to be completely replaced by self-imposed discipline
    D. elimination of formal discipline in favor of informal discipline

22. At the first interview between a supervisor and a newly appointed investigator, GREATEST care should be taken to

    A. build toward a satisfactory personal relationship even if some other objectives of the interview must be postponed
    B. cover a predetermined list of specific objectives so as to make a further orientation interview unnecessary

C. create an image of a forceful, determined supervisor whose wishes cannot be imposed by a subordinate without great risk
D. create an impression of efficiency and control of operation free from interpersonal relationships

23. In teaching the job to an investigator recently assigned to a unit, many teaching methods must be used.
    In general, however, the BEST way for the supervisor to train such an investigator is by having him

    A. do the job under proper supervision
    B. listen to lectures
    C. observe the work of other investigators
    D. study written material

24. A recently appointed investigator has reached the stage in learning his job where he is just beginning to be able to make decisions, although he still makes numerous mistakes and frequently does not know how to handle a situation.
    When the supervisor finds that the investigator has handled a certain situation in an acceptable manner, but not in the best manner, it would be BEST for the supervisor to

    A. explain to the investigator how he could have handled the situation better
    B. indicate approval of the way the situation was handled and explain how it could have been handled better
    C. say nothing about the situation
    D. show dissatisfaction with the way the situation was handled and explain how it could have been handled better

25. A supervisor has a job to be done of a type usually done by an investigator. The job is an important and recurring one, but not urgent at the moment. He knows that it would take more time to tell the investigator how to do the job than to do it himself, and that it would take still more time to make the investigator understand the situation, decide how to handle it, and then get the job done.
    In such a case, it would generally be BEST for the supervisor to

    A. assign the job to the investigator without explaining it
    B. do the job himself
    C. explain the situation and help the investigator to decide how to handle it
    D. tell the investigator exactly what to do

KEY (CORRECT ANSWERS)

1. A
2. D
3. A
4. B
5. B

6. C
7. A
8. B
9. D
10. A

11. A
12. C
13. A
14. A
15. B

16. A
17. B
18. C
19. D
20. D

21. A
22. A
23. A
24. B
25. C

TEST 2

DIRECTIONS: Each question or incomplete statement is followed by several suggested answers or completions. Select the one that BEST answers the question or completes the statement. *PRINT THE LETTER OF THE CORRECT ANSWER IN THE SPACE AT THE RIGHT.*

1. In order to improve the work of an experienced investigator who usually does average work, the one of the following actions which it would generally be BEST for the supervisor to take is to

    A. allow the investigator to be self-directed and unsupervised except where there is a large outlay of money involved
    B. apply strict discipline to any signs of laxness or inattention to duty
    C. carefully list and document every error made by the investigator and inform him of them
    D. use praise as a device to motivate the investigator to do better work

2. The one of the following guiding principles to which a supervisor should give MOST consideration when it becomes necessary to discipline an investigator is that

    A. rules should be applied in a fixed and inflexible manner
    B. the discipline should be applied for the purpose of improving the morale of all his investigators
    C. the main benefit to be derived from disciplining one offender is to deter other potential offenders
    D. the nature of the discipline should be such as to improve the future work of the offender

3. A unit supervisor notices one of his investigators reading a novel at his desk during working hours. This is the first time that this has happened. The investigator is an experienced employee who does above-average work.
For the unit supervisor to ignore the situation is GENERALLY

    A. *wise*, since it is never desirable to penalize a good employee because of any single incident
    B. *unwise*, since it may be interpreted by the staff as condoning inattention to work
    C. *wise*, since democratic supervision allows employees leeway to apportion their workday as they see fit
    D. *unwise*, since it is necessary to take strong action at the first sign of insubordination

4. When investigators in a particular unit are guilty of infractions, it is the practice of the unit supervisor to give necessary warnings or reprimands in a jocular manner. This practice is GENERALLY

    A. *unwise*, because humorous or jocular aspects should be kept from relationships between supervisors and investigators
    B. *unwise*, because it leaves the investigator unsure of the true intent or extent of the discipline
    C. *wise*, because it makes the investigator realize that there is no personal animosity involved
    D. *wise*, because it reduces the severity of the warning or reprimand

5. An experienced investigator complains to his unit supervisor that the latter's continual very close supervision of his work is unnecessary and annoying. The unit supervisor is a recently appointed supervisor.
In this case, it would generally be BEST for the unit supervisor to

   A. ask the investigator to explain his complaint further, telling him that it will receive consideration, and then re-evaluate his supervisory practices, seeking advice from his own supervisor if necessary
   B. assure the investigator that there had been no intention of singling him out but that, as a subordinate, he will have to get used to new supervisory methods employed by new, wide-awake supervisors
   C. explain to the investigator that it is the job of the unit supervisor to supervise him and that he should understand his role and be able to overcome his annoyance
   D. promise the investigator that the annoying supervisory methods will be discontinued but remind him that the unit supervisor must be respected and looked to for assistance, training, and supervision

5.____

6. A unit supervisor becomes aware that one of his investigators has a personal problem which is causing the subordinate considerable concern and is beginning to affect his work.
Of the following, the action which it would generally be BEST for the unit supervisor to take is to

   A. ignore the matter but, if the investigator brings the matter up, politely tell him that it is not proper for a unit supervisor to discuss personal problems of subordinates
   B. make the investigator aware that he may discuss personal problems with his unit supervisor who will offer whatever assistance he can, compatible with the duties of his job
   C. refer the matter to his own supervisor
   D. indicate that he would like to help solve the problem and insist that the investigator provide full details

6.____

7. An investigator who has many personal problems frequently introduces one or more of them into the discussion at conferences with his unit supervisor. He talks of them at some length.
It would generally be BEST for the unit supervisor to

   A. discuss the problems with the investigator and, as a helping person, assist with their solution
   B. explain that he would like to help solve the problems but that the repeated introduction of them in conferences is interfering with the work of the unit
   C. inform the investigator that his personal problems should not be brought to the office and that it would be improper for the unit supervisor to try to help with them
   D. listen silently to the exposition of the problems made by the investigator and then return to the business at hand without commenting on the problem

7.____

8. For the investigator to understand the culture of a family is important CHIEFLY because the

   A. client tends to react to the situation largely in ways derived from attitudes learned at home

8.____

B. needs of the entire family cannot be satisfied unless the individual needs of each member are satisfied first
C. client can be treated more effectively when considered as a member of a cultural group rather than a separate individual
D. family can be understood much more readily if the dominant individual motivating it is understood first

9. Emphasis in the practice of casework has shifted from merely providing the client with a practical service, to involving the client in using the service or treatment.
This statement implies MOST NEARLY that, at present,

   A. casework will attempt to help the client only when it is felt that he will profit from the service
   B. casework is no longer deeply involved in assisting the client in a direct and realistic way
   C. the most important change in casework today has been its shift from helping the client in a practical way to planning for him in a theoretical way
   D. the caseworker or investigator attempts to mobilize the client to active participation in decision-making

9._____

10. In all casework practice, whether it be in an agency or in an institution, the properly prepared case history record is of great importance in the treatment of the client and his problem CHIEFLY because it

   A. gives the supervisory and administrative casework staff reviewing the case a keener understanding of the general sociological and psychological causes underlying dependency and other factors which make it necessary for clients to seek casework assistance
   B. furnishes the agency or institution involved in the case with a factual record as a basis for determining whether or not continuing treatment of the client is justified
   C. assists the caseworkers or investigators involved in the case by providing them, on a continuous basis, with a clear picture of the various factors underlying the client's problems and of what has been done to help resolve the situation
   D. provides the caseworker or investigator responsible for the case with the basic facts which will enable her to determine whether the client is really trying to help himself or whether he is passing his responsibility on to the caseworker or investigator

10._____

11. When comparing the narrative form with the summary form of a casework recording, the narrative form is usually the BEST way to record

   A. objective material obtained from investigations of the client's statements, while the summary form is best to record worker's detailed observations of client's reactions to his present problem
   B. both social data and eligibility material, while the summary form is best to record material dealing with feelings, attitudes and client-worker relationships
   C. material relating to prognosis, treatment given, and the results obtained, while the summary form is best to record a verbatim report of primary evidence obtained from personal worker-client contacts
   D. material dealing with feelings, attitudes, and client-worker relationships, while the summary form is best to record both social data and eligibility material

11._____

12. A problem in recording is to decide how much detail to have in a case record. The case history should GENERALLY include

    A. a more detailed description of the client's reaction to practical matters than to psychological conflicts
    B. a verbatim account of worker-client interaction in significant interviews and a detailed description of the client's feelings toward the treatment plan
    C. only as much data, whether it be sociological or psychological, as will enable the worker to understand the client, the problem to be solved, and the main factors in its solution
    D. the full details of the client's personality development and emotional relationships regardless of the type or complexity of the problem

13. Interviewing is always directed to the client and his situation. The one of the following which is the MOST accurate statement with respect to the proper focus of an interview is that the

    A. investigator limits the client to concentration on objective data
    B. client is generally permitted to talk about facts and feelings with no direction from the investigator
    C. main focus in interviews is on feelings rather than facts
    D. investigator is responsible for helping the client focus on any material which seems to be related to his problems or difficulties

14. Assume that you are conducting a training program for the investigators under your supervision. At one of the sessions, you discuss the problem of interviewing a dull and stupid client who gives a slow and disconnected case history.
    The BEST of the following interviewing methods for you to recommend in such a case in order to ascertain the facts is for the investigator to

    A. ask the client leading questions requiring *yes* or *no* answers
    B. request the client to limit his narration to the essential facts so that the interview can be kept as brief as possible
    C. review the story with the client, patiently asking simple questions
    D. tell the client that unless he is more cooperative, he cannot be helped to solve his problem

15. A recent development in interviewing procedure, known as multiple-client interviewing, consists of interviews of the entire family at the same time. However, this may not be an effective method in certain situations.
    Of the following, the situation in which the standard individual interview would be PREFERABLE is when

    A. family members derive consistent and major gratification from assisting each other in their destructive responses
    B. there is a crucial family conflict to which the members are reacting
    C. the family is overwhelmed by interpersonal anxieties which have not been explored
    D. the investigator wants to determine the pattern of family interaction to further his diagnostic understanding

5 (#2)

16. The one of the following which is the CHIEF value of verbatim recording of all or a portion of an important interview is the possibility it offers for

   A. careful study and clarification of psychological goals in treatment
   B. a prompt solution to the problem by preservation, in an orderly and concise fashion of the full psychological and economic picture of the client's situation
   C. quick determination of the more obvious social goals and offering of concrete services by presentation of the essential facts
   D. supervision of experienced investigators by showing the emotional overtones, subtle reactions, and intricate investigator-client interchanges

17. Experts in the field of casework recording generally agree that the kind of material for which the narrative form of recording is MOST suitable is

   A. material that deals with feelings, attitudes, and client-investigator relationships, because this style permits the use of primary evidence in the form of verbal material and behavior observed in the interview
   B. social data, including eligibility material and family background history, because it can then be presented in a chronological, orderly fashion to enable the investigator to select the desired facts
   C. personal facts concerning the individual's personality patterns and their growth and development, because they can be seen in an orderly progression from primal immaturity until their ultimate stage of completion
   D. selectively chosen and documented material essential to a quicker and clearer understanding of the various ramifications of the case by a new investigator when responsibility for handling the client is reassigned

18. A case record includes relevant social and psychological facts about the client, the nature of his request, his feeling about his situation, his attitude towards the agency and his use of and reaction to treatment.
    In addition, it should always contain

   A. routine history
   B. complete details of personality development and emotional relationships
   C. detailed process accounts of all contacts
   D. data necessary for understanding the problem and the factors important in arriving at a solution

19. The CHIEF basis for the inability of a troubled client to express his problem clearly to the investigator is that the client

   A. sees his problem in complex terms and does not think it possible to give the investigator the whole picture
   B. has erected defenses against emotions that seem to him inadmissible or intolerable
   C. cannot describe how he feels about his problem
   D. views the situation as unlikely to be solved and is blocked in self-expression

20. In aggressive casework, when an investigator visits a multi-problem family, he should begin by

   A. arranging individual interviews with the children
   B. outlining the steps to be taken in the solution of their problems

C. inviting the family to visit the agency so that a normal casework situation may be created
D. explaining what points of risk or danger exist in their situation and inviting an expression of their feelings

21. The job of the supervisory investigator may be considered in part an administrative one CHIEFLY because it 21.____

   A. requires administrative training or experience
   B. involves a direct relationship with the executive office of the department
   C. entails responsibility for staff development
   D. calls for planning, organizing, and coordinating

22. If a supervisory investigator discovers that the amount of the grant in a particular case is inaccurate, he should 22.____

   A. make the necessary adjustments and assign another investigator to the case
   B. caution all investigators in the unit to be more careful in the future
   C. assume that the investigator's computation was correct when it was made
   D. arrange to have the investigator review the budget with the client and make the necessary adjustments

23. If, in the process of investigating eligibility for assistance, discrepancies occur between the applicant's statement of his situation and that given by a relative interviewed, the investigator should USUALLY 23.____

   A. accept the relative's statement since the relative has less interest in falsifying the facts
   B. return to the client for clarification of the situation
   C. immediately discount the relative's statement since he may be motivated by his legal responsibility for supporting the applicant
   D. point out the discrepancies to the relative and ask him for any explanation he can give

24. In evaluating the adequacy of an individual's income, an investigator should place PRIMARY emphasis on 24.____

   A. its value in relation to the average income
   B. the source of the income
   C. its relation to the earning capacity of the individual
   D. its purchasing power

25. The length of residence required to make a person eligible for the various forms of public assistance available in the United States 25.____

   A. is the same in all states but is different among public assistance programs in a given state
   B. is the same in all states and among different public assistance programs in a given state
   C. is the same in all states for different categories
   D. varies among states and among different public assistance programs in a given state

KEY (CORRECT ANSWERS)

1. D
2. D
3. B
4. B
5. A

6. B
7. B
8. A
9. D
10. C

11. D
12. C
13. D
14. C
15. A

16. A
17. A
18. D
19. B
20. D

21. D
22. D
23. B
24. D
25. D

———

TEST 3

DIRECTIONS: Each question or incomplete statement is followed by several suggested answers or completions. Select the one that BEST answers the question or completes the statement. *PRINT THE LETTER OF THE CORRECT ANSWER IN THE SPACE AT THE RIGHT.*

1. A person who knowingly brings a needy person from another state into the state for the purpose of making him a public charge is guilty of

   A. violation of the Displaced Persons Act
   B. violation of the Mann Act
   C. a felony
   D. a misdemeanor

2. An aged person who is unable to produce immediate proof of age has made an application for assistance. He states that it will take about a week to obtain the necessary proof and that he does not have enough money to provide meals for himself until then.
   If it appears that he is in immediate need, he should be told that

   A. temporary assistance will be provided pending the completion of the investigation
   B. a personal loan will be made to him from a revolving fund
   C. he should arrange for a small loan from private sources
   D. he will have to produce an affidavit witnessed by two relatives who will vouch for the accuracy of his statements before any assistance can be provided

3. If the investigator learns during an interview that the client has applied for assistance without the knowledge of her husband, even though he is a member of the same household, the investigator should

   A. appear not to notice this oversight but watch for other evidences of marital discord
   B. make no mention of this to the applicant but, before taking final action, send a note to the husband asking him to come in
   C. discuss this situation with the client and help her recognize the value of her husband's participation in the application
   D. point out to the applicant the implications of her behavior and ask for an explanation of her motives

4. Of the sources through which an agency can seek information about the family background and economic needs of a particular client, the MOST important consists of

   A. records and documents covering the client
   B. interviews with the client's relatives
   C. the client's own story
   D. direct contacts with former employers

5. The one of the following sources of evidence which would be MOST likely to give information needed to verify residence is

   A. family affidavits
   B. medical and hospital bills
   C. an original birth certificate
   D. rental receipts

6. Vital statistics are a resource used by investigators to

   A. help establish eligibility through verification of births, deaths, and marriages
   B. help establish eligibility through verification of divorce proceedings
   C. secure proof of unemployment and eligibility for unemployment compensation
   D. secure indices of the cost of living in the larger cities

7. Case records should be considered confidential in order to

   A. permit investigators to make objective, rather than subjective, comments
   B. prevent recipients from comparing amounts of assistance given to other recipients
   C. keep pertinent information from other investigators
   D. protect clients and their families

8. Because the investigator generally is not trained as a psychiatrist, he should, when encountering psychiatric problems in the performance of his departmental duties,

   A. ignore such problems because they are beyond the scope of his responsibilities
   B. inform the affected persons that he recognizes their problems personally but will take no official cognizance of them
   C. ask to be relieved of the cases in which these problems are met and recommend that they be assigned to a psychiatrist
   D. recognize such problems where they exist and make referrals to the proper sources for treatment

9. Inasmuch as periodic visits to clients at home are required by the department, according to good work practice, it is MOST desirable for the investigator to

   A. visit without appointment as this gives him a chance to see the person and the house *as they really are* and forestalls changing things to create a different impression
   B. write giving an appointment time as this saves the investigator from visiting when people are not at home and helps him to plan his work more efficiently
   C. write suggesting an appointment time so that the client may be prepared for the interview and the investigator uses his time economically
   D. advise all applicants during their first interview that they will be visited periodically but will not be given definite appointments

10. Assuming that careful interpretation has been given but an applicant for assistance refuses to accede to the necessary procedures to establish his eligibility, the MOST preferable of the following courses of action for the investigator to take would be to

    A. do nothing further
    B. grant a temporary delay in the hope that the applicant will change his mind
    C. try to ascertain why the applicant feels as he does, but to respect his decision if he refuses to change his mind
    D. proceed to check on all the facts possible even though the applicant has not given his permission

11. The PRIMARY purpose in discussing with an applicant the steps in determining his eligibility and the kind of verification of facts which the agency will need is to

    A. enable the applicant to understand the basis of eligibility and participate in determining it
    B. protect the position of the agency so that there will be no comeback if the application is not granted
    C. give the applicant an opportunity to modify any statement he may have made previously
    D. promote public relations for the agency since the applicant will tell others how the agency is operating

12. Of the following, the LEAST valid reason for the maintenance of the case record is to

    A. furnish reference material for other investigators
    B. improve the quality of service to the client
    C. show how the funds are being expended
    D. reduce the complexities of the case to manageable proportions

13. A public agency will lean more on forms than a private agency in the same field of activity because

    A. forms simplify the recording responsibilities of newly appointed investigators
    B. public records are of the family agency type
    C. the governmental framework requires a greater degree of standardization
    D. more interviews and visits are made in connection with public cases

14. In spite of the need which most of us have of finding rules and procedures to guide us, we must face the difficulty at the outset that there is no such thing as a model case record.
    Of the following, the BEST justification for this statement is that

    A. records should be written to suit the case
    B. case recording should be patterned after the best models obtainable
    C. rules cannot be applied to case work because each case requires individual treatment
    D. the establishment of routine and procedures in investigatory work is an ideal which cannot be realized

15. In attempting to discover whether an applicant for aid has had any previous experience as a recipient through other agencies in the community, the investigator should

    A. check the application with the social service exchange
    B. send the fingerprints of the applicant to the Police Department
    C. consult the latest records of the department
    D. ask the applicant to submit a notarized statement to the effect that such aid has not been received from any other source

16. Suppose a client whom you are investigating has borrowed $250 in order to purchase an evening gown for one of her children who is being graduated from high school. She is planning to repay the loan at the rate of ten dollars a week and presents verification of this transaction as well as the purchase.
    As an investigator, you would be complying with the BEST casework principles by

A. telling the client her grant will be reduced in view of her ability to manage on ten dollars less each week
B. telling the client that she must never do this again
C. explaining to the client how her action will make it more difficult for the family to get along on their limited grant
D. suggesting that she return the dress and repay the borrowed money in this way

17. An investigator determined, while investigating an applicant for Medical Assistance for the Aged, that the applicant's income and resources are over and above the limits permitted under the Medical Assistance for the Aged program. However, the applicant's medical needs seem to be extensive, and the applicant insists that he cannot pay for his needed medical care.
The investigator should

   A. accept the case for Medical Assistance for the Aged in the normal manner and await a determination of the cost of the medical care in order to determine if there is actually a budget deficit
   B. have the cost of the medical care determined prior to making any decision as to acceptance or rejection of the case
   C. handle the case exactly as he would the case of an applicant for any other type of assistance who does not have a budget deficit
   D. reject the case for Medical Assistance for the Aged until the applicant can obtain verification of the cost of his needed medical care

17._____

18. Of the following, the choice of method to be used in the supervisory process should be influenced MOST by the

   A. number and type of cases carried by each investigator
   B. emotional maturity of the investigator
   C. number of investigators supervised and their past experience
   D. subject matter to be learned and the long range goals of supervision

18._____

19. In an evaluation conference with an investigator, the BEST approach for the supervisor to take is to

   A. help the investigator to identify his strengths, as a basis for working on his weaknesses
   B. identify the investigator's weaknesses and help him overcome them
   C. allow the investigator to identify his weaknesses first and then suggest ways of overcoming them
   D. discuss the investigator's weaknesses but emphasize his strengths

19._____

20. Assume that an investigator is discouraged about the progress of his work and feels that it is futile to attempt to cope with many of his cases.
Of the following, it would be BEST for the supervisor to

   A. suggest to the investigator that such feelings are inappropriate for a professional worker
   B. tell the investigator that he must seek professional help in order to overcome these feelings
   C. reduce the investigator's caseload and give him cases that are less complex
   D. review with the investigator several of his cases in which there were obvious accomplishments

20._____

21. The supervisor is responsible for providing the investigator with the following means of support, with the EXCEPTION of

    A. interest and advice on his personal problems
    B. instruction on community resources
    C. inspiration for carrying out the work of the agency
    D. understanding his strengths and limitations

22. When an investigator frequently takes the initiative in asking questions and discussing problems during a supervisory conference, this is probably an indication that the

    A. supervisor is not sufficiently interested in the investigator
    B. conference is a positive learning experience for the investigator
    C. worker is hostile and resists supervision
    D. supervisor's position of authority is in question

23. When a supervisor finds that one of his investigators cannot accept criticism, of the following, it would be BEST for the supervisor to

    A. have the investigator transferred to another supervisor
    B. warn the investigator of disciplinary proceedings unless his attitude changes
    C. have the investigator suspended after explaining the reason
    D. explore with the investigator his attitude toward authority

24. Of the following, the condition which the inexperienced investigator is LEAST likely to be aware of, without the guidance of the supervisor, is

    A. when he is successful in helping a client
    B. when he is not making progress in helping a client
    C. that he has a personal bias toward certain clients
    D. that he feels insecure because of lack of experience

25. The supervisor should provide an inexperienced investigator with controls as well as freedom MAINLY because controls will

    A. enable him to set up his own controls sooner
    B. put him in a situation which is closer to the realities of life
    C. help him to use authority in handling a casework problem
    D. give him a feeling of security and lay the foundation for future self-direction

KEY (CORRECT ANSWERS)

1.	D		11.	A
2.	A		12.	D
3.	C		13.	C
4.	C		14.	A
5.	D		15.	A
6.	A		16.	C
7.	D		17.	A
8.	D		18.	D
9.	C		19.	A
10.	C		20.	D

21. A
22. B
23. D
24. C
25. D

EXAMINATION SECTION
TEST 1

DIRECTIONS: Each question or incomplete statement is followed by several suggested answers or completions. Select the one that BEST answers the question or completes the statement. *PRINT THE LETTER OF THE CORRECT ANSWER IN THE SPACE AT THE RIGHT.*

1. The one of the following which is the BEST description of a properly objective investigator is one who
    A. is friendly and sensitive to the client's feelings, without becoming emotionally involved
    B. is distant and impersonal, remaining unaffected by what the client says
    C. lets personal emotions enter as far as the client's situation calls for them
    D. becomes emotionally involved with the client's situation but without showing involvement

1._____

2. The one of the following which is MOST necessary for successfully interviewing a person who belongs to a culture different from that of the investigator is for the investigator to
    A. have some appreciation of the other culture
    B. ignore those cultural differences which lead to bias
    C. stay away from sensitive, touchy issues
    D. assume the mannerisms of people in the other culture

2._____

3. In fact-finding interviews, it is generally assumed that the smaller the number of interviewees, the greater the increase of reliability with the addition of others. The PROPER number of interviewees need to insure the accuracy of information obtain generally depends upon the
    A. educational level of those interviewed
    B. number of people who have the required information
    C. directness of the questions asked
    D. variability of the information received

3._____

4. The one of the following which is generally MOST likely to be accurately described in an interview by an interviewee is
    A. the presence of a large painting in the investigator's office
    B. the number of people in the investigator's waiting room
    C. space relations
    D. duration of time

4._____

5. The one of the following which is generally the BEST course of action for an investigator to take when interviewing a person who is reluctant to tell what he knows about a matter under investigation is to
    A. be curt and abrupt, and threaten the person with the consequences of his withholding information

5._____

31

B. be firm and severe, and pressure the person into telling the needed information
C. be patient and candid with the person being questioned about the investigation since doing otherwise is not ethical
D. give the person false information about the investigation so he will give the needed information without realizing its importance

6. It is often recommended that an investigator prepare in advance a list of questions or topics to be covered in an interview.
The MAIN reason for such a checklist is to
   A. allow investigations to be assigned to less efficient investigators
   B. eliminate a large amount of follow-up paperwork
   C. aid the investigator in remembering to cover all important documents
   D. aid the investigator in maintaining an objective distance from the person interviewed

6._____

7. Usually, the CHIEF advantage of a directive approach in an interview is that the
   A. investigator maintains control over the course of the interview
   B. person interviewed is more likely to be put at ease
   C. person interviewed is generally left free to direct the interview
   D. investigator will not suggest answers to the person interviewed

7._____

8. Usually, the CHIEF advantage of a non-directive approach by an investigator in conducting an interview is that the
   A. investigator generally conceals what he is looking for in the interview
   B. person interviewed is more likely to express his true feelings about the topic under discussion
   C. person interviewed is more likely to follow an idea introduced by the investigator
   D. investigator can keep the discussion limited to topics he believes to be relevant

8._____

9. The one of the following which is generally the LEAST likely to be accurate in a description of an event given to an investigator is a statement about
   A. the presence of an object
   B. the number of people, when their number is small
   C. locations of people
   D. duration of time

9._____

10. Assume that you, an investigator, are conducting a character investigation. In an interview, the one of the following character traits of the person being interviewed which can USUALLY be determined with a good degree of reliability is
    A. honesty   B. dependability
    C. forcefulness   D. perseverance

10._____

11. As an investigator, you have been assigned the task of obtaining a family's social history.
    The BEST place for you to interview members of the family while obtaining this social history would generally be in
    A. the family's home
    B. your agency's general offices
    C. the home of a friend of the family
    D. your own private office

12. You, an investigator, are checking someone's work history.
    The way for you to get the MOST reliable information from a previous employer is to
    A. send personal letters; the employer will respond to the personal attention
    B. send form letters; the employer will cooperate readily since little time or effort is asked of him
    C. arrange a personal interview; the employer may offer information he would not care to put in a letter or speak over the phone
    D. telephone; this method is as effective as a personal interview and is much more convenient

13. The effect that attestation, or the formal taking of an oath, has on witness testimony is to
    A. decrease accuracy, since a witness under oath is more nervous about what is said
    B. makes little difference, since the witness is not too swayed by an oath
    C. increase accuracy, since a witness under oath feels more responsibility for what is said
    D. eliminate inaccuracy unless there is deliberate perjury on the part of the witness

14. If an investigator obtains testimony from persons in interviews by means of interrogation or asking questions rather than by letting the person freely relate the testimony, what is said will GENERALLY be
    A. greater in range and less accurate
    B. greater in range and more accurate
    C. about the same in range and less accurate
    D. about the same in range and more accurate

15. Experienced investigators have learned to phrase their questions carefully in order to obtain the desired response.
    Of the following, the question which would usually elicit the MOST accurate answer is:
    A. "How old are you?"
    B. "What is your income?"
    C. "How are you today?"
    D. "What is your date of birth?"

16. The one of the following questions which would generally lead to the LEAST reliable answer is:
    A. "Did you see a wallet?"
    B. "Was the German Shepherd gray?"
    C. "Didn't you see the stop sign?"
    D. "Did you see the guard on duty?"

17. Some investigators may make a practice of observing details of the surroundings when interviewing in someone's home or office.
Such a practice is GENERALLY considered
    A. *undesirable*, mainly because such snooping is unwarranted, unethical invasion of privacy
    B. *undesirable*, mainly because useful information is rarely, if ever, gained this way
    C. *desirable*, mainly because useful insights into the character of the person interviewed may be gained
    D. *desirable*, mainly because it is impossible to evaluate a person adequately without such observation of his environment

17.____

18. The one of the following questions which MOST often lead to a reliable answer is:
    A. "Was his hair very dark?"
    B. "Wasn't there a clock on the wall?"
    C. "Was the automobile white or gray?"
    D. "Did you see a motorcycle?"

18.____

19. The one of the following which can MOST accurately be determined by an investigator by means of interviewing is
    A. a person's intelligence
    B. factual information about an event
    C. a person's aptitude for a specific task
    D. a person's perceptions of his own abilities

19.____

20. The one of the following which is MOST likely to help a person being interviewed feel at ease is for the investigator to
    A. let him start the conversation
    B. give him an abundance of time
    C. be relaxed himself
    D. open the interview by telling a joke

20.____

21. If the interviewee is to perceive some goal for himself in the interview and thus be motivated to participate in it, it is important that he clearly understands some of the aspects of the interview.
Of the following aspects, the one the interviewee needs LEAST to understand is
    A. the purpose of the interview
    B. the mechanics of interviewing
    C. the use made of the information he contributes
    D. what will be expected of him in the interview

21.____

22. As an investigator working on a project requiring inter-agency cooperation, you find that employees of an agency involved in the project are constantly making it difficult for you to obtain necessary information.
Of the following, the BEST action for you to take FIRST is to
    A. discuss the problem with your supervisor
    B. speak with your counterpart in the other agency

22.____

5 (#1)

C. discuss the problem with the head of the uncooperative agency
D. contact the head of your agency

23. The investigator is justified in misleading the interviewee only when, in the investigator's judgment, this is clearly required by the problem being investigated.
Such a practice is
   A. *necessary*; there are times when complete honesty will impede a successful investigation
   B. *unnecessary*; such a tactic is unethical and should never be employed
   C. *necessary*; an investigator must be guided by success rather than ethical considerations in an investigation
   D. *unnecessary*; it is clearly doubtful whether such a practice will help the investigator conclude the investigation successfully

23.____

24. Assume that, in investigating a case of possible welfare fraud, it becomes necessary to hold an interview in the client's home in order to observe family interaction and conditions. Upon arriving, the investigator finds that the client's living room is noisy and crowded, with neighbors present and children running in and out.
Of the following, the BEST course of action for the investigator to take is to
   A. conduct the interview in the living room after telling the children to behave and asking the neighbors to leave
   B. tell the client that it is impossible to conduct the interview in the apartment and make an appointment for the next day in the investigators office
   C. suggest that they move from the living room into the kitchen where there is a table on which he can write
   D. try his best to conduct the interview in the noisy and crowded living room

24.____

25. You, an investigator, are giving testimony in court about a matter you have investigated. An attorney is questioning you in an abrasive, badgering way and, in an insulting manner, calls into doubt your ability as an investigator. You lose your temper and respond angrily, telling the attorney to stop harassing and insulting you.
Of the following, the BEST description of such a response is that it is generally
   A. *appropriate*; as a witness in court, you do not have to take insults from anybody, including an attorney
   B. *inappropriate*; losing your temper will show that you are weak and cannot be trusted as an investigator
   C. *appropriate*; a judge and jury will usually respect someone who responds strongly to unjust provocation
   D. *inappropriate*; such conduct is unprofessional and may unfavorably impress a judge and jury

25.____

KEY (CORRECT ANSWERS)

1.	A		11.	A
2.	A		12.	C
3.	D		13.	C
4.	A		14.	A
5.	C		15.	D
6.	C		16.	B
7.	A		17.	C
8.	B		18.	D
9.	D		19.	D
10.	C		20.	C

21. B
22. A
23. A
24. C
25. D

TEST 2

DIRECTIONS: Each question or incomplete statement is followed by several suggested answers or completions. Select the one that BEST answers the question or completes the statement. *PRINT THE LETTER OF THE CORRECT ANSWER IN THE SPACE AT THE RIGHT.*

1. An investigator may have problems in obtaining information from persons who have a history of mental disturbance CHIEFLY because such persons are
    A. usually highly unstable so that they cannot give a coherent account of anything they have experienced
    B. usually very withdrawn so that they generally are unwilling to talk to anyone they do not know well
    C. often normal in manner so that an investigator may be unaware that their condition may bias information they provide
    D. often violent and may try to attack an investigator who questions them intensively about a topic which is sensitive

1.____

2. Empathy can be defined as the ability of one individual to respond sensitively and imaginatively to another's feelings.
    For an investigator to be empathetic during an interview is USUALLY
    A. *undesirable*, mainly because an investigator should never be influenced by the feelings of the one being interviewed
    B. *desirable*, mainly because an interview will not be productive unless the investigator takes the side of the person interviewed
    C. *undesirable*, mainly because empathy usually leads an investigator to be biased in favor of the person being interviewed
    D. *desirable*, mainly because this ability allows the investigator to direct his questions more effectively to the person interviewed

2.____

3. Assume that an investigator must, in the course of an investigation, question several people who know each other.
    To gather them all in one group and question them together is GENERALLY
    A. *good practice*, since any inaccurate information offered by one person would be corrected by others in the group
    B. *poor practice*, since people in a group rarely pay adequate attention to questions
    C. *good practice*, since the investigator will save much time and effort in this way
    D. *poor practice*, since the presence of several people can inhibit an individual from speaking

3.____

4. While conducting a character investigation of a potential employee, you, as an investigator, notice that most community members interviewed have negative opinions of the candidate.
    Of the following statements about the usefulness of community opinions in such a matter, the one which is LEAST accurate is that

4.____

A. prudence should be exercised in evaluating information received in a community contact
B. a community investigation sometimes elicits gossip which may present an exaggerated picture
C. community opinion is reliable when used to assess an individual's character
D. opinions which cannot be supported by facts must be considered as such

5. An effective investigator should know that the one of the following which LEAST describes why there is a wide range of individual behavior in human relations is that
   A. socio-economic status influences human behavior
   B. physical characteristics do not influence human behavior
   C. education influences human behavior
   D. childhood experience influences human behavior

6. In your investigative unit, you discern a growing friction between two co-workers which is beginning to impede the work of the unit.
   Of the following, the approach you should FIRST adopt is to
   A. mediate the friction yourself; if unsuccessful, then inform your supervisor
   B. ignore the friction; although detrimental, it is beyond your authority to settle
   C. promptly discuss the friction and possible course of action with other members of your unit
   D. promptly inform your supervisor of the friction and let him handle the matter

7. In certain cases, in order that an investigation be conducted successfully, an investigator must have the cooperation of people in the community.
   The one of the following which BEST describes how an investigator may gain community cooperation in an investigation is by
   A. using persuasion
   B. using authority
   C. spending many hours in the community
   D. being friendly with community leaders

8. During a field investigation, an investigator encounters an uncooperative interviewee.
   Of the following, the FIRST thing the investigator should do in such a situation is to
   A. try various appeals to win the interviewee over to a cooperative attitude
   B. try to ascertain the reason for non-cooperation
   C. promise the interviewee that all data will be kept confidential
   D. alter his interviewing technique with the uncooperative interviewee

9. You, as an investigator, discover that an interviewee who was requested to bring with him specific documents for his initial employment interview has forgotten the documents.

Of the following, the BEST course of action to take is to
- A. give the person a reasonable amount of time to furnish the document
- B. tell the person you will let him know how much additional time he could receive
- C. mark the person disqualified for employment; he has failed to provide reasonably requested data on time
- D. mark the person provisionally qualified for employment; upon receipt of the documents, he will be permanently qualified

10. As an investigator checking interviewees' work experience, you realize that the person whom you are to interview is only marginally fluent in English and has, therefore, requested permission to bring a translator with him.
Of the following, the BEST course of action is to inform the interviewee that
    - A. outside translators may not be used
    - B. only city translators may be used
    - C. state law requires fluency in English of all civil servants
    - D. he may be assisted in the interview by his translator

11. Assume that during the course of an interview, an investigator is verbally attacked by the person being interview.
Of the following, it would be MOST advisable for the investigator to
    - A. answer back in a matter-of-fact manner
    - B. ask the person to apologize and discontinue the interview
    - C. ignore the attack but adjourn the interview to another day
    - D. use restraint and continue the interview

12. Assume that an investigator finds that the person he is interviewing has difficulty finishing his sentences and seems to be groping for words.
In such a case, the BEST approach for the investigator to take is to
    - A. say what he thinks the person has in mind
    - B. proceed patiently without calling attention to the problem
    - C. ask the person why he finds it difficult to finish his sentence
    - D. interrupt the interview until the person feels more relaxed

13. The one of the following which BEST describes the effect of the sympathetic approach in interviewing on the interviewee is that it will
    - A. have no discernible effect on the interviewee
    - B. calm the interviewee
    - C. lead the interviewee to understate his problems
    - D. mislead the interviewee

14. The one of the following characteristics which is a PRIMARY requisite for a successful investigative interview is
    - A. total curiosity
    - B. total sympathy
    - C. complete attention
    - D. complete dedication

15. Assume that you, an investigator, become aware that one of your colleagues has a drinking problem which is affecting the operations of your unit.
Of the following, the action which you should take FIRST is to
    A. give your colleague time to resolve the problem himself
    B. discuss the problem with your colleague
    C. inform your supervisor of the problem
    D. not involve yourself in your colleague's problem

16. Assume that an Assistant District Attorney has asked you, the investigator of an alleged welfare fraud, to conduct a follow-up interview with a primary state witness.
The one of the following which is MOST important in arranging such an interview is to
    A. keep the witness cooperative
    B. conduct the matter in secret
    C. allow the witness to determine where and when the interview takes place
    D. conduct the interview as soon as possible to insure a strong case

17. Assume that an investigative unit has received a complex task requiring team work.
Of the following, the one which is LEAST essential to the operations of a team effort is
    A. a small group
    B. a leader
    C. regular interaction between team members
    D. separate office space for each team member

18. By examining a candidate's employment record, an investigator can determine many things about the candidate.
Of the following, the one which is LEAST apparent from an employment record is the candidate's
    A. character
    B. willingness to work
    C. capacity to get along with co-workers
    D. potential for advancing in civil service

19. Assume that you, an investigator, are conducting an investigative interview in which the person being interviewed is using the interview as a forum for venting his anti-civil service feelings.
Of the following, the FIRST thing that you should do is to
    A. agree with the person; perhaps that will shorten the outburst
    B. respectfully disagree with the person; the decorum of the interview has already been disrupted
    C. courteously and objectively direct the interview to the relevant issue
    D. reschedule the interview to another mutually agreeable time

20. The pattern of an investigative interview is LARGELY set by the 20.____
    A. person being interviewed
    B. person conducting the interview
    C. nature of the investigation
    D. policy of the agency employing the interviewer

21. Assume that a person being interviewed, who had been talking freely, suddenly 21.____
    tries to change the subject.
    To a trained interviewer, this behavior would mean that the person PROBABLY
    A. knew very little about the subject
    B. realized that he was telling too much
    C. decided that his privacy was being violated
    D. realized that he was becoming confused

22. Assume that you, an investigator, receive a telephone call from an unknown 22.____
    individual requesting information about a case you are currently investigating.
    In such a situation, the BEST course of action for you to take is to
    A. give him the information over the telephone
    B. tell him to write to your department for the information
    C. send him the information, retaining a copy for your files
    D. tell him to call back, giving you additional time to check into the matter

23. Assume that you, an investigator, are responding to a written query from a 23.____
    member of the public protesting a certain procedure employed by your agency.
    In such a case, your response should stress MOST the
    A. difficulty that a large agency encounters in trying to treat all members of
       the public fairly
    B. idea that the procedure in question will be discontinued if enough
       complaints are received
    C. necessity for the procedure
    D. origin of the procedure

Questions 24-25.

DIRECTIONS: Questions 24 and 25 are to be answered in the light of the information given in
             the following passage.

Assume that a certain agency is having a problem at one of its work locations because a sizable portion of the staff at that location is regularly tardy in reporting to work. The management of the agency is primarily concerned about eliminating the problem and is not yet too concerned about taking any disciplinary action. You are an investigator working for this agency, and though you have never had any contact with this location, you are assigned to investigate to determine, if possible, what might be causing this problem.

After several interviews, you see that low morale created by poor supervision at this location is at least part of the problem. Then, the last person you will interview before submitting your report tells you, when asked the reason for his tardiness, "*Well, I don't know; I just can't get up in the morning. So when I do get going, I've got to rush to get here. And just between you and me, I've lost interest in the job. Working conditions are bad, and it's hard for me to be enthusiastic about working here."*

24. Given the goals of the investigation and assuming that the investor was using a non-directive approach in this interview, of the following, the investigator's MOST effective response should be:
    A. "You know, you are building a bad record of tardiness."
    B. "Can you tell me more about this situation?"
    C. "What kind of person is your superior?"
    D. "Do you think you are acting fairly towards the agency by being late so often?"

25. Given the goals of the investigation and assuming the investigator was using a directed approach in this interview, of the following, the investigator's response should be
    A. "That doesn't seem like much of an excuse to me."
    B. "What do you mean by saying that you've lost interest?"
    C. What problems are there with the supervision you are getting?"
    D. "How do you think your tardiness looks in your personnel record?"

KEY (CORRECT ANSWERS)

1.	C		11.	D
2.	D		12.	B
3.	D		13.	B
4.	C		14.	C
5.	B		15.	C
6.	D		16.	A
7.	A		17.	D
8.	B		18.	D
9.	A		19.	C
10.	D		20.	B

21.	B
22.	B
23.	C
24.	B
25.	C

EXAMINATION SECTION
TEST 1

DIRECTIONS: Each question or incomplete statement is followed by several suggested answers or completions. Select the one that BEST answers the question or completes the statement. *PRINT THE LETTER OF THE CORRECT ANSWER IN THE SPACE AT THE RIGHT.*

1. An investigator uses Forms A, B, and C in filling out his investigation reports. He uses Form B five times as often as Form A, and he uses Form C three times as often as Form B.
   If the total number of all forms used by the investigator in a month equal 735, how many times was Form B used?
   A. 150 B. 175 C. 205 D. 235

   1._____

2. Of all the investigators in one agency, 25% work in a particular building. Of these, 12% have desks on the 14th floor.
   What percentage of the investigators work in this building but do NOT have desks on the 14th floor?
   A. 12% B. 13% C. 22% D. 23%

   2._____

3. An investigator is given two reports to read. Report P is 160 pages long and takes the investigator 3 hours and 20 minutes to read.
   If Report S is 254 pages long and the investigator reads it at the same rate as he reads Report P, how long will it take him to read Report S? _____ hours _____ minutes.
   A. 4; 15 B. 4; 50 C. 5; 10 D. 5; 30

   3._____

4. A team of 6 investigators was assigned to interview 234 people.
   If half the investigators conduct twice as many interviews as the other half, and the slow group interviews 12 persons a day, how many days would it take to complete this assignment? _____ days.
   A. 4½ B. 5 C. 6 D. 6½

   4._____

5. The investigators in one agency conduct an average of 12 interviews an hour from 10 A.M. to 12 noon and from 1 P.M. to 5 P.M. daily. The director of his agency knows from past experience that 20% of those called in to be interviewed are unable to keep the appointments that were scheduled.
   If the director wants his staff to be kept occupied with interviews for the entire time period that has been set aside for this function, how many appointments should be scheduled for each day?
   A. 86 B. 90 C. 96 D. 101

   5._____

6. An investigator has a 430-page report to read. The first day, he is able to read 20 pages. The second day, he reads 10 pages more than the first day, and the third day, he reads 15 pages more than the second day.

   6._____

43

If, on the following days, he continues to read at the same rate as he was reading on the third day, he will complete the report on the _____ day.
A. 7th   B. 8th   C. 10th   D. 11th

7. The 36 investigators in an agency are each required to submit 25 investigation reports a week. These reports are filled out on a certain form, and only one copy of the form is needed per report.
Allowing 20% for waste, how many packages of 45 forms a piece should be ordered for each weekly period?
A. 15   B. 20   C. 25   D. 30

7.____

8. During the fiscal year, an investigative unit received $260 for stationery and telephone expenditures. It spent 43% for stationery and 1/3 of the balance for telephone service.
The amount of money that was left at the end of the fiscal year was MOST NEARLY
A. $49   B. $50   C. $99   D. $109

8.____

Questions 9-10.

DIRECTIONS: Questions 9 and 10 are to be answered SOLELY on the data given below.

Number of days absent per worker (sickness)	1	2	3	4	5	6	7	8 or Over
Number of Workers	96	45	16	3	1	0	1	0

Total Number of Workers: 500

9. The TOTAL number of man days lost due to illness in 2020 was
A. 137   B. 154   C. 162   D. 258

9.____

10. Of the 500 workers studied, the number who lost NO days due to sickness in 2020 was
A. 230   B. 298   C. 338   D. 372

10.____

Questions 11-13.

DIRECTIONS: Questions 11 through 13 are to be answered SOLELY on the basis of the following passage.

The rise of urban-industrial society has complicated the social arrangements needed to regulate contacts between people. As a consequence, there has been an unprecedented increase in the volume of laws and regulations designed to control individual conduct and to govern the relationship of the individual to others. In a century, there has been an eight-fold increase in the crimes for which one may be prosecuted.

For these offenses, the courts have the ultimate responsibility for redressing wrongs and convicting the guilty. The body of legal precepts gives the impression of an abstract and evenhanded dispensation of justice. Actually, the personnel of the agencies applying these precepts are faced with the difficulties of fitting abstract principles to highly variable situations emerging from the dynamics of everyday life. It is inevitable that discrepancies should exist between precept and practice.

The legal institutions serve as a framework for the social order by their slowness to respond to the caprices of transitory fad. This valuable contribution exacts a price in terms of the inflexibility of legal institutions in responding to new circumstances. This possibility is promoted by the changes in values and norms of the dynamic larger culture of which the legal precepts are a part.

11. According to the above passage, the increase in the number of laws and regulations during the twentieth century can be attributed to the
    A. complexity of modern industrial society
    B. increased seriousness of offenses committed
    C. growth of individualism
    D. anonymity of urban living

11.____

12. According to the above passage, which of the following presents a problem to the staff of legal agencies? The
    A. need to eliminate the discrepancy between precept and practice
    B. necessity to apply abstract legal precepts to rapidly changing conditions
    C. responsibility for reducing the number of abstract legal principles
    D. responsibility for understanding offenses in terms of the real-life situations from which they emerge

12.____

13. According to the above passage, it can be concluded that legal institutions affect social institutions by
    A. preventing change
    B. keeping pace with its norms and values
    C. changing its norms and values
    D. providing stability

13.____

Questions 14-16.

DIRECTIONS: Questions 14 through 16 are to be answered SOLELY on the basis of information given in the following passage.

A personnel interviewer, selecting job applicants, may find that he reacts badly to some people even on first contact. This reaction cannot usually be explained by things that the interviewee has done or said. Most of us have had the experience of liking or disliking, of feeling comfortable and uncomfortable with people on first acquaintance, long before we have had a chance to make a conscious, rational decision about them. Often, too, our liking or disliking is transmitted to the other person by subtle processes such as gestures, posture, voice intonations, or choice of words. The point to be kept in mind is this: the relations between people are complex and occur at several levels, from the conscious to the unconscious. This is true whether the relationship is brief or long, formal or informal.

Some of the major dynamics of personality which operate on the unconscious level are projection, sublimation, rationalization, and repression. Encountering these for the first time, one is apt to think of them as representing pathological states. In the extreme, they undoubtedly are, but they exist so universally that we must consider them also to be parts of normal personality.

Without necessarily subscribing to any of the numerous theories of personality, it is possible to describe personality in terms of certain important aspects or elements. We are all aware of ourselves as thinking organisms.

This aspect of personality, the conscious part, is important for understanding human behavior, but it is not enough. Many find it hard to accept the notion that each person also has an unconscious. The existence of the unconscious is no longer a matter of debate. It is not possible to estimate at all precisely what proportion of our total psychological life is conscious, what proportion unconscious. Everyone who has studied the problem, however, agrees that consciousness is the smaller part of personality. Most of what we are and do is a result of unconscious processes. To ignore this is to risk mistakes.

14. The above passage suggests that an interviewer can be MOST effective if he
    A. learns how to determine other peoples' unconscious motivations
    B. learns how to repress his own unconsciously motivated mannerisms and behavior
    C. can keep others from feeling that he either likes or dislikes them
    D. gains an understanding of how the unconscious operates in himself and in others

15. It may be inferred from the above passage that the *subtle processes*, such as gestures, posture, voice intonation, or choice of words referred to in the first paragraph are USUALLY
    A. in the complete control of an expert investigator
    B. the determining factors in the friendships a person establishes
    C. controlled by a person's unconscious
    D. not capable of being consciously controlled

16. The above passage implies that various different personality theories are USUALLY
    A. so numerous and different as to be valueless to an investigator
    B. in basic agreement about the importance of the unconscious
    C. understood by the investigator who strives to be effective
    D. in agreement that personality factors such as projection and repression are pathological

Questions 17-19.

DIRECTIONS: Questions 17 through 19 are to be answered SOLELY on the basis of information contained in the following passage.

No matter how well the interrogator adjusts himself to the witness and how precisely he induces the witness to describe his observations, mistakes still can be made. The mistakes made by an experienced interrogator may be comparatively few, but as far as the witness is concerned, his path is full of pitfalls. Modern "witness psychology" has shown that even the most honest and trustworthy witnesses are apt to make grave mistakes in good faith. It is, therefore, necessary that the interrogator get an idea of the weak links in the testimony in order to check up on them in the event that something appears to be strange or not quite satisfactory.

Unfortunately, modern witness psychology does not yet offer any means of directly testing the credibility of testimony. It lacks precision and method, in spite of worthwhile attempts on the part of learned men. At the same time, witness psychology, through the gathering of many experience concerning the weaknesses of human testimony, has been of invaluable service. It shows clearly that only evidence of a technical nature has absolute value as proof.

Testimony may be separated into the following stages: (1) perception; (2) observation; (3) mind fixation of the observed occurrences, in which fantasy, association of ideas, and personal judgment participate; (4) expression in oral or written form, where the testimony is transferred from one witness to another or to the interrogator. Each of these stages offers innumerable possibilities for the distortion of testimony.

17. The above passage indicates that having witnesses talk to each other before testifying is a practice which is GENERALLY
    A. *desirable*, since the witnesses will be able to correct each other's errors in observation before testimony
    B. *undesirable*, since the witnesses will collaborate on one story to tell the investigator
    C. *undesirable*, since one witness may distort his testimony because of what another witness may erroneously say
    D. *desirable*, since witnesses will become aware of discrepancies in their own testimony and can point out the discrepancies to the investigator

18. According to the above passage, the one of the following which would be the MOST reliable for use as evidence would be the testimony of a
    A. handwriting expert about a signature on a forged check
    B. trained police officer about the identity of a criminal
    C. laboratory technician about an accident he has observed
    D. psychologist who has interviewed any witness who relate conflicting stories

19. Concerning the validity of evidence, it is clear from the above passage that
    A. only evidence of a technical nature is at all valuable
    B. the testimony of witnesses is so flawed that it is usually valueless
    C. an investigator, by knowing modern witness psychology, will usually be able to perceive mistaken testimony
    D. an investigator ought to expect mistakes in even the most reliable witness testimony

Questions 20-21.

DIRECTIONS: Questions 20 and 21 are to be answered SOLELY on the basis of information given in the following passage.

Since we generally assure informants that what they say is confidential, we are not free to tell one informant what the other has told us. Even if the informant says, "*I don't care who knows it; tell anybody you want to,*" we find it wise to treat the interview as confidential. An interviewer who relates to some informants what other informants have told him is likely to stir up anxiety and suspicion. Of course, the interviewer may be able to tell an informant what he has heard without revealing the source of his information. This may be perfectly appropriate where a story has wide currency so that an informant cannot infer the source of the information. But if an event is not widely known, the mere mention of it may reveal to one informant what another informant has said about the situation. How can the data be cross-checked in these circumstances.

20. The above passage IMPLIES that the anxiety and suspicion an interviewer may arouse by telling what has been learned in other interviews is due to the
    A. lack of trust the person interviewed may have in the interviewer's honesty
    B. troublesome nature of the material which the interviewer has learned in other interviews
    C. fact that the person interviewed may not believe that permission was given to repeat the information
    D. fear of the person interviewed that what he is telling the interviewer will be repeated

20.____

21. The above passage is MOST likely part of a longer passage dealing with
    A. ways to verify data gathered in interviews
    B. the various anxieties a person being interviewed may feel
    C. the notion that people sometimes say things they do not mean
    D. ways an interview can avoid seeming suspicious

21.____

Questions 22-23.

DIRECTIONS: Questions 22 and 23 are to be answered SOLELY on the basis of information given below.

The ability to interview rests not on any single trait, but on a vast complex of them. Habits, skills, techniques, and attitudes are all involved. Competence in interviewing is acquired only after careful and diligent study, prolonged practice (preferably under supervision), and a good bit of trial and error; for interviewing is not an exact science; it is an art. Like many other arts, however, it can and must draw on science in several of its aspects.

There is always a place for individual initiative, for imaginative innovations, and for new combinations of old approaches. The skilled interviewer cannot be bound by a set of rules. Likewise, there is not a set of rules which can guarantee to the novice that his interviewing will be successful. There are, however, some accepted, general guideposts which may help the beginner to avoid mistakes, learn how to conserve this efforts, and establish effective working relationships with interviewees; to accomplish, in short, what he sets out to do.

22. According to the above passage, rules and standard techniques for interviewing are 22.____
    A. helpful for the beginner, but useless for the experienced, innovative interviewer
    B. destructive of the innovation and initiative needed for a good interviewer
    C. useful for even the experienced interviewer who may, however, sometimes go beyond them
    D. the means by which nearly anybody can become an effective interviewer

23. According to the above passage, the one of the following which is a prerequisite to competent interviewing is 23.____
    A. avoid mistakes
    B. study and practice
    C. imaginative innovation
    D. natural aptitude

Questions 24-27.

DIRECTIONS: Questions 24 through 27 are to be answered SOLELY on the basis of information given in the following passage.

The question of what material is relevant is not as simple as it might seem. Frequently, material which seems irrelevant to the inexperienced has, because of the common tendency to disguise and distort and misplace one's feelings, considerable significance. It may be necessary to let the client "ramble on" for a while in order to clear the decks, as it were, so that he may get down to things that really are on his mind. On the other hand, with an already disturbed person, it may be important for the interviewer to know when to discourage further elaboration of upsetting material. This is especially the case where the worker would be unable to do anything about it. An inexperienced interviewer might, for instance, be intrigued with the bizarre elaboration of material that the psychotic produces, but further elaboration of this might encourage the client in his instability. A too random discussion may indicate that the interviewee is not certain in what areas the interviewer is prepared to help him, and he may be seeking some direction. Or again, satisfying though it may be for the interviewer to have the interviewee tell him intimate details, such revelations sometimes need to be checked or encouraged only in small doses. An interviewee who has "talked too much" often reveals subsequent anxiety. This is illustrated by the fact that frequently after a "confessional" interview, the interviewee surprises the interviewer by being withdrawn, inarticulate, or hostile, or by breaking the next appointment.

24. Sometimes a client may reveal certain personal information to an interviewer and subsequently may feel anxious about this revelation. 24.____
    If, during an interview, a client begins to discuss very personal matters, it would be BEST to
    A. tell the client, in no uncertain terms, that you're not interested in personal details
    B. ignore the client at this point
    C. encourage the client to elaborate further on the details
    D. inform the client that the information seems to be very personal

25. The author indicates that clients with severe psychological disturbances pose an especially difficult problem for the inexperienced interviewer. The difficulty lies in the possibility of the client
    A. becoming physically violent and harming the interviewer
    B. rambling on for a while
    C. revealing irrelevant details which may be followed by cancelled appointments
    D. reverting to an unstable state as a result of interview material

26. An interviewer should be constantly alert to the possibility of obtaining clues from the client as to the problem areas.
    According to the above passage, a client who discusses topics at random may be
    A. unsure of what problems the interviewer can provide help with
    B. reluctant to discuss intimate details
    C. trying to impress the interviewer with his knowledge
    D. deciding what relevant material to elaborate on

27. The evaluation of a client's responses may reveal substantial information that may aid the interviewer in assessing the problem areas that are of concern to the client. Responses that seemed irrelevant at the time of the interview may be of significance because
    A. considerable significance is attached to all relevant material
    B. emotional feelings are frequently masked
    C. an initial *rambling on* is often a prelude to what is actually bothering the client
    D. disturbed clients often reveal subsequent anxiety

Questions 28-30.

DIRECTIONS: Questions 28 through 30 are to be answered SOLELY on the basis of the following passage.

The physical setting of the interview may determine its entire potentiality. Some degree of privacy and a comfortable relaxed atmosphere are important. The interviewee is not encouraged to give much more than his name and address if the interviewer seems busy with other things, if people are rushing about, if there are distracting noises. He has a right to feel that, whether the interview lasts five minutes or an hour, he has, for that time, the undivided attention of the interviewer. Interruptions, telephone calls, and so on, should be reduced to a minimum. If the interviewee has waited in a crowded room for what seems to him an interminably long period, he is naturally in mood to sit down and discuss what is on his mind. Indeed, by that time, the primary thing on his mind may be his irritation at being kept waiting, and he frequently feels it would be impolite to express this. If a wait or interruptions have been unavoidable, it is always helpful to give the client some recognition that these are disturbing and that we can naturally understand that they make it more difficult for him to proceed. At the same time, if he protests that they have not troubled him, the interviewer can best accept his statements at their face value, as further insistence that they must have been disturbing may be interpreted by him as accusing, and he may conclude that the interviewer has been personally hurt by his irritation.

28. Distraction during an interview may tend to limit the client's responses. In a case where an interruption has occurred, it would be BEST for the investigator to
    A. terminate this interview and have it rescheduled for another time period
    B. ignore the interruption since it is not continuous
    C. express his understanding that the distraction can cause the client to feel disturbed
    D. accept the client's protests that he has been troubled by the interruption

29. To maximize the rapport that can be established with the client, an appropriate physical setting is necessary. At the very least, some privacy would be necessary.
    In addition, the interviewer should
    A. always appear to be busy in order to impress the client
    B. focus his attention only on the client
    C. accept all the client's statements as being valid
    D. stress the importance of the interview to the client

30. Clients who have been waiting quite some time for their interview may, justifiably, become upset.
    However, a client may initially attempt to mask these feelings because he may
    A. personally hurt the interviewer
    B. want to be civil
    C. feel that the wait was unavoidable
    D. fear the consequences of his statement

KEY (CORRECT ANSWERS)

1.	B	11.	A	21.	A
2.	C	12.	B	22.	C
3.	D	13.	D	23.	B
4.	D	14.	D	24.	D
5.	B	15.	C	25.	D
6.	D	16.	B	26.	A
7.	C	17.	C	27.	B
8.	C	18.	A	28.	C
9.	D	19.	D	29.	B
10.	C	20.	D	30.	B

TEST 2

DIRECTIONS: Each question or incomplete statement is followed by several suggested answers or completions. Select the one that BEST answers the question or completes the statement. *PRINT THE LETTER OF THE CORRECT ANSWER IN THE SPACE AT THE RIGHT.*

Questions 1-5.

DIRECTIONS: In Questions 1 through 5, choose the statement which is BEST from the point of view of English usage suitable for a business report.

1. A. The client's receiving of public assistance checks at two different addresses were disclosed by the investigation.
   B. The investigation disclosed that the client was receiving public assistance checks at two different addresses.
   C. The client was found out by the investigator to be receiving public assistance checks at two different addresses.
   D. The client has been receiving public assistance checks at two different addresses, disclosed the investigation

   1.____

2. A. The investigation of complaints are usually handled by this unit, which deals with internal security problems in the department.
   B. This unit deals with internal security problems in the department; usually investigating complaints.
   C. Investigating complaints is this unit's job, being that it handles internal security problems in the department
   D. This unit deals with internal security problems in the department and usually investigates complaints.

   2.____

3. A. The delay in completing this investigation was caused by difficulty in obtaining the required documents from the candidate.
   B. Because of difficulty in obtaining the required documents from the candidate is the reason that there was a delay in completing this investigation.
   C. Having had difficulty in obtaining the required documents from the candidate, there was a delay in completing this investigation.
   D. Difficulty in obtaining the required documents from the candidate had the affect of delaying the completion of this investigation.

   3.____

4. A. This report, together with documents supporting our recommendation, are being submitted for your approval.
   B. Documents supporting our recommendation is being submitted with the report for your approval.
   C. This report, together with documents supporting our documentation, is being submitted for your approval.
   D. The report and documents supporting our recommendation is being submitted for your approval.

   4.____

5. A. Several people were interviewed and numerous letters were sent before this case was completed.
    B. Completing this case, interviewing several people and sending numerous letters were necessary.
    C. To complete this case needed interviewing several people and sending numerous letters.
    D. Interviewing several people and sending numerous letters was necessary to complete the case.

Questions 6-20.

DIRECTIONS: For each of the sentences numbered 6 to 20, select from the options given below the MOST applicable choice, and mark your answer accordingly.
   A. The sentence is correct.
   B. The sentence contains a spelling error only.
   C. The sentence contains an English grammar error only.
   D. The sentence contains both a spelling error and an English grammar error.

6. He is a very dependible person whom we expect will be an asset to this division.

7. An investigator often finds it necessary to be very diplomatic when conducting an interview.

8. Accurate detail is especially important if court action results from an investigation.

9. The report was signed by him and I since we conducted the investigation jointly.

10. Upon receipt of the complaint, an inquiry was begun.

11. An employee has to organize his time so that he can handle his workload efficiantly.

12. It was not apparent that anyone was living at the address given by the client.

13. According to regulations, there is to be at least three attempts made to locate the client.

14. Neither the inmate nor the correction officer was willing to sign a formal statement.

15. It is our opinion that one of the persons interviewed were lying.

16. We interviewed both clients and departmental personel in the course of this investigation.

17. It is concievable that further research might produce additional evidence.

18. There are too many occurences of this nature to ignore.

19. We cannot accede to the candidate's request. 19.____

20. The submission of overdue reports is the reason that there was a delay in completion of this investigation. 20.____

Questions 21-2.

DIRECTIONS: Each of Questions 21 through 25 consists of three sentences lettered A, B, and C. In each of these questions, one of the sentences may contain an error in grammar, sentence structure, or punctuation, or all three sentences may be correct. If one of the sentences in a question contains an error in grammar, sentence structure, or punctuation, print in the space at the right the capital letter preceding the sentence which contains the error. If all three sentences are correct, print the letter D.

21. A. Mr. Smith appears to be less competent than I in performing these duties. 21.____
    B. The supervisor spoke to the employee, who had made the error, but did not reprimand him.
    C. When he found the book lying on the table, he immediately notified the owner.

22. A. Being locked in the desk, we were certain that the papers would not be taken. 22.____
    B. It wasn't I who dictated the telegram; I believe it was Eleanor.
    C. You should interview whoever comes to the office today.

23. A. The clerk was instructed to set the machine on the table before summoning the manager. 23.____
    B. He said that he was not familiar with those kind of activities.
    C. A box of pencils, in addition to erasers and blotters, was included in the shipment.

24. A. The supervisor remarked, "Assigning an employee to the proper type of work is not always easy." 24.____
    B. The employer found that each of the applicants were qualified to perform the duties of the position.
    C. Any competent student is permitted to take this course if he obtains the consent of the instructor.

25. A. The prize was awarded to the employee whom the judges believed to be most deserving. 25.____
    B. Since the instructor believes this book is the better of the two, he is recommending it for use in the school.
    C. It was obvious to the employees that the completion of the task by the scheduled date would require their working overtime.

KEY (CORRECT ANSWERS)

1.	B	11.	B
2.	D	12.	B
3.	A	13.	C
4.	C	14.	A
5.	A	15.	C
6.	D	16.	B
7.	A	17.	B
8.	A	18.	B
9.	C	19.	A
10.	A	20.	C

21. B
22. A
23. B
24. B
25. D

READING COMPREHENSION
UNDERSTANDING AND INTERPRETING WRITTEN MATERIAL
EXAMINATION SECTION
TEST 1

DIRECTIONS: Each question or incomplete statement is followed by several suggested answers or completions. Select the one that BEST answers the question or completes the statement. *PRINT THE LETTER OF THE CORRECT ANSWER IN THE SPACE AT THE RIGHT.*

Questions 1-4.

DIRECTIONS: Questions 1 through 4 are to be answered SOLELY on the basis of the information in the following paragraphs.

Some authorities have questioned whether the term *culture of poverty* should be used since *culture* means a design for living which is passed down from generation to generation. The culture of poverty is, however, a very useful concept if it is used with care, with recognition that poverty is a subculture, and with avoidance of the *cookie-cutter* approached. With regard to the individual, the cookie-cutter view assumes that all individuals in a culture turn out exactly alike, as if they were so many cookies. It overlooks the fact that, at least in our urban society, every individual is a member of more than one subculture; and which subculture most strongly influences his response in a given situation depends on the interaction of a great many factors, including his individual make-up and history, the specifics of the various subcultures to which he belongs, and the specifics of the given situation. It is always important to avoid the cookie-cutter view of culture, with regard to the individual and to the culture or subculture involved.

With regard to the culture as a whole, the cookie-cutter concept again assumes homogeneity and consistency. It forgets that within any one culture or subculture there are conflicts and contradictions, and that at any given moment an individual may have to choose, consciously, between conflicting values or patterns. Also, most individuals, in varying degrees, have a dual set of values—those by which they live and those they cherish as best. This point has been made and documented repeatedly about the culture of poverty.

1. The *cookie-cutter* approach assumes that
   A. members of the same *culture* are all alike
   B. *culture* stays the same from generation to generation
   C. the term *culture* should not be applied to groups who are poor
   D. there are value conflicts within most *cultures*

2. According to the above passage, every person in our cities
   A. is involved in the conflicts of urban culture
   B. recognizes that poverty is a subculture
   C. lives by those values too which he is exposed
   D. belongs to more than one subculture

3. The above passage emphasizes that a culture is likely to contain within it
   A. one dominant set of values
   B. a number of contradictions
   C. one subculture to which everyone belongs
   D. members who are exactly alike

4. According to the above passage, individuals are sometimes forced to choose BETWEEN
   A. cultures
   B. subcultures
   C. different sets of values
   D. a new culture and an old culture

Questions 5-8.

DIRECTIONS: Questions 5 through 8 are to be answered SOLELY on the basis of the following passage.

There are approximately 33 million poor people in the United States; 14.3 million of them are children, 5.3 million are old people, and the remainder are in other categories. Altogether, 6.5 million families live in poverty because the head of household cannot work; they are either too old or too sick or too severely handicapped, or they are widowed or deserted mothers of young children. There are the working poor: the low-paid workers, the workers in seasonal industries, and soldiers with no additional income who are heads of families. There are the underemployed: those who would like full-time jobs but cannot find them, those employees who would like year-round work but lack of opportunity, and those who are employed below their level of training. There are the non-working poor: the older men and women with small retirement incomes and those with no income, the disabled, the physically and mentally handicapped, and the chronically sick.

5. According to the above passage, approximately what percent of the poor people in the United States are children?
   A. 33   B. 16   C. 20   D. 44

6. According to the above passage, people who work in seasonal industries are LIKELY to be classified as
   A. working poor
   B. underemployed
   C. non-working poor
   D. low-paid workers

7. According to the above passage, the category of non-working poor includes people who
   A. receive unemployment insurance
   B. cannot find full-time work
   C. are disabled or mentally handicapped
   D. are soldiers with wives and children

8. According to the above passage, among the underemployed are those who
   A. can find only part-time work
   B. are looking for their first jobs
   C. are inadequately trained
   D. depend on insufficient retirement incomes

Questions 9-13.

DIRECTIONS: Read the Inter-office Memo below. Then, answer Questions 9 through 13 SOLELY on the basis of the memo.

INTER-OFFICE MEMORANDUM

To: Alma Robinson, Human Resources Aide

From: Frank Shields, Social Worker

I would like to have you help Mr. Edward Tunney, who is trying to raise his two children by himself. He needs to learn to improve the physical care of his children and especially of his daughter Helen, age 9. She is avoided and ridiculed at school because her hair is uncombed, her teeth not properly cleaned, her clothing torn, wrinkled and dirty, as well as shabby and poorly fitted. The teachers and school officials have contacted the Department and the social worker for two years about Helen. She is not able to make friends because of these problems. I have talked to Mr. Tunney about improvements for the child's clothing, hair, and hygiene. He tends to deny these things are problems, but is cooperative, and a second person showing him the importance of better physical care for Helen would be helpful.

Perhaps you could teach Helen how to fix her own hair. She has all the materials. I would also like you to form your own opinion of the sanitary conditions in the home and how they could be improved.

Mr. Tunney is expecting your visit and is willing to talk with you about ways he can help with these problems.

9. In the above memorandum, the Human Resources Aide is being asked to help Mr. Tunney to
    A. improve the learning habits of his children
    B. enable his children to make friends at school
    C. take responsibility for the upbringing of his children
    D. give attention to the grooming and cleanliness of his children

10. This case was brought to the attention of the social worker by
    A. government officials
    B. teachers and school officials
    C. the Department
    D. Mr. Tunney

11. In general, Mr. Tunney's attitude with regard to his children could BEST be described as
    A. interested in correcting the obvious problem, but unable to do so alone
    B. unwilling to follow the advice of those who are trying to help
    C. concerned but unaware of the seriousness of these problems
    D. interested in helping them, but afraid of taking the advice of the social worker

12. Which of the following actions has NOT been suggested as a possible step for the Human Resource Aide to take?
    A. Help Helen to learn to care for herself by teaching her grooming skills
    B. Determine was of improvement gathered on a home visit
    C. Discuss her own views on Helen's problems with school officials
    D. Ask Mr. Tunney in what ways he believes the physical care may be improved

13. According to the above memo, the Human Resources Aide is ESPECIALLY being asked to observe and form her own opinions about
    A. the relationship between Mr. Tunney and the school officials
    B. Helen's attitude toward her classmates and teacher
    C. the sanitary conditions in the home
    D. the reasons Mr. Tunney is not cooperative with the agency

Questions 14-16.

DIRECTIONS: Questions 14 through 16 are to be answered SOLELY on the basis of the following paragraph.

In social work, professional responsibility and accountability extend to a larger segment of the general community than is true of the older professions which have more limited and more specialized areas of community responsibility and public trust. Advances in knowledge about both the nature of human institutions and the nature of the individual have placed social work in the center of a vast complex of interrelationships. The situations that come to the attention of the social worker, whatever his functions, may be the circumstances of an individual client or of a group or of a community which may or may not be socially sanctioned, and the proposed remedy may be considered desirable or questionable. When there is agreement between the client group and the community on the nature of the problem and on the validity of the proposed remedy, such agreement may lead to the establishment of social institutions. Complication arise when the client or client group, or the community, does not accept the need for change or is not in agreement with the social worker about the direction it should take. The social worker has the obligation to pursue his objective regardless of the difficulties. Even if social work, as it is practiced today, were to achieve the degree of acceptance afforded the older professions, it would still find itself, with every new development, holding unorthodox and not very respectful views on many aspects of personal and social relationships.

14. The MOST accurate of the following statements about the relationship between social work and the other professions is:
    A. Advances in knowledge have placed social work in a central position among the professions
    B. Although younger, social work has become basic to the older professions in their responsibility and accountability in the community
    C. It is the responsibility of social workers to hold unorthodox views on social relationships
    D. The areas of responsibility of social work within the community are more extensive than those of the older professions

15. When, because of an existing problem, a social worker has advocated a change in a social institution which has been opposed by the community, the social worker should

    A. attempt to surmount the opposition, continuing to seek to reach his objective
    B. change his position to gain the support of the community
    C. review the position that he has taken to see whether he cannot revise his objective to the point where it may gain community support
    D. work to achieve for his profession the degree of acceptance which is afforded the older professions

15.____

16. Of the following, the BEST title for the above paragraph is

    A. DANGERS OF SOCIAL RESPONSIBILITY
    B. SOCIAL WORK AND THE OLDER PROFESSION COMPARED
    C. SOCIAL WORKERS' RESPONSIBILITY IN SOCIAL CHANGE
    D. UNORTHODOX SOCIAL WORK

16.____

Questions 17-19.

DIRECTIONS: Questions 17 through 19 are to be answered SOLELY on the basis of the following paragraphs.

Toward the end of the 19th century, as social work principles and theories took form, areas of conflict between the responsibility of the social worker to the client group and to the status quo of social and economic institutions became highlighted. The lay public's attitude toward the individual poor was one of emphasis on betterment through the development of the individual's capacity for self-maintenance. They hoped to maintain this end both by helping the client to rely on his unused capacities for self-help and by facilitating is access to what were assumed to be the natural sources of help family, relatives, churches, and other charitable associations. Professional social workers were fast becoming aware of the need for social reform. They perceived that traditional methods of help were largely inadequate to cope with the factors that were creating poverty and maladjustment for a large number of the population faster than the charity societies could relieve such problems through individual effort. The critical view, held by social workers, of the character of many social institutions was not shared by other groups in the community who had not reached the same point of awareness about the deficiencies in the functioning of these institutions. Thus, the views of the social worker were beginning to differ, sometimes radically, from the basic views of large sections of the population.

17. The social workers of the late 19th century found themselves in conflict with the status quo CHIEFLY because they

    A. had become professionalized through the development of a body of theory and principles
    B. became aware that many social ills could not be cured through existing institutions
    C. felt that traditional methods of helping the poor must be expanded regardless of the cost to the public
    D. believed that the right of the individual to be self-determining should be emphasized

17.____

18. It was becoming apparent, by the end of the 19th century, that in relation to the needs of the poor, existing social institutions
    A. did not sufficiently emphasize the ability of the poor to utilize their natural sources of help
    B. were using the proper methods of helping the poor, but were hindered by the work of social workers who had broken with tradition
    C. were no longer capable of meeting the needs of the poor because the causes of poverty had changed
    D. were capable of meeting the needs of the poor, but needed more financial aid from the general public since the number of people in need had increased

18.____

19. Social workers at the end of the 19th century may be PROPERLY classified as
    A. growing in awareness that many social ills could be alleviated through social reform
    B. very perceptive individuals who realized that traditional methods of help were humiliating to the poor
    C. strong advocates of expanding the existing traditional sources of relief
    D. too radical because they favored easing life for the poor at the expense of increased taxation to the public at large

19.____

Questions 20-24.

DIRECTIONS: Questions 20 through 24 are to be answered SOLELY on the basis of the following paragraphs.

With the generation gap yawning before us, it is well to remember that 20 years ago teenagers produced a larger proportion of unwedlock births than today, and that the illegitimacy rate among teenagers is lower than among women in their twenties and thirties. In addition, the illegitimacy rate has risen less among teenagers than among older women.

It is helpful to note the difference between illegitimacy rate and illegitimacy ratio. The ratio is the number of illegitimate babies per 1,000 live births. The rate is the number of illegitimate births per 1,000 unmarried women of childbearing age. The ratio talks about babies; the rate talks about mothers. The ratio is useful for planning services, but worse than useless for considering trends since it depends on the age and marital composition of the population, illegitimacy rate, and the fertility of married women. For example, the ratio among girls under 18 is bound to be high in comparison with older women since few are married mothers. However, the illegitimacy rate is relatively low.

20. Of the following, the MOST suitable title for the above passage would be
    A. THE GENERATION GAP
    B. MORAL STANDARDS AND TEENAGE ILLEGITIMACY RATIO
    C. A COMPARISON OF ILLEGITIMACY RATE AND ILLEGITIMACY RATIO
    D. CAUSES OF HIGH ILLEGITIMACY RATES

20.____

21. According to the above passage, which of the following statements is CORRECT?
The illegitimacy
    A. rate has fallen among women in their thirties
    B. ratio is the number of illegitimate births per 1,000 unmarried women of childbearing age
    C. ratio is partially dependent on the illegitimacy rate
    D. rate is more useful than the ratio for planning services

22. According to the above passage, of the following age groups, the illegitimacy ratio would be expected to be HIGHEST in comparison with the other groups for the group aged
    A. 17   B. 21   C. 25   D. 29

23. According to the above passage, of the following age groups, the illegitimacy rate would be expected to be LOWEST in comparison with the other groups for the group aged
    A. 17   B. 21   C. 25   D. 29

24. As used in the above passage, the underlined word *composition* means MOST NEARLY
    A. essay   B. makeup   C. security   D. happiness

25. A document was published by a public agency and distributed for discussion. The document contained data showing trends in the level of reading among freshmen college students and suggested that the high schools were not investing enough effort in overcoming retardation. It compared the costs of intensifying reading instruction in the secondary schools as compared to costs in colleges for such instruction.
According to the above statement, it is REASONABLE to conclude that
    A. the document proposed new programs
    B. the college students read better than high school students
    C. some college students need remedial reading
    D. the study was done by a consultant

KEY (CORRECT ANSWERS)

1.	A		11.	C
2.	D		12.	C
3.	B		13.	C
4.	C		14.	D
5.	D		15.	A
6.	A		16.	C
7.	C		17.	B
8.	A		18.	C
9.	D		19.	A
10.	B		20.	C

21.	C
22.	A
23.	A
24.	B
25.	C

TEST 2

DIRECTIONS: Each question or incomplete statement is followed by several suggested answers or completions. Select the one that BEST answers the question or completes the statement. *PRINT THE LETTER OF THE CORRECT ANSWER IN THE SPACE AT THE RIGHT.*

Questions 1-4.

DIRECTIONS: Questions 1 through 4 are to be answered SOLELY on the basis of the following paragraph.

Form W-280 provides a uniform standard for estimating family expenses and is used as a basis for determining eligibility for the care of children at public expense. The extent to which legally responsible relatives can pay for the care of a child must be computed. The minimum amount of the payment required from legally responsible relatives shall be 50% of the budget surplus as computed on Form W-281, plus any governmental benefits, such as OASDI benefits, or Railroad Retirement benefits being paid to a family member for the child receiving care or services. Because of the kinds and quantities of services included in the budget schedule (W-280) and because only 50% of the budget surplus is required as payment, no allowances for special needs are made, except for verified payments into civil service pension funds, amounts paid to a garnishee, or amounts paid to another agency for the care of other relatives for whom the relative is legally responsible, or for other such expenses if approval has been granted after Form W-278 has been submitted. In determining the income of the legally responsible relative, income from wages, self-employment, unemployment insurance benefits, and any such portion of governmental benefits as is not specifically designated for children already receiving care is to be included. Should 50% of the family's surplus meet the child care expenses, the case shall not be processed. Form W-279, an agreement to support, shall be signed by the legally responsible relative when 50% of the surplus is $1.00 or more a week.

1. A family is required to sign an agreement to support
   A. whenever they are legally responsible for the support of the child under care
   B. before any care at public expense is given to the child
   C. when their income surplus is at least $2.00/week
   D. when 50% of their income surplus meets the full needs of the child

1.____

2. The reason for allowing a family to deduct only certain specified expenses when computing the amount they are able to contribute to the support of a child being cared for at public expense is that the family
   A. should not be permitted to have a higher standard of living than the child being cared for
   B. the budget schedule is sufficiently generous and includes an allowance for other unusual expenses
   C. may not be able to verify their extraordinary expenses
   D. may meet other unusual expenses from the remainder of their surplus

2.____

3. Mrs. B. wishes to have her daughter, Mary, cared for at public expense. Her income includes her wages and OASDI benefits of $250 a month, of which $50 a month is paid for Mary and $50 a month for another minor member of the family who is already being cared for at public expense.
In order to determine the amount of Mrs. B.'s budget surplus, it is necessary to consider as income her wages and
   A. $50 of OASDI received for Mary
   B. $150 of the OASDI benefits
   C. $200 of the OASDI benefits
   D. $200 of the OASDI benefits if she is legally responsible for the care of the other child in placement

4. In order to determine a family's ability to contribute to the support of a child, the worker should
   A. have the legally responsible member sign Form W-279 agreeing to support the child, and then compute the family surplus on W-281 in accordance with public assistance standards
   B. compute the family's income in accordance with the allowance included on Form W-280 and the expenses included on Form W-279 and have Form W-279 signed if necessary
   C. use Form W-278 to work out a budget schedule for the family and compute their surplus on W-281 and then have them sign W-279 if necessary
   D. compute income and expenses on Form W-281, based on Form W-280, and have Form W-279 signed if necessary

Questions 5-10.

DIRECTIONS: Questions 5 through 10 are to be answered SOLELY on the basis of the following passage.

Too often in the past, society has accepted the existing social welfare programs, preferring to tinker with refinements when fundamental reform was in order. It has been a <u>demeaning</u> degrading welfare system in which the instrument of government was wrongfully and <u>ineptly</u> used. It has been a system which has only alienated those forced to benefit from it and demoralized those who had to administer it at the level where the pain was clearly visible.

There is a need to put this nation on a course in which cash benefits, providing a basic level of support, are conferred in such a way as to intrude as little as possible into privacy and self-respect. It is difficult to define a basic level of support, no matter how high or low it might be set. In the end, however, the design is not determined so much by how much is truly adequate for a family to meet all of its needs, but by the resources available to carry out the promise. That may be a harsh fact of life but it is also just that—a fact of life

5. Of the following, the MOST suitable title for the above passage would be
   A. THE NEED FOR GOVERNMENT CONTROL OF WELFARE
   B. DETERMINING THE BASIC LEVEL OF SUPPORT
   C. THE NEED FOR WELFARE REFORM
   D. THE ELIMINATION OF WELFARE PROGRAMS

6. In the above passage, the author's GREATEST criticism of the welfare system is that it is too
   A. disrespectful of recipients
   B. expensive to administer
   C. limited by regulations
   D. widespread in application

   6._____

7. According to the above passage, the BASIC level of support is actually determined by
   A. how much is required for a family to meet all of its needs
   B. the age of the recipients
   C. how difficult it is to administer the program
   D. the economic resources of the nation

   7._____

8. In the above passage, the author does NOT argue for
   A. a work incentive system
   B. a basic level of support
   C. cash benefits
   D. the privacy of recipients

   8._____

9. As used in the above passage, the underlined word demeaning means MOST NEARLY
   A. ineffective
   B. expensive
   C. overburdened
   D. humiliating

   9._____

10. As used in the above passage, the underlined word ineptly means MOST NEARLY
    A. foolishly
    B. unsuccessfully
    C. unskillfully
    D. unhappily

    10._____

Questions 11-14.

DIRECTIONS: Questions 11 through 14 are to be answered SOLELY on the basis of the following paragraph.

The employment rate, which counts those unemployed in the sense that they are actively looking for work and unable to find it, gives a relatively superficial index of economic conditions in a community. A better index is the subemployment rate which includes the unemployment rate and also includes those working part-time while they are trying to get full-time work; those heads of households under 65 years of age who earn less than $240 per week working full-time, and those individuals under 65 who are not heads of households and earn less than $224 per week in a full-time job; and an estimate of the males *not counted*, which is a very real concern in ghetto areas.

11. Of the following, the MOST suitable title for the above paragraph would be
    A. EMPLOYMENT IN THE UNITED STATES
    B. PART-TIME WORKERS AND THE ECONOMY
    C. THE LABOR MARKET AND THE COMMUNITY
    D. TWO INDICATORS OF ECONOMIC CONDITIONS

    11._____

12. On the basis of the above paragraph, which of the following statements is CORRECT? 12.____
    A. The unemployment rate includes everyone who is not fully employed.
    B. The subemployment rate is higher than the unemployment rate.
    C. The unemployment rate gives a more complete picture of the economic situation than the subemployment rate.
    D. The subemployment rate indicates how many part-time workers are dissatisfied with the number of hours they work per week.

13. As used in the above paragraph, the underlined word superficial means MOST NEARLY 13.____
    A. exaggerated   B. official   C. surface   D. current

14. According to the above paragraph, which of the following is included in the subemployment rate? 14.____
    A. Everyone who is unemployed
    B. All part-time workers
    C. Everyone under 65 who earns less than $220 per week in a full-time job
    D. All heads of households who earn less than $240 per week in a full-time job

Questions 15-16.

DIRECTIONS: Questions 15 and 16 are to be answered SOLELY on the basis of the following paragraphs.

The city's economy has its own dynamics, and there is only so much the government can do to shape it. But that margin is critically important. If the city uses its points of leverage, it can generate a large number of jobs—and good jobs, jobs that lead to advancement.

As a major employer itself, the city can upgrade the jobs it offers and greatly improve its services to the public if it does so. Since highly skilled professionals will always be in short supply, the city must train more paraprofessionals to take over routine tasks. Equally important, it must provide them with a realistic job ladder so they can move on up—nurse's aide to certified nurse, for example, teacher's aide to teacher. The training programs for such upgrading will require a substantial public investment but the cost-benefit return should be excellent.

As a major purchaser of goods and services, the city can stimulate business enterprise in the ghetto. The growth of Blacks and Puerto Rican firms will produce more local jobs; it will also create the kind of managerial talent the ghetto needs.

New kinds of enterprise can be set up. In housing, for example, there is a huge backlog of rehabilitation work to be done and a large pool of unskilled manpower to be trained for it. Corporations can be formed to take over tenements, remodel, and operate them, as in the Brownsville Home Maintenance Program. Grocery cooperatives to bring food prices down are another possibility.

15. According to the above paragraphs, the city is the major employer and by using its capacity it can 15.____
    A. assist unskilled people with talent to move up on the job ladder
    B. create private enterprises that will renew all areas of the city in need of renewal
    C. eliminate poverty in the ghetto areas by selective purchase of goods and services
    D. have no influence on the economy of the city

16. According to the above paragraph, one may REASONABLY conclude that 16.____
    A. the city has no power to influence the job market
    B. a byproduct of strategic purchasing and employment and training practices can be the rehabilitation of housing and the lowering of food prices
    C. highly skilled professions, which are now in short supply, will no longer be needed after paraprofessionals are trained to take over routine jobs
    D. the city's major objective is to bring down food prices

Questions 17-21.

DIRECTIONS: Questions 17 through 21 are to be answered SOLELY on the basis of the following paragraphs.
For each question, there are two statements.
Based on the information in the paragraphs, mark your answer:
A. If only statement is correct;
B. If only statement 2 is correct;
C. If both statements are correct;
D. if the excerpt do not contain sufficient evidence for concluding whether either or both statements are correct.

Upstate, 35% of the AFDC families lived in districts suburban to New York City, 43% in upstate urban districts, and 22% in the rest of upstate. Among white families, 28% resided in suburban districts, 40% in upstate urban districts, and 32% in the rest of upstate. Among non-white families, 43% lived in suburban districts, 47% in upstate urban districts, and 10% in the rest of upstate.

Upstate, 78.7% of the AFDC families resided in SMSA (Standard Metropolitan Statistical Area) counties, including 68.7% of the whites and 90.4% of the non-whites. In Buffalo, 83.3% of the families were non-white; in Rochester, 57.9% were non-whites; in cities of 100,000 to 250,000 (Albany, Syracuse, and Utica), 55.2% were white; and the rest of the upstate urban counties, 86.5% were white.

The two most frequent underlying reasons for a family requiring AFDC were desertion of the father (31.3% of the cases) and *father not married to mother* (30.%). Desertions were proportionately highest among Puerto Rican families (38.6%), compared with 29.4% for Blacks and 23.6% for white families. Unmarried mothers comprised 39.4% of the Black cases, compared with 26.6% for Puerto Ricans and 14.8% for white cases.

6 (#2)

White families had substantially higher proportions in the separated and divorce categories than non-whites. When the deserted, separated, and divorced categories are combined, marital breakdown occurred in 59% of the white AFDC families, compared with 52.3% for Puerto Ricans and 44.4% for Blacks.

Substantial ethnic differences existed in the proportions of incapacitated fathers; overall, the rate was 7.5%, but among white families the rate was 14.8%, compared with 9.4% for Puerto Ricans and only 3.0% for Blacks. Families where the father was deceased comprised 5.9% of the AFDC cases.

In New York City, desertion rates (35.3% of all cases) were substantially higher than upstate (18.9%), particularly among white families, as ethnic differences in New York City diminished considerably. Unmarried mother rates closely paralleled the statewide figures.

Incapacity of the father occurred more frequently among white families upstate (17.5%) than among white families in New York City (104%). Deceased fathers were proportionately highest among the New York City Black and Puerto Rican caseload, possibly reflecting fewer remarriage and employment opportunities among these groups in the event of the death of the father.

17. 1. The most frequent underlying reason for a family requiring AFDC was *father not married to mother*. 17.____
    2. Three-fourths of New York State's AFDC families lived in New York City.

18. 1. There were more cases of desertion among AFDC cases upstate than there were of incapacity of the father among white AFDC families upstate. 18.____
    2. There was a higher percentage of marital breakdowns among white AFDC families compared to Puerto Rican for Black families.

19. 1. Desertion of the father accounted for more AFDC cases than all other reasons combined. 19.____
    2. The proportion of incapacitated fathers in Puerto Rican families was higher than the overall rate of incapacitated fathers.

20. 1. Non-white families had substantially higher proportions in the divorced and separated categories than white families. 20.____
    2. Among AFDC families in New York State, there were more Puerto Ricans than Blacks in the combined deserted, separated, and divorced categories

21. 1. In New York City, there was a higher percentage of unmarried mothers among Puerto Rican AFDC families than among white cases. 21.____
    2. Among white families, desertion rates were considerably higher upstate than in New York City.

Questions 22-25.

DIRECTIONS: Questions 22 through 25 are to be answered SOLELY on the basis of the information in the following paragraph.

The question of what material is relevant is not as simple as it might seem. Frequently, material which seems irrelevant to the inexperienced has, because of the common tendency to disguise and distort and misplace one's feelings, considerable significance. It may be necessary to let the client *ramble on* for a while in order to clear the decks, as it were, so that he may get down to things that really are on his mind. On the other hand, with an already disturbed person, it may be important for the interviewer to know when to discourage further elaboration of upsetting material. This is especially the case where the worker would be unable to do anything about it. An inexperienced interviewer might, for instance, be intrigued with the bizarre elaboration of material that the psychotic produces, but further elaboration of this might encourage the client in his instability. A too random discussion may indicate that the interviewee is not certain in what areas the interviewer is prepared to help him, and he may be seeking some direction. Or again, satisfying though it may be for the interviewer to have the interviewee tell him intimate details, such revelations sometimes need to be checked or encouraged only in small doses. An interviewee who has *talked too much* often reveals subsequent anxiety. This is illustrated by the fact that frequently after a *confessional* interview, the interviewee surprises the interviewer by being withdrawn, inarticulate, or hostile, or by breaking the next appointment.

22. Sometimes a client may reveal certain personal information to an interviewer and subsequently may feel anxious about this revelation.
    If, during an interview, a client begins to discuss very personal matters, it would be BEST to
    A. tell the client, in no uncertain terms, that you're not interested in personal details
    B. ignore the client at this point
    C. encourage the client to elaborate further on the details
    D. inform the client that the information seems to be very personal

23. The author indicates that clients with severe psychological disturbances pose an especially difficult problem for the inexperienced interviewer.
    The DIFFICULTY lies in the possibility of the client
    A. becoming physically violent and harming the interviewer
    B. rambling on for a while
    C. revealing irrelevant details which may be followed by cancelled appointments
    D. reverting to an unstable state as a result of interview material

24. An interviewer should be constantly alert to the possibility of obtaining clues from the client as to the problem areas.
    According to the above passage, a client who discusses topics at random may be
    A. unsure of what problems the interviewer can provide help
    B. reluctant to discuss intimate details
    C. trying to impress the interviewer with his knowledge
    D. deciding what relevant material to elaborate on

25. The evaluation of a client's responses may reveal substantial information that may aid the interviewer in assessing the problem areas that are of concern to the client. Responses that seemed irrelevant at the time of the interview may be of significance because
    A. considerable significance is attached to all irrelevant material
    B. emotional feelings are frequently masked
    C. an initial rambling on is often a prelude to what is actually bothering the client
    D. disturbed clients often reveal subsequent anxiety

25.____

KEY (CORRECT ANSWERS)

1.	C	11.	D
2.	D	12.	B
3.	B	13.	C
4.	D	14.	C
5.	C	15.	A
6.	A	16.	B
7.	D	17.	D
8.	A	18.	C
9.	D	19.	B
10.	C	20.	D

21.	A
22.	D
23.	D
24.	A
25.	B

PREPARING WRITTEN MATERIAL

PARAGRAPH REARRANGEMENT
COMMENTARY

The sentences that follow are in scrambled order. You are to rearrange them in proper order and indicate the letter choice containing the correct answer at the space at the right.

Each group of sentences in this section is actually a paragraph presented in scrambled order. Each sentence in the group has a place in that paragraph; no sentence is to be left out. You are to read each group of sentences and decide upon the best order in which to put the sentences so as to form a well-organized paragraph.

The questions in this section measure the ability to solve a problem when all the facts relevant to its solution are not given.

More specifically, certain positions of responsibility and authority require the employee to discover connection between events sometimes, apparently, unrelated. In order to do this, the employee will find it necessary to correctly infer that unspecified events have probably occurred or are likely to occur. This ability becomes especially important when action must be taken on incomplete information.

Accordingly, these questions require competitors to choose among several suggested alternatives, each of which presents a different sequential arrangement of the events. Competitors must choose the MOST logical of the suggested sequences.

In order to do so, they may be required to draw on general knowledge to infer missing concepts or events that are essential to sequencing the given events. Competitors should be careful to infer only what is essential to the sequence. The plausibility of the wrong alternatives will always require the inclusion of unlikely events or of additional chains of events which are NOT essential to sequencing the given events.

It's very important to remember that you are looking for the best of the four possible choices, and that the best choice of all may not even be one of the answers you're given to choose from.

There is no one right way to solve these problems. Many people have found it helpful to first write out the order of the sentences, as they would have arranged them, on their scrap paper before looking at the possible answers. If their optimum answer is there, this can save them some time. If it isn't, this method can still give insight into solving the problem. Others find it most helpful to just go through each of the possible choices, contrasting each as they go along. You should use whatever method feels comfortable and works for you.

While most of these types of questions are not that difficult, we've added a higher percentage of the difficult type, just to give you more practice. Usually there are only one or two questions on this section that contain such subtle distinctions that you're unable to answer confidently. And you then may find yourself stuck deciding between two possible choices, neither of which you're sure about.

EXAMINATION SECTION
TEST 1

DIRECTIONS: The sentences that follow are in scrambled order. You are to rearrange them in proper order and indicate the letter choice containing the correct answer. *PRINT THE LETTER OF THE CORRECT ANSWER IN THE SPACE AT THE RIGHT.*

1. Below are four statements labeled W, X, Y and Z. 1.____
   W. He was a strict and fanatic drillmaster.
   X. The word is always used in a derogatory sense and generally shows resentment and anger on the part of the user.
   Y. It is from the name of this Frenchman that we derive our English word, martinet.
   Z. Jean Martinet was the Inspector-General of Infantry during the reign of King Louis XIV.

   The PROPER order in which these sentences should be placed in a paragraph is:
   A. X, Z, W, Y   B. X, Z, Y, W   C. Z, W, Y, X   D. Z, Y, W, X

2. In the following paragraph, the sentences, which are numbered, have been jumbled. 2.____
   I. Since then it has undergone changes.
   II. It was incorporated in 1955 under the laws of the State of New York.
   III. Its primary purposes, a cleaner city, has, however, remained the same.
   IV. The Citizens Committee works in cooperation with the Mayor's Inter-departmental Committee for a Clean City.

   3.____

   The order in which these sentences should be arranged to form a well-organized paragraph is:
   A. II, IV, I, III   B. III, IV, I, II   C. IV, II, I, III   D. IV, III, II, I

Questions 3-5.

DIRECTIONS: The sentences listed below are part of a meaningful paragraph but they are not given in their proper order. You are to decide what would be the BEST order in which to put the sentences so as to form a well-organized paragraph. Each sentence has a place in the paragraph; there are no extra sentences. You are then to answer Questions 3 through 5 inclusive on the basis of your rearrangements of these scrambled sentences into a properly organized paragraph.

In 1887 some insurance companies organized an Inspection Department to advise their clients on all phases of fire prevention and protection. Probably this has been due to the smaller annual fire losses in Great Britain than in the United States. It tests various fire prevention devices and appliances and determines manufacturing hazards and their safeguards. Fire research began earlier in the United States and is more advanced than in Great Britain. Later they established a laboratory specializing in electrical, mechanical, hydraulic, and chemical fields.

75

3. When the five sentences are arranged in proper order, the paragraph starts with the sentence which begins
   A. "In 1887..."   B. "Probably this..."   C. "It tests..."
   D. "Fire research..."   E. "Later they..."

3.____

4. In the last sentence listed above, "they" refers to
   A. the insurance companies
   B. the United States and Great Britain
   C. the Inspection Department
   D. clients
   E. technicians

4.____

5. When the above paragraph is properly arranged, it ends with the words
   A. "...and protection."
   B. "...the United States."
   C. "...their safeguards."
   D. "...in Great Britain."
   E. "...chemical fields."

5.____

KEY (CORRECT ANSWERS)

1. C
2. C
3. D
4. A
5. C

TEST 2

DIRECTIONS: In each of the questions numbered I through V, several sentences are given. For each question, choose as your answer the group of number that represents the MOST logical order of these sentences if they were arranged in paragraph form. *PRINT THE LETTER OF THE CORRECT ANSWER IN THE SPACE AT THE RIGHT.*

1.
   I. It is established when one shows that the landlord has prevented the tenant's enjoyment of his interest in the property leased.
   II. Constructive eviction is the result of a breach of the covenant of quiet enjoyment implied in all leases.
   III. In some parts of the United States, it is not complete until the tenant vacates within a reasonable time.
   IV. Generally, the acts must be of such serious and permanent character as to deny the tenant the enjoyment of his possessing rights.
   V. In this event, upon abandonment of the premises, the tenant's liability for that ceases.
   The CORRECT answer is:
   A. II, I, IV, III, V
   B. V, II, III, I, IV
   C. IV, III, I, II, V
   D. I, III, V, IV, II

   1.____

2.
   I. The powerlessness before private and public authorities that is the typical experience of the slum tenant is reminiscent of the situation of blue-collar workers all through the nineteenth century.
   II. Similarly, in recent years, this chapter of history has been reopened by anti-poverty groups which have attempted to organize slum tenants to enable them to bargain collectively with their landlords about the conditions of their tenancies.
   III. It is familiar history that many of the worker remedied their condition by joining together and presenting their demands collectively.
   IV. Like the workers, tenants are forced by the conditions of modern life into substantial dependence on these who possess great political aid and economic power.
   V. What's more, the very fact of dependence coupled with an absence of education and self-confidence makes them hesitant and unable to stand up for what they need from those in power.
   The CORRECT answer is:
   A. V, IV, I, II, III
   B. II, III, I, V, IV
   C. III, I, V, IV, II
   D. I, IV, V, III, II

   2.____

3.
   I. A railroad, for example, when not acting as a common carrier may contract away responsibility for its own negligence.
   II. As to a landlord, however, no decision has been found relating to the legal effect of a clause shifting the statutory duty of repair to the tenant.
   III. The courts have not passed on the validity of clauses relieving the landlord of this duty and liability.
   IV. They have, however, upheld the validity of exculpatory clauses in other types of contracts.

   3.____

77

V. Housing regulations impose a duty upon the landlord to maintain leased premises in safe condition.
VI. As another example, a bailee may limit his liability except for gross negligence, willful acts, or fraud.

The CORRECT answer is:
A. II, I, VI, IV, III, V
B. I, III, IV, V, VI, II
C. III, V, I, IV, II, VI
D. V, III, IV, I, VI, II

4.
I. Since there are only samples in the building, retail or consumer sales are generally eschewed by mart occupants, and in some instances, rigid controls are maintained to limit entrance to the mart only to those persons engaged in retailing.
II. Since World War I, in many larger cities, there has developed a new type of property, called the mart building.
III. It can, therefore, be used by wholesalers and jobbers for the display of sample merchandise.
IV. This type of building is most frequently a multi-storied, finished interior property which is a cross between a retail arcade and a loft building.
V. This limitation enables the mart occupants to ship the orders from another location after the retailer or dealer makes his selection from the samples.

The CORRECT answer is:
A. II, IV, III, I, V
B. IV, III, V, I, II
C. I, III, II, IV, V
D. I, IV, II, III, V

5.
I. In general, staff-line friction reduces the distinctive contribution of staff personnel.
II. The conflicts, however, introduce an uncontrolled element into the managerial system.
III. On the other hand, the natural resistance of the line to staff innovations probably usefully restrains over-eager efforts to apply untested procedures on a large scale.
IV. Under such conditions, it is difficult to know when valuable ideas are being sacrificed.
V. The relatively weak position of staff, requiring accommodation to the line, tends to restrict their ability to engage in free, experimental innovation.

The CORRECT answer is:
A. IV, II, III, I, V
B. I, V, III, II, IV
C. V, III, I, II, IV
D. II, I, IV, V, III

KEY (CORRECT ANSWERS)

1. A
2. D
3. D
4. A
5. B

TEST 3

DIRECTIONS: Questions 1 through 4 consist of six sentences which can be arranged in a logical sequence. For each question, select the choice which places the numbered sentences in the MOST logical sequent. *PRINT THE LETTER OF THE CORRECT ANSWER IN THE SPACE AT THE RIGHT.*

1. I. The burden of proof as to each issue is determined before trial and remains upon the same party throughout the trial.
    II. The jury is at liberty to believe one witness' testimony as against a number of contradictory witnesses.
    III. In a civil case, the party bearing the burden of proof is required to prove his contention by a fair preponderance of the evidence.
    IV. However, it must be noted that a fair preponderance of evidence does not necessarily mean a greater number of witnesses.
    V. The burden of proof is the burden which rests upon one of the parties to an action to persuade the trier of the facts, generally the jury, that a proposition he asserts is true.
    VI. If the evidence is equally balanced, or if it leaves the jury in such doubt as to be unable to decide the controversy either way, judgment must be given against the party upon whom the burden of proof rests.
    The CORRECT answer is:
    A. III, II, V, IV, I, VI
    B. I, II, VI, V, III, IV
    C. III, IV, V, I, II, VI
    D. V, I, III, VI, IV, II

    1.____

2. I. If a parent is without assets and is unemployed, he cannot be convicted of the crime of non-support of a child.
    II. The term "sufficient ability" has been held to mean sufficient financial ability.
    III. It does not matter if his unemployment is by choice or unavoidable circumstances.
    IV. If he fails to take any steps at all, he may be liable to prosecution for endangering the welfare of a child.
    V. Under the penal law, a parent is responsible for the support of his minor child only if the parent is "of sufficient ability."
    VI. An indigent parent may meet his obligation by borrowing money or by seeking aid under the provisions of the Social Welfare Law.
    The CORRECT answer is:
    A. VI, I, V, III, II, IV
    B. I, III, V, II, IV, VI
    C. V, II, I, III, VI, IV
    D. I, VI, IV, V, II, III

    2.____

3. I. Consider, for example, the case of a rabble rouser who urges a group of twenty people to go out and break the windows of a nearby factory.
    II. Therefore, the law fills the indicated gap with the crime of inciting to riot.
    III. A person is considered guilty of inciting to riot when he urges ten or more persons to engage in tumultuous and violent conduct of a kind likely to create public alarm.
    IV. However, if he has not obtained the cooperation of at least four people, he cannot be charged with unlawful assembly.

    3.____

V. The charge of inciting to riot was added to the law to cover types of conduct which cannot be classified as either the crime of "riot" or the crime of "unlawful assembly."
VI. If he acquires the acquiescence of at least four of them, he is guilty of unlawful assembly even if the project does not materialize.

The CORRECT answer is:
- A. III, V, I, VI, IV, II
- B. V, I, IV, VI, II, III
- C. III, IV, I, V, II, VI
- D. V, I, IV, VI, III, II

4.
I. If, however, the rebuttal evidence presents an issue of credibility, it is for the jury to determine whether the presumption has, in fact, been destroyed.
II. Once sufficient evidence to the contrary is introduced, the presumption disappears from the trial.
III. The effect of a presumption is to place the burden upon the adversary to come forward with evidence to rebut the presumption.
IV. When a presumption is overcome and ceases to exist in the case, the fact or facts which gave rise to the presumption still remain.
V. Whether a presumption has been overcome is ordinarily a question for the court.
VI. Such information may furnish a basis for a logical inference.

The CORRECT answer is:
- A. IV, VI, II, V, I, III
- B. III, II, V, I, IV, VI
- C. V, III, VI, IV, II, I
- D. V, IV, I, II, VI, III

KEY (CORRECT ANSWERS)

1. D
2. C
3. A
4. B

PREPARING WRITTEN MATERIAL
EXAMINATION SECTION
TEST 1

DIRECTIONS: Each of Questions 1 through 5 consists of a sentence which may or may not be an example of good formal English usage. Examine each sentence, considering grammar, punctuation, spelling, capitalization, and awkwardness. Then choose the correct statement about it from the four options below it. If the English usage in the sentence given is better than any of the changes suggested in options B, C, or D, pick option A. (Do not pick an option that will change the meaning of the sentence.) *PRINT THE LETTER OF THE CORRECT ANSWER IN THE SPACE AT THE RIGHT.*

1. I don't know who could possibly of broken it. 1.____
   A. This is an example of good formal English usage.
   B. The word "who" should be replaced by the word "whom."
   C. The word "of" should be replaced by the word "have."
   D. The word "broken" should be replaced by the word "broke."

2. Telephoning is easier than to write. 2.____
   A. This is an example of good formal English usage.
   B. The word "telephoning" should be spelled "telephoneing."
   C. The word "than" should be replaced by the word "then."
   D. The words "to write" should be replaced by the word "writing."

3. The two operators who have been assigned to these consoles are on vacation. 3.____
   A. This is an example of good formal English usage.
   B. A comma should be placed after the word "operators."
   C. The word "who" should be replaced by the word "whom."
   D. The word "are" should be replaced by the word "is."

4. You were suppose to teach me how to operate a plugboard. 4.____
   A. This is an example of good formal English usage.
   B. The word "were" should be replaced by the word "was."
   C. The word "suppose" should be replaced by the word "supposed."
   D. The word "teach" should be replaced by the word "learn."

5. If you had taken my advice; you would have spoken with him. 5.____
   A. This is an example of good formal English usage.
   B. The word "advice" should be spelled "advise."
   C. The words "had taken" should be replaced by the word "take."
   D. The semicolon should be changed to a comma.

KEY (CORRECT ANSWERS)

1. C
2. D
3. A
4. C
5. D

TEST 2

DIRECTIONS: Select the correct answer. *PRINT THE LETTER OF THE CORRECT ANSWER IN THE SPACE AT THE RIGHT.*

1. The one of the following sentences which is MOST acceptable from the viewpoint of correct grammatical usage is:
    A. I do not know which action will have worser results.
    B. He should of known better.
    C. Both the officer on the scene, and his immediate supervisor, is charged with the responsibility.
    D. An officer must have initiative because his supervisor will not always be available to answer questions.

    1.____

2. The one of the following sentences which is MOST acceptable from the viewpoint of correct grammatical usage is:
    A. Of all the officers available, the better one for the job will be picked.
    B. Strict orders were given to all the officers, except he.
    C. Study of the law will enable you to perform your duties more efficiently.
    D. It seems to me that you was wrong in failing to search the two men.

    2.____

3. The one of the following sentences which does NOT contain a misspelled word is:
    A. The duties you will perform are similar to the duties of a patrolman.
    B. Officers must be constantly alert to sieze the initiative.
    C. Officers in this organization are not entitled to special privileges.
    D. Any changes in procedure will be announced publically.

    3.____

4. The one of the following sentences which does NOT contain a misspelled word is:
    A. It will be to your advantage to keep your firearm in good working condition.
    B. There are approximately fourty men on sick leave.
    C. Your first duty will be to pursuade the person to obey the law.
    D. Fires often begin in flameable material kept in lockers.

    4.____

5. The one of the following sentences which does NOT contain a misspelled word is:
    A. Offices are not required to perform technical maintainance.
    B. He violated the regulations on two occasions.
    C. Every employee will be held responable for errors.
    D. This was his nineth absence in a year.

    5.____

KEY (CORRECT ANSWERS)

1. D
2. C
3. C
4. A
5. B

TEST 3

DIRECTIONS: Select the correct answer. *PRINT THE LETTER OF THE CORRECT ANSWER IN THE SPACE AT THE RIGHT.*

1. You are answering a letter that was written on the letterhead of the ABC Company and signed by James H. Wood, Treasurer.
   What is usually considered to be the correct salutation to use in your reply?
   A. Dear ABC Company:
   B. Dear Sirs:
   C. Dear Mr. Wood:
   D. Dear Mr. Treasurer:

   1.____

2. Assume that one of your duties is to handle routine letters of inquiry from the public.
   The one of the following which is usually considered to be MOST desirable in replying to such a letter is a
   A. detailed answer handwritten on the original letter of inquiry
   B. phone call, since you can cover details more easily over the phone than in a letter
   C. short letter giving the specific information requested
   D. long letter discussing all possible aspects of the question raised

   2.____

3. The CHIEF reason for dividing a letter into paragraphs is to
   A. make the message clear to the reader by starting a new paragraph for each new topic
   B. make a short letter occupy as much of the page as possible
   C. keep the reader's attention by providing a pause from time to time
   D. make the letter look neat and businesslike

   3.____

4. Your superior has asked you to send an e-mail from your agency to a government agency in another city. He has written out the message and has indicated the name of the government agency.
   When you dictate the message to your secretary, which of the following items that your superior has NOT mentioned must you be sure to include?
   A. Today's date
   B. The full address of the government agency
   C. A polite opening such as "Dear Sirs"
   D. A final sentence such as "We would appreciate hearing from your agency in reply as soon as is convenient for you"

   4.____

5. The one of the following sentences which is grammatically preferable to the others is:
   A. Our engineers will go over your blueprints so that you may have no problems in construction.
   B. For a long time he had been arguing that we, not he, are to blame for the confusion.
   C. I worked on this automobile for two hours and still cannot find out what is wrong with it.
   D. Accustomed to all kinds of hardships, fatigue seldom bothers veteran policemen.

   5.____

KEY (CORRECT ANSWERS)

1. C
2. C
3. A
4. B
5. A

TEST 4

DIRECTIONS: Select the correct answer. *PRINT THE LETTER OF THE CORRECT ANSWER IN THE SPACE AT THE RIGHT.*

1. Suppose that an applicant for a job as snow laborer presents a letter from a former employer stating: "John Smith has a pleasing manner and never got into an argument with his fellow employees. He was never late or absent."
   This letter
   A. indicates that with some training Smith will make a good snow gang boss
   B. presents no definite evidence of Smith's ability to do snow work
   C. proves definitely that Smith has never done any snow work before
   D. proves definitely that Smith will do better than average work as a snow laborer

   1.____

2. Suppose you must write a letter to a local organization in your section refusing a request in connection with collection of their refuse.
   You should start the letter by
   A. explaining in detail the consideration you gave the request
   B. praising the organization for its service to the community
   C. quoting the regulation which forbids granting the request
   D. stating your regret that the request cannot be granted

   2.____

3. Suppose a citizen writes in for information as to whether or not he may sweep refuse into the gutter. A Sanitation officer answers as follows:
   Dear Sir:
      No person is permitted to litter, sweep, throw or cast, or direct, suffer or permit any person under his control to litter, sweep, throw or cast any ashes, garbage, paper, dust, or other rubbish or refuse into any public street or place, vacant lot, air shaft, areaway, backyard or court.
                                 Very truly yours,
                                 John Doe
   This letter is *poorly* written CHIEFLY because
   A. the opening is not indented   B. the thought is not clear
   C. the tone is too formal and cold   D. there are too many commas used

   3.____

4. A section of a disciplinary report written by a Sanitation officer states: "It is requested that subject Sanitation man be advised that his future activities be directed towards reducing his recurrent tardiness else disciplinary action will be initiated which may result in summary discharge."
   This section of the report is *poorly* written MAINLY because
   A. at least one word is misspelled   B. it is not simply expressed
   C. more than one idea is expressed   D. the purpose is not stated

   4.____

5. A section of a disciplinary report written by an officer states: "He comes in late. He takes too much time for lunch. He is lazy. I recommend his services be dispensed with."
   This section of the report is *poorly* written MAINLY because
   A. it ends with a preposition   B. it is not well organized
   C. no supporting facts are stated   D. the sentences are too simple

   5.____

KEY (CORRECT ANSWERS)

1. B
2. D
3. C
4. B
5. C

ARITHMETICAL REASONING
EXAMINATION SECTION
TEST 1

DIRECTIONS: Each question or incomplete statement is followed by several suggested answers or completions. Select the one that BEST answers the question or completes the statement. *PRINT THE LETTER OF THE CORRECT ANSWER IN THE SPACE AT THE RIGHT.*

1. On January 1, a family was receiving supplementary monthly public assistance of $280 for food, $240 for rent, and $140 for other necessities. In the spring, their rent rose by 10%, and their rent allotment was adjusted accordingly. In the summer, due to the death of a family member, their allotments for food and other necessities were reduced by 1/7.
   Their monthly allowance check in the fall should be
   A. $623 B. $644 C. $664 D. $684

   1.____

2. Twice a month, a certain family receives a $340 general allowance for rent, food, and clothing expense. In addition, the family receives a specific supplementary allotment for utilities of $384 a year, which is added to their semi-monthly check.
   If the general allowance alone is reduced by 5%, what will be the TOTAL amount of their next semi-monthly check?
   A. $323 B. $339 C. $340 D. $355

   2.____

3. If each supervising clerk in a certain unit sees an average of 9 clients in a 7-hour day and there are 15 supervising clerks in the unit, APPROXIMATELY how many clients will be seen in a 35-hour week?
   A. 315 B. 405 C. 675 D. 945

   3.____

4. In one day, an aide receives 18 inquiries by phone and 27 inquiries in person. What percentage of the inquiries received that day were by phone?
   A. 33% B. 40% C. 45% D. 60%

   4.____

5. If the weekly paychecks for 5 employees are $258.64, $325.48, $287.50, and $313.12, then the combined weekly income for the 5 employee is
   A. $1,455.68 B. $1,456.08 C. $1,462.68 D. $1,474.08

   5.____

6. Suppose that there are 17 aides working in an office where many community complaints are received by telephone. In one ten-day period, 4,250 calls were received.
   If the same number of calls were received each day and the aides divided the work load equally, about how many calls did each aide respond to daily?
   A. 25 B. 35 C. 75 D. 250

   6.____

7. Suppose that an assignment was divided among 5 aides.
    If the first aide spent 67 hours on the assignment, the second aide spent 95 hours, the third aide spent 52 hours, the fourth aide spent 78 hours, and the fifth aide spent 103 hours, what was the AVERAGE amount of time spent by each aide on the assignment? _____ hours.
    A. 71 B. 75 C. 79 D. 83

8. If there are 240 employees in a center and 1/3 are absent on the day of a bad snowstorm, how many employees were at work in the center on that day?
    A. 80 B. 120 C. 160 D. 200

9. Suppose that an aide takes 25 minutes to prepare a letter to a client.
    If the aide is assigned to prepare 9 letters on a certain day, how much time should be set aside for this task? _____ hours.
    A. 3¾ B. 4¼ C. 4¾ D. 5¼

10. Suppose that a certain center uses both Form A and Form B in the course of its daily work and that Form A is used 4 times as often as Form B.
    If the total number of both forms used in one week is 750, how many times was Form A used?
    A. 100 B. 200 C. 400 D. 600

11. Suppose a center has a budget of $2,185.40 from which 8 desks costing $156.10 apiece must be bought.
    How many additional desks can be ordered from this budget after the 8 desks have been purchased?
    A. 4 B. 6 C. 9 D. 14

12. When researching a particular case, a team of 16 aides was asked to check through 234 folders to obtain the necessary information.
    If half the aides worked twice as fast as the other half, and the slow group checked through 12 folders each hour, about how long would it take to complete the assignment? _____ hours.
    A. 4¼ B. 5 C. 6 D. 6½

13. The difference in the cost of two typewriters is $56.64.
    If the less expensive typewriter costs $307.22, what is the cost of the other typewriter?
    A. $343.86 B. $344.06 C. $363.86 D. $364.06

14. At the start of a year, a family was receiving a public assistance grant of $382 twice a month, on the first and fifteenth of each month. On March 1, their rent allowance was decreased from $150 to $142 a month since they had moved to a smaller apartment. On August 1 their semi-monthly food allowance, which had been $80.40, was raised by 10%.
    In that year, the TOTAL amount of money disbursed to this family was
    A. $4,544.20 B. $6,581.40 C. $9,088.40 D. $9,168.40

3 (#1)

15. It is discovered that a client has received double public assistance for 2 months by having been enrolled at two service centers of the Department of Social Services. The client should have received $168 twice a month instead of the double amount. He now agrees to repay the money by equal deductions from his public assistance check over a period of 12 months.
What will the amount of his NEXT check be?
   A. $112   B. $140   C. $154   D. $160

16. Suppose a study is being made of the composition of 3,550 families receiving public assistance. Of the first 1,050 families reviewed, 18% had four or more children.
If, in the remaining number of families, the percentage with four or more children is half as high as the percentage in the group already reviewed, then the percentage of families with four or more children in the entire group of families is MOST NEARLY
   A. 12   B. 14   C. 16   D. 17

17. Suppose that food prices have risen 13%, and an increase of the same amount has been granted in the food allotment given to people receiving public assistance.
If a family has been receiving $810 a month, 35% of which is allotted for food, then the TOTAL amount of public assistance this family receives per month will be changed to
   A. $805.42   B. $840.06   C. $846.86   D. $899.42

18. Assume that the food allowance is to be raised 5% in August but will be retroactive for four months to April.
The retroactive allowance is to be divided into equal sections and added to the public assistance checks for August, September, October, November, and December.
A family which has been receiving $840 monthly, 40% of which was allotted for food, will receive what size check in August?
   A. $853.44   B. $856.80   C. $861.00   D. $870.24

19. A blind client, who receives $210 public assistance twice a month, inherits 14 shares of stock worth $180 each. The client is required to sell the stock and spend his inheritance before receiving more public assistance.
Using his public assistance allowance as a guide, how many months are his new assets expected to last?
   A. 6   B. 7   C. 8   D. 12

20. The Department of Social Services has 16 service centers. These centers may be divided into those which are downtown and those which are uptown. Two of the centers are special service centers and are downtown, while the remainder of the centers are general service centers. There is a total of 7 service centers downtown.
The percentage of the general service centers which are uptown is MOST NEARLY
   A. 56   B. 64   C. 69   D. 79

21. For six months, a family lived in a 4-room apartment where they paid $380 a month. They made an intrasite move to a 4-room apartment where they paid $85 per room a month for six months.
Comparing the two six-month periods, the TOTAL amount of money the family saved by making the intrasite was
    A. $240 B. $290 C. $430 D. $590

22. To calculate a tenant's usable income, you should make Social Security deductions of 4.4 percent on salary up to a maximum of $9,000 and State Disability deductions of .5 percent on salary up to $3,000.
What does a tenant's combined deduction amount to if his annual salary is $13,400?
    A. $411.00 B. $568.60 C. $619.60 D. $700.00

23. If the temporary relocation expenses for housing are set at $18 per day for one adult and $10 per day for each additional person in a room, how much money is allowed for a woman and four children temporarily relocated in one room for a period of six days?
    A. $168 B. $348 C. $378 D. $518

24. According to relocation policy, a family relocating to private housing from federally-aided or certain other sites will be granted a relocation payment. This payment equals the difference between 1/5 of the family's yearly income and the scheduled yearly rent for a standard apartment for their size family.
Suppose a 2-person family whose yearly income is $12,900 has been unable to obtain public housing and so finds a one-bedroom private apartment. The scheduled rent for a one-bedroom apartment appropriate for their occupancy is $240 a month.
What payment will they receive?
    A. $240 B. $288 C. $300 D. $410

25. A family on a housing relocation site is paying $410 per month for rent. This represents 25% of their gross monthly income.
If the husband earns 4/5 of their total combined monthly income, how much does the wife earn per month?
    A. $328 B. $540 C. $1,280 D. $1,500

KEY (CORRECT ANSWERS)

1.	A	11.	B
2.	B	12.	D
3.	C	13.	C
4.	B	14.	D
5.	B	15.	B
6.	A	16.	A
7.	C	17.	C
8.	C	18.	D
9.	A	19.	A
10.	D	20.	B

21. A
22. A
23. B
24. C
25. A

SOLUTIONS TO PROBLEMS

1. After spring, the rent allotment should be $(240+24) = $264. After the summer, the reduced allotment for food and other necessities should be $[(280+140) − 1/7(280+140)] = $(420-1/7(420)] = $(420-60) = $360. The monthly check in the fall including rent, food, and other necessities should be $360 + $264 = $624.

2. Amount of general allowance in the family's semi-monthly check = $340. Amount of utilities allotment in the family's semi-monthly check: ($$\frac{384}{12}$ × ½) = $16. Amount of general allowance in family' semi-monthly check after a 5% reduction = $340 less 5% of $340 = $(340-17) = $3223. Total amount of the next month's semi-monthly check: Reduced general allowance + utilities allotment = $323 + $16 = $339.

3. During 7 hours, a total of (15)(9) = 135 clients can be seen. Thus, in 35 hours, a total of (135)(5) = 675 clients will be seen.

4. 18(18+27) = .40 = 40%

5. $258.64 + $325.48 + $287.34 + $271.50 + $313.12 = $1,456.08

6. 4250/10 = 425 calls per day. Then, 425/17 = 25

7. (67+95+52+78+103)/5 = 79 hours

8. Number present = (240)(2/3) = 160

9. (25)(9) = 225 min. = 3 hrs. 45 min. = 3 ¾ hours

10. Let x, 1/4x = number of forms A, B, respectively. Then, x + 1/4x = 750. Solving, x = 600

11. $2,185.40 − (8)($156.10) = $936.60. Then, $936.60 ÷ $156.10 = 6 desks

12. Since the slow group did 12 folders each hour, the faster group did 24 folders each hour. Then, 234/(12+24) = 6 ½ hrs.

13. Expensive typewriter costs $307.22 + $56.64 = $363.86

14. For months of January and February, the amount the family receives is $(382×2×2) = $1528
    For months of March through July, the family receives $(764-8) × 5 = $3780
    For months August through December, the family receives $(756+16.08) × 5 = $3860.40
    The total amount of money disbursed to this family is $1528 + $3780 + $3860.40 = $9,168.40

15. The overpayment for 2 months = ($168)(4) = $672. If this is paid back over 12 months, each month's amount is reduced by $672/12 = $56. Then, each check (semi-monthly) is reduced by $28. His next check will be $168 - $28 = $140

7 (#1)

16. $(1050)(.18) + (2500)(.09) = 414$. Then, $414/3550 = 12\%$

17. $(\$810)(.35) = \$283.50$ originally allotted for food. The new food allotment = $(\$283.50)(1.13) = \$320.355$. The total assistance now = $\$810 - \$283.50 + \$320.355 = \$846.855$ or $\$846.86$

18. $(\$840)(.40) = \$336$ per month for food. The new food allowance = $(\$336)(1.05) = \$352.80$ per month. The difference of $16.80 is retroactive to April, which means $(\$16.80)(9) = \$151.20$ additional money for August through December. Each check for these 5 months will be increased by $\$15.20/5 = 30.24$. Thus, the check in August = $\$840 + 30.24 = \$840 + 30.24 = \$870.24$

19. $(\$180)(14) = \$2520$. Then, $\$2520/\$420 = 6$ months

20. 5 general are downtown; 9 of 14 general are uptown; $9/14 \approx 64\%$

21. $(\$85)(4) = \$340$ per month. Savings per month = $\$380 - \$340 = \$40$ For six months, the savings = $\$240$

22. $(\$9000(.044) + (\$3000)(.005) = \$411$ total deductions

23. $(\$18+\$40)(6) = \$348$ relocation expenses

24. $(\$240)(12) - (1/5)(\$12,900) = \$300$ relocation payment

25. $\$410 \div .25 = \$1640$. The wife earns $(1640)(1/5) = \$328$ each month

TEST 2

DIRECTIONS: Each question or incomplete statement is followed by several suggested answers or completions. Select the one that BEST answers the question or completes the statement. *PRINT THE LETTER OF THE CORRECT ANSWER IN THE SPACE AT THE RIGHT.*

1. A project tenant who owns and drives a taxicab for living, reports for a three-month period an income of $6,250 after operating expenses of $1,300 have been considered. In addition, his tips are valued at 12% of his income before operating expenses.
   An estimate of his yearly income is MOST NEARLY
   A. $22,000 B. $23,000 C. $28,000
   D. $28,500 E. $29,000

   1._____

2. The maximum annual subsidy which can be paid by the State toward the operation of any low-rent housing project is the sum of the annual interest on the total original loan or building the project and 1% of the portion of the loan actually spent.
   If the original loan for a project was $8,000,000 at 1¾% interest, but only $7,500,000 was actually spent, then the MAXIMUM annual subsidy is
   A. $140,000 B. $145,000 C. $215,000
   D. $220,000 E. $271,250

   2._____

3. In 2020, the cost of repairs and maintenance at a certain housing project was $5,589 more than in 2019, representing an increase of 4.6%. A further increase at the same rate was anticipated for 2021.
   The cost of repairs and maintenance in 2021 was MOST NEARLY
   A. $127,100
   B. $132,700
   C. $132,900
   D. $133,000
   E. an amount which cannot be determined from the given data

   3._____

4. Each day a delivery truck used by the Housing Authority travels 25 miles from a project to a storehouse and 25 miles on the return trip. It travels at the rate of 30 miles per hour going to the storehouse and at the rate of 20 miles per hour returning.
   The average rate, in miles per hour, for the roundtrip is MOST NEARLY
   A. 24
   B. 25
   C. 26
   D. the square root of 600
   E. an amount which cannot be determined from the given data

   4._____

5. A report on the first 6,000 applications for apartments in a certain project containing 1,400 apartments indicated that those who were ineligible fell into four categories: 2,800 ineligible for reason A, 600 ineligible for reason B, 1,200 ineligible for reason C, and 400 ineligible for reason D.

   5._____

If the same proportions continue for the remaining 21,500 applications, then the percentage of eligible applicants who can be given apartments in the project is MOST NEARLY
A. 25   B. 30   C. 33   D. 40   E. 60

6. The number of applications for apartments in low-rent housing projects was 40,000 in 2019. The number of applications increased 5% in 2020, and increased again in 2021 by 6% over the 2,000 total.
The percentage by which the 2021 figures exceed the 2019 figures is
A. 5.3   B. 6.0   C. 11.0   D. 11.3   E. 30.0

7. A rectangular lot, 75 feet by 11.0 feet, was purchased as part of a project site for $28,500.
The price per square foot of this lot is MOST NEARLY
A. $2.85   B. $3.45   C. $3.95   D. $30.00   E. $30.95

8. It has been estimated that 125 kilowatt-hours of electricity are used each month in one average Housing Authority apartment at a cost of 14.8 cents per kilowatt-hour.
On this basis, the total cost of the electricity used in one year in a project containing 1,400 apartments is MOST NEARLY
A. $20,000   B. $25,000   C. $200,000
D. $250,000   E. $2,000,000

9. The walls and ceilings of 20 rooms are to be painted with the same kind of paint, each room being 15 feet long, 12 feet wide, and 10 feet high. Each room contains two windows, each 3 feet by 6 feet, and a door 3 feet by 8 feet, which are not to be painted. One gallon of paint covers 400 square feet of surface.
The number of gallons of paint needed is MOST NEARLY
A. 33   B. 34   C. 35   D. 36   E. 75

10. A group of buildings is valued at $11,500,000. Assume that the cos of fire insurance for these buildings is 5.3 cents per $100 of valuation per year.
The cost of fire insurance for one year is MOST NEARLY
A. $600   B. $6,000   C. $20,000
D. $60,000   E. $2,000,000

11. Of the 15 employees in a certain unit, one-third earn $27,600 per year, three earn $32,600, one earns $46,400, and the rest earn $33,800.
The average salary of the employees of this unit is MOST NEARLY
A. $31,000   B. $32,000   C. $33,000   D. $34,000   E. $35,000

12. Four pieces, each 2'8½" long, are cut from a piece of pipe 16½' long.
The length of the remaining piece of pipe is
A. 6'8½"   B. 6'10"   C. 6'10⅜"   D. 6'11⅛"   E. 9'9½"

13. A tenant ears E dollars a month, spends S dollars a week, and saves the rest. 13.____
    The tenant's yearly savings can be expressed by
    A. 12(E-4S)   B. 12E – 52S   C. 12(E-S)
    D. 52(E-4S)   E. E - S

14. A unit of fifteen Housing Assistants has been assigned the job of interviewing 14.____
    applicants. Each interview takes 35 minutes, and an additional 10 minutes is
    needed for making entries and notes. The last interview each day is always
    scheduled so that it can be completed that day.
    The number of applicants who can be interviewed in a week, consisting of five
    7-hour days, is MOST NEARLY
    A. 375   B. 525   C. 675   D. 700   E. 725

15. A review of the 14,000 applications for apartments in a certain project 15.____
    containing 1,200 apartments indicated that 4,800 applicants were eligible and
    6,400 were ineligible. No decision could be reached on the remaining
    applications because certain necessary information was omitted by the
    applicants, but it was assumed that the proportion of eligible and ineligible
    applicants would remain the same as in those already decided.
    On the basis of these figures, the percentage of eligible applicants who can be
    given apartments in the project is
    A. under 17%   B. 17%   C. 20%
    D. 25%   E. 33 1/3%

16. An oil burner in a housing development burns 76 gallons of fuel oil per hour. 16.____
    At 9 A.M. on a very cold day, the superintendent asks the Housing Manager to
    put in an emergency order for more fuel oil. At that time, he reports that he has
    on hand 266 gallons. At noon, he again comes to the manager, notifying him
    that no oil has been delivered.
    The MAXIMUM amount of time that he can continue to furnish heat without
    receiving more oil is
    A. no more time   B. ½ hour   C. 1 hour
    D. 1½ hours   E. 2 hours

17. As a result of reports received by the Housing Authority concerning the reputed 17.____
    ineligibility of 756 tenants because of above-standard incomes, an intensive
    check of their employers has been ordered. Four housing assistants have
    been assigned to this task. At the end of 6 days at 7 hours each, they have
    checked on 336 tenants. In order to speed up the investigation, two more
    housing assistants are assigned to this point.
    If they worked at the same rate, the number of additional 7-hour days it would
    take to complete the job is MOST NEARLY
    A. 1   B. 3   C. 5   D. 7   E. 9

4 (#2)

18. A municipal aide on a special trip is returning to his office from a point 17½ miles away, and makes the return trip to his office at an average speed of 25 miles an hour, except for a 15-minute stopover at one point to get a flat tire fixed. The time it should take him to reach his office is MOST NEARLY _____ minutes.
   A. 12   B. 22   C. 36   D. 42   E. 57

19. A district office has an assigned staff of 320 employees. Of this number, 25% are not available for duty due to illness, vacations, and other reasons. Of those who are available for duty, 1/8 are assigned to auditing and special projects, and the rest to handling the workload.
The ACTUAL number of employees available for handling the workload is
   A. 350   B. 310   C. 270   D. 210   E. 180

20. Two dozen shuttlecocks and four badminton rackets are to be purchased for a playground. The shuttlecocks are priced at $3.60 each, and the rackets at $27.50 each. The playground receives a discount of 30% from these prices.
The TOTAL cost of this equipment is
   A. $72.90   B. $114.30   C. $137.48   D. $186.00   E. $220.70

21. On January 1, a family was receiving public assistance allowance of $185 for food, $53 for clothing, $17.50 for utilities, and $22 for personal needs, all semi-monthly, and a monthly allowance of $550 for rent. On May 1, the rent allowance was increased by 12% but all other allowances remained the same for the rest of the year.
The TOTAL amount of money granted this family during the year was
   A. $10,528   B. $13,262   C. $13,788
   D. $21,056   E. $27,676

22. It has been decided to make changes in food allotments to clients receiving public assistance to conform to changes in food costs. Of the food allowance, 30% is intended for meat, 30% for fruits and vegetables, 25% for groceries, and 15% for dairy products. Assume that meat prices have gone up 5%, and dairy prices have remained the same.
For a family that has been receiving $400 per month for food, the new monthly food allowance will be
   A. $333   B. $375   C. $393   D. $403.50   E. $420

23. On January 1, a family was receiving a public assistance allowance of $195 for food, $63 for clothing, $27.50 for utilities, and $32 for personal needs, all semi-monthly, and a monthly allowance of $510 for rent. On June 1, the rent allowance was increased by 12%, but all other allowances remained the same for the rest of the year.
The TOTAL amount of money granted this family during the year was
   A. $13,843.40   B. $14,107.20   C. $14,168.40
   D. $14,474.40   E. $16,886.80

24. A member of a family receiving public assistance amounting to $600 monthly has obtained a part-time job, for which he is paid $40 a day. He is employed 3 days a week. His carfare costs $3.00 per day and his lunches $2.00 per day. Assume that there are $4^1/_3$ weeks per month. The Department of Welfare requires that net earnings be deducted from relief allowances.
The family's semi-monthly public assistance allowances should be reduced to
   A. $40.00   B. $72.50   C. $96.25   D. $123.75   E. $145.00

25. A couple living in a furnished room has been receiving a public assistance grant of $375 semi-monthly and has been paying a weekly rent of $75. The landlord has been granted a 12% increase in rent. Assume that a month consists of $4^1/_3$ weeks.
The amount of the new semi-monthly grant, including this rent increase, that the couple will receive will be MOST NEARLY
   A. $394.50   B. $397   C. $409   D. $514   E. $557

KEY (CORRECT ANSWERS)

1.	D		11.	B
2.	C		12.	A
3.	C		13.	B
4.	A		14.	C
5.	B		15.	C
6.	D		16.	B
7.	B		17.	C
8.	D		18.	E
9.	A		19.	D
10.	B		20.	C

21. C
22. C
23. C
24. B
25. A

SOLUTIONS TO PROBLEMS

1. For 3 months, income = $6,250 + (.12)($7550) = $7156. Then, annual income = ($7154)(4) = $28,624, closest to $28,500.

2. Maximum annual subsidy = ($8,000,000)(.0175) + (.01)($7,500,000) = $215,000

3. Cost in 2019 = $5589/.046 = $121,500. The cost in 2020 = $121,500 + $5589 = $127,089. This means the cost in 2021 = ($127,089)(1.046) = $132,900

4. Average rate = total distance/total time = (25+25) ÷ (25/30 + 25/20) = 24 mph

5. Out of 600, number of eligible = 6000 – 2800 – 600 – 1200 – 400 = 1000. Thus, for 27,500 applications, (1/6)(27,500) = 4583 would be eligible. Finally, 1400 ÷ 4583 ≈ 30%

6. Number of applications in 2020 = (40,000)(1.05) = 42,000. Number of applications in 2021 = (42,000)(1.06) = 44,520. Then, (44,520–40,000) ÷ 40,000 = 11.3%

7. $28,500 ÷ [(75×110)] = $3.45 per sq. ft.

8. Total cost = (125)(.148)(12)(1400) = $310,800; closest to choice D of $250,000

9. Painted area of each room = (2)(15)(10) + (2)(12)(10) + (15)(12) – (2)(3)(6) – (3)(8) = 660 sq. ft. So, (20)(660) = 13,200 sq. ft. to be painted in all rooms. Finally, 13,200/400 = 33 gallons of paint needed

10. Insurance cost = (.053)($11,500,000)/$100 = $6095, closest to $6000

11. [(5)($27,600) + (3)($32,600) + (1)($46,400) + (6)($33,800)]/15 = $32,233 closest to $32,000

12. 16½ - (4)(2'5³/₈") = 16'6" – 8'21½" = 16'6" – 9'9½" = 6'8½"

13. Annual savings = 12E – 52S

14. 7 ÷ ¾ = 9.$\overline{3}$, which means each interviewer can interview a maximum of 9 applicants each day. Then, (5)(9)(15) = 675 applicants

15. 4800/(4800+6400) = 3/7 eligible. On that assumption, there would be (3/7)(14,000) = 6000 eligible applicants. Then, 1200/6000 = 20%

16. 266 – (3)(76) = 38 gallons of oil left. Then, 38/76 = ½ hour

17. (6)(7)(4) = 168 hours to check on 336 tenants. This means 2 tenants require 1 man-hour. Now, (6)(7)(x days) = man-hours would be needed to check the remaining 420 tenants. This requires 210 man-hours. So, (6)(7)(x) = 210. Solving, x = 5

18. $\frac{17.5}{25}$ = .7 hr. = 42 min. Total time = 42 + 15 = 57 minutes.

19. Number available = 320[1−.25(1/8)(.75) = 210

20. Total cost = (.70)[(24)($3.60)+(4)(27.50)] = $137.48

21. From January through April, amount = (8)($185+$53+$17.50+$22) + (4)($550) = $4420. From May through December, amount = (16)($185+$53+17.50+$22) + (8)($550)(1.12) = $9368. Total annual amount = $4420 + $9368 = $13,788

22. Meat allowance = ($400)(.30)(1.10) = $132; fruit and vegetable allowance = ($400)(.30)(.80) = $96; grocery allowance = ($400)(.25)(1.05) = $105; dairy allowance = ($400)(.15) = $60. New monthly allowance = $132 + $96 + $105 + $.60 = $393

23. From January through May, amount = (10)($195+$63+$27.50+$32) + (5)($510) = $5725. From June through December, amount = (14)($195+$63+$27.50+$32) + (7)($510)(1.12) = $8443.40. Total annual amount = $5725 + $8443.40 = $14,168.40

24. Monthly assistance should be reduced to $600 − [(40)(3)($4^{1}/_{3}$) − ($5)(3)($4^{1}/_{3}$)] = $145. So, the semi-monthly amount is now $145/2 = $72.50

25. ($75)($4^{1}/_{3}$)/2 = original semi-monthly rent.
    New semi-monthly rent = (162.50)(1.12) = $182. Since this represents an increase of $19.50, the new semi-monthly grant will be increased to $375 + $19.50 = $394.50

PLANNING, CONDUCTING AND RECORDING AN INTERVIEW

"Talk is cheap because supply exceeds demand."

The above statement may be true in many situations, but when it comes to an investigator trying to get answers out of a witness, the opposite will probably happen. One of the most important skills investigators can develop is the ability to get people to open up and talk to them. In this chapter, you will learn about the "art" of interviewing. Yes, it is an art because those who do it well are more successful than those who shrug interviewing off as just "asking questions and writing down answers."

An interview is more than just going to someone's house, knocking on the door, and then asking questions. It takes planning. If you come across in a threatening manner or can't adequately explain why you need to interview a witness, you'll never get any voluntary cooperation. If you ask complex questions or don't allow witnesses to tell their story in their own words, you're not going to get what it is you are after. And, finally, if you cannot adequately convey to others what you found out during the interview, it may as well not have taken place. The "art" of interviewing consists of three phases—planning, conducting, and recording—all of which are discussed in this chapter.

- State the purpose of a financial interview.
- List the objectives of a financial interview.
- Describe the elements that must be considered when planning an interview
- Describe techniques used when conducting an interview.
- Identify and describe methods used to record an interview.

"Just the facts." Remember Sergeant Joe Friday's famous phrase from the television Show *Dragnet*? For years, every week like clockwork, Joe had the uncanny ability to detect, investigate, and resolve criminal matters in 30 minutes or less.

Television makes it look easy. Unfortunately, it isn't. Detecting and investigating a financial crime can take weeks, months, and even years. So, while reality significantly differs from what happens on television, one thing remains the same—financial investigators, just like Joe Friday, search for facts by interviewing people.

Few skills are as important to the financial investigator as the ability to talk to people and successfully gather information from them. Yet, law enforcement officers are not empowered to force people to talk to them. These powers are granted only to courts, grand juries, and certain judicial and legislative bodies. Consequently, investigators face the double duty of convincing the interviewee (hereafter called the **witness**) to agree to be interviewed and then getting the witness to talk after getting inside the door.

WHAT IS AN INTERVIEW?

Phone interviews. Employment interviews. Counseling interviews. Investigatory interviews. As you can see, there are many types of interviews. And though they all serve different purposes, they are founded on the same definition: an interview is a specialized form of oral, face-to-face communication between people that is entered into for a specific task-related purpose associated with a particular subject matter.

For the financial investigator, two aspects of this definition should be noted. The first one is that an interview is a face-to-face communication. Not only will investigators listed to what witnesses say, they will be able to see what the witnesses do. The visual and non-verbal aspects of an interview are very important and should not be overlooked. Secondly, the interview has a specific task-related purpose. This task-related purpose is what makes an interview different from mere conversation. A conversation can take off in many directions; an interview must be focused on relevant content.

INTRODUCTION TO THE FINANCIAL INTERVIEW

Before we get into a general discussion of the interview process, we should look at some specifics of the financial interview. The purpose of a financial interview, its objectives, and the type of question to be asked during a financial interview are discussed below.

Purpose and Objectives

For the financial investigator, the interview is a tool used to determine what knowledge a witness has concerning an investigation. Knowledge in this context includes information about the allegation or crime in question, and any relevant records in a witness's possession. The information and documents provided to the investigator form the basis of the witness's testimony.

A financial interview is different from a financial interrogation. Financial interviews are conducted to obtain information and documentation from witnesses. Financial interrogations are conducted with suspects and hostile witnesses to elicit confessions or admissions of culpability. An investigator may plan on conducting an interview and have it turn into an interrogation. Conversely, interrogation can commenced only to discover that the witness appears to be innocent, and with that, an interrogation turns into an interview.

The financial interview is not something that investigators undertake haphazardly. Prior to each interview, they must decide what they hope to accomplish by interviewing a particular witness. In other words, they must determine the interview's objective(s).

The objectives of a financial interview are:

- To obtain information that establishes or refutes the allegation or crime under investigation.
- To obtain leads for further development of the case
- To obtain all information and documents in the witness's possession relative to the financial investigation
- To obtain background and personal information about the witness and motivation for involvement in the crime

Type of Question Asked

A financial interview is a special type of investigatory interview. During most investigations, people are interviewed to obtain their recollections of events. For example:

- "Can you describe the person who came into the bank?"
- "Do you remember if anyone was with him?"
- "What color was the car she purchased?"

Financial interviews go beyond recollection questions. Like the financial investigation itself, they are concerned with specific details of financial transactions and the movement of money. For example:

- "Why did you have this check cashed?"
- "You notarized two signatures on this document. One is the suspect's. Who is the other individual?"
- "How did she pay for the car?"

THE THREE PHASES OF AN INTERVIEW

For any investigator, an interview is more than just asking a witness some questions. Who should be interviewed? What questions should be asked? In what order should the questions be asked? Where should the interview take place? How can the witness be put at ease so that he or she cooperates? What happens to the information collected? These are just some of the questions an investigator must ask before, during, and after the interview.

A good interview requires a lot of forethought, skillful execution, and an ability to convey what happened during the interview to others. The interview process is comprised of the following three phases:

- Planning
- Conducting
- Recording

Planning an Interview

Prior to planning any interview, the investigator is usually faced with one or more of the following conditions:

- A crime has been alleged or committed, but the facts relating to the situation have not yet been established.
- A complainant or victim has been identified. This could be an individual, business, or governmental entity.
- Records or documents reflecting financial transactions relating to the suspected criminal activity have surfaced.
- Rumors, innuendo, or factual information pointing to a specific suspect have emerged.

The investigator uses the interview to develop information about these existing conditions. The information collected will be used to support or dispel the allegations.

Selecting Witnesses

When an investigation begins, investigators must determine who they want to interview and in what order. Traditional criminal cases are generally investigated by first contacting the outer circle of honest, disinterested witnesses and then working inward to the co-conspirators and ultimately to the target. Law enforcement normally starts the interview process with the complaining witness and after exhausting his or her knowledge of the facts and reasons for suspicion, proceeds in a similar manner around the outer circle of witnesses.

In a financial investigation, this traditional sequence is often altered. Following the movement of money dictates talking to witnesses that have knowledge of financial transactions. Accordingly, the hierarchy of interviews is determined by the degree of knowledge or participation in financial activities created by the alleged criminal event or crime at issue. For example, in a political corruption investigation, documents showing the movement of money from the payer of the bribe to the taker of the bribe would be of paramount importance to the investigator. People with documents (bankers, money couriers, business associates) would be priority contacts. In an embezzlement or tax evasion investigation, the key interviews would be with custodians of accounting records and internal audit files, and tax return preparers. Even in a drug case, financial transactions decide the order of contacts for the investigator. The priority witnesses will have records reflecting the suspect's use of proceeds from the drug trade. While each investigation offers a different set of interview options and priorities, the bottom line in a financial investigation is that every person who has documents pertaining to financial transactions, or knowledge about them, should be interviewed.

Types of Witnesses

One of the things an investigator must consider prior to contacting an individual for an interview is what type of witness will that person be. Will he or she be cooperative, hostile, or have no feelings one way or the other? Prospective witnesses can be categorized into three general types.

Neutral
This is an uninterested third party such as a custodian of public or financial records. This person has no interest in the outcome of the investigation and provides documents and/or unbiased information.

Friendly
A friendly witness is one who cooperates. Witnesses are friendly for a variety of reasons. Certain people naturally tell anybody everything. Others realize that they stand to benefit from providing information about the suspect to authorities. Also, many people seem to enjoy "playing detective" and get caught up in the excitement of being a part of an important investigation.

Reluctant or Hostile
This is an uncooperative party who is typically a friend or associate of the suspect. This witness may also be hostile due to his or her own culpability in the criminal activity under investigation.

Neutral and friendly witnesses usually agree to interviews upon request. No more than proper identification and introduction by the investigator opens the door. Interviewing hostile witnesses often presents greater challenges. Most likely, these witnesses will not voluntarily submit to an interview. They refuse to provide information and documents.
Since law enforcement cannot, on its own, compel any witness to say or do anything, investigators need assistance from the legal system. With approval from a government attorney (i.e., city or district attorney, or U.S. Attorney), the investigator can be issued a document (i.e., summons, subpoena) which commands a witness to appear and submit to an interview. The investigator serves this document on the witness and, if the witness disregards the document, contempt charges and incarceration possibly could result. But even an investigative tool that can command appearance before the investigator does not override a witness's constitutional

guarantees. So, while a hostile witness can be ordered to open the door and submit to an interview, he or she cannot be compelled to say anything incriminating.

Contacting the Suspect

The suspect is a valuable source of information. It follows then that deciding when to interview the suspect is an important decision. Should he or she be contacted at the start of the investigation or confronted upon its completion? Should the investigator contact the suspect at all? The decision is determined by the investigator and is different for each investigation. Interviewing the suspect during the early stages of the investigation makes good sense if it is feared that records in his or her possession may be destroyed or an alibi may be concocted. Often, catching the suspect off guard results in a more responsive interview filled with more answers and more documents. Also, early interviews have resulted in quick confessions and/or early indications of innocence.

On the other hand, delaying contact with the suspect may be advantageous if information and documents gathered from other witnesses can be used to refute the suspect's alibis and lies. Additionally, confessions sometimes occur when the suspect is confronted face to face with the evidence of guilt.

In certain situations, the suspect may not be interviewed at all. He or she may be beyond the reach of law enforcement (i.e., out of the country) or may be represented by an attorney who refuses to allow his or her client to be interviewed on constitutional grounds.

Method of Questioning

While planning an interview, the investigator must determine the method of questioning to use. Questioning can be organized in a number of ways:

- **Chronological Method.** The witness is questioned about the events in the order that they occurred from beginning to end. This is the usual organization of questioning.

- **Questioning According to Documents.** In this type of interview format, a particular document (financial statement, canceled check, tax return) is the focus. The witness may be the legal custodian of the record and have no other involvement in the investigation.

- **Questioning According to Transactions or Events.** The witness may have sold the subject of a house or delivered a package for him or her. The questions in this situation would center on the event and radiate from there.

During the planning phase, the investigator should prepare a written outline that lists main topics to be covered in the interview. An outline allows the investigator to concentrate on important ideas and areas to be covered. However, writing down every specific question to be asked and in a specified order should be avoided as this has the tendency to make the investigator inflexible and tied to the next question. The investigator unwittingly becomes guided by what is written on the sheet of paper instead of what is being said by the witness. Also, the witness may catch a glimpse of the upcoming questions and prepare responses in advance. The following page contains a simplified example of an interview outline. The outline used for an actual interview would be more extensive.

Sample Interview Outline

Ray Austin Interview

Introduction: Identify Self
State Purpose

Background: DOB
SSN
Address
Married
Wife (Maiden Name)
Children
Source of Income
Parents
Education
Military
Prior Arrest, Convictions

Assets
Liabilities
Cash-on-Hand

Associates: Adkins HTB Inc.
Allen Cleveland
Massey TB Trust
Rosemary Westbury
Tony Idaho
Toni Boise
Marc Fresno

Conducting an Interview

Once an investigator is finished with the planning phase, he or she is ready to conduct the interview. The interview itself is composed of three distinct parts:

- Introduction
- Body
- Close

Introduction

The introduction is critical as it sets the tone for the whole interview. It serves the following two purposes:

- Allows the investigator to identify himself or herself to the witness
- Allows the investigator to state the purpose of the contact

The following shows right and wrong ways for an investigator to introduce himself or herself.

Wrong
"Mr. Smith, my name is John Jones and this is Mary Adams. We're with the government. We're investigating Jim Dealer and we need to talk to you."

Right
"Mr. Smith, my name is John Jones. I am a Special Agent with the Internal Revenue Service's Criminal Investigation Division. This is Special Agent Mary Adams from the Drug Enforcement Administration. We are currently conducting an investigation involving alleged violations of money laundering laws by Jim Dealer. May we speak to you for a few moments?"

The objective of the introduction is to put witnesses at ease and to get them to agree to answer questions. However, once the investigator identifies himself or herself, the next question normally is asked by the witness.

Witness: "Why are you contacting me?"
Investigator: "We would like to ask some questions about your financial dealings with Jim Dealer and his associates."

Since the investigator's goal is to put the witness in a frame-of-mind to answer questions, he or she must supply a reason which leads the witness to perceive that he or she will benefit from cooperating with the investigator. If the witness believes that the investigator represents a threat, voluntary cooperation is generally lost. The next page shows some right and wrong ways to gain the cooperation of a hesitant witness.

During the introduction, the investigator should ask general, almost generic, questions such as name, address, telephone number, and date of birth. Since many witnesses are apprehensive, the investigator needs to be patient and avoid rushing into important questions. Through reassuring the witness that his or her cooperation will not cause any undue hardships, inconveniences, or embarrassment, a rapport can be established that will assist both the witness and the investigator during the interview process. When the introduction has been completed and the witness is ready to talk, the investigator moves on to the second part of the actual interview—the body.

Right and Wrong Ways to Gain the Cooperation of a Witness

Wrong
Witness: "Why should I talk to you? I don't want to get involved."
Investigator: "You should have thought of that sooner; it's too late now. We can talk here or we can talk downtown. It's your choice."

Right
Witness: "Why should I talk to you? I don't want to get involved."
Investigator: "You certainly are not required to talk to me. I am just seeking some information on a serious matter which may or may not result in legal action. By speaking informally with me now, it may save you the trouble of having to testify later, depending on the information you have. Is that okay?"

Or

Witness: "I don't want to answer any questions at this time without first talking to my lawyer."

Investigator: "You certainly don't have to talk to me, with or without your lawyer. Let's do it this way. Let me ask you a few questions; and if you don't want to answer them, just say so. I'm not trying to get you into trouble. I'm just trying to do my job and get some answers. Is that okay?"

The Body

The body of the interview is the fact finding part of the interview process. Questions are asked and answers are provided. The structure of the interview is determined by the method of questioning (chronological, by document, or by transaction or event) which should have been pre-determined and outlined by the investigator.

In this stage of the interview, witnesses should be allowed to tell their story in their own words. Recognizing that a witness's story will usually be disjointed and rambling, the investigator must be prepared to put order to the material—find the details, focus for clarity, and ensure the accuracy. For the investigator, conducting an interview is much more than just asking questions and writing down answers. This process requires concentration and active participation by the investigator if his or her objectives are going to be achieved.

The time-honored questioning devices of *who, what, where, why, why,* and *how* allow investigators to push witnesses for details. Investigators should continue the questions until they are convinced that a witness's knowledge of a topic is exhausted. Details, details, details! Whether recollections or records, it is the detail provided by the witness that lays the foundation for a successful financial investigation. The following exchange between an investigator and a witness illustrates how to pursue the detail in a line of questioning.

Investigator: "How was the kickback payment made?"
Witness: "At a meeting."
Investigator: "Where did this meeting take place?"
Witness: "In Mr. X's office."
Investigator: "How many people were there?"
Witness: "There were three of us."
Investigator: "Who were they?"
Witness: "Mr. X, Bill Baker, and me."
Investigator: "How was the kickback divided?"
Witness: "Mr. X split it into three piles."
Investigator: "How much did each of you get?"
Witness: "I don't know. Mr. X didn't count the money. He just estimated the size of each pile."
Investigator: "Did you all get the same size piles?"
Witness: "Yes. I counted it at my office. I had just a little over $100,000."
Investigator: "Would you say that Mr. X received about $100,000 also?"
Witness: "That would seem about right."

A witness's opinion of events often clouds the facts. Although there is nothing wrong with requesting an opinion from a witness, the investigator, through proper questioning, needs to separate the facts (what was said) from the opinions (what was talked about). The goal is a verbatim recollection from the witness. For example:

Wrong
"What did you and Jim Dealer talk about?"

Right
"What did Jim Dealer say to you? What did you say to him?"

As was stated earlier, an investigator must actively participate in the interview process. It's not as simple as ask a question, write down a response. The investigator must constantly analyze responses, and continually check for inconsistencies, and incompleteness. For example:

Investigator:	"How long did your meeting with Mr. Grey last?"
Witness:	"It lasted all day."
Investigator:	"What did Mr. Grey say?"
Witness:	"Not much."

An all-day meeting with not much said should raise a red flag in the investigator's mind. This line of questioning needs to be pursued.

During an interview, investigators have a multitude of tasks to handle simultaneously. From listening to a response and recording it, to formulating the next question, they have a lot to do. There are some general "do's and don'ts" that investigators should consider when performing an interview.

Interview Do's and Don'ts

- *Do* interviews as a team. One investigator listens and controls the questioning while the second records the responses.

- *Do* interview witnesses individually. Attempting to interview two witnesses in the same room at the same time results in one of two things—one witness influences the other's responses or one witness becomes mute, thereby allowing the second witness to answer all the questions. Always separate witnesses and conduct their interviews simultaneously.

- *Do* control the interview. For example, don't let an attorney who is present disrupt the interview. Before beginning the interview, advise each participant of their role in the process. This should help eliminate any control problems.

- *Do* provide the witness with an "out". If a witness has previously denied knowledge, or has supplied false information, there is often reluctance to admit it. The investigator should provide this witness an "out". It normally will be taken. For example:
"Mr. Smith, I know when we talked before you denied knowing Mr. Dealer. You probably forgot about meeting him. Can we start over?"

- *Don't* ask compound/complex or negatively phrased questions (i.e., "you didn't see the money, did you?"). Questions should be simple, to the point, and positively phrased.

- *Don't* make threats and avoid threatening remarks. Threats rarely work, so overbearing tactics should be avoided. The "good cop/bad cop" interview technique looks good on television, but is usually inappropriate in financial investigations.

In our legal system, documents cannot speak for themselves, either figuratively or literally. A witness must identify, explain, and introduce every financial document to give it meaning in any legal proceeding or court action. So what does interviewing have to do with the introduction of documents into a legal proceeding? Plenty! Successful interviewing creates cooperative witnesses who breathe life into financial records involving the movement of money.

Technical areas such as accounting procedures or business specialties should be covered in detail during the body of an interview. The investigator should ask questions concerning the document's entries, meanings, and purposes. The investigator should also determine the identity of the document's custodian and solicit the authenticity of the document. Investigators should not be afraid to ask questions and should keep that old saying, "There is no such thing as a stupid question" in mind. Any question can lead to a surprising answer.

The investigator's job during the interview process is not complete until he or she has exhausted the witness's knowledge on the important topics relative to the ongoing investigation. Successful interviews obtain information and financial leads, as opposed to solving the case. If enough interviews are conducted and enough information is uncovered, the case will solve itself.

The Close

After the witness has provided information, the investigator should review the key points gathered during the body of the interview. This process of summing up the important facts serves the following two purposes:

- It allows the investigator to clarify the facts.
- It provides an opportunity for the investigator and witness to agree with the investigator's summation.

Once the summation has been agreed on, the investigator should ask the following three questions:

- **"Is there anything that I have forgotten to ask?"**
  Probably the number one reason investigators fail to get the answers they seek is that they simply fail to ask the question. Using this "catch-all" question allows the witness the opportunity to play detective.

- **"Is there anyone else you think I should speak with?"**
  This question is designed to find more leads. If the witness is hesitant, it's okay to say that his or her name will not be revealed to the person(s) suggested.

- **"Is there anything else that you would like to say?"**
  This should be the investigator's last question. It gives the witness one final chance to say anything that he or she wishes.

Exit gracefully, even after encounters with hostile witnesses. Soothe the apprehensive witness by mentioning that all the information that he or she provided will be held in confidence and/or for official purposes only. If the witness was cooperative, thank him or her for the cooperation; if nothing was said, express regrets and leave the door open for future contacts.

Recording an Interview

Investigators conduct interviews to obtain information and documents in an attempt to resolve financial crimes. It is also necessary to prepare a permanent record of each interview for future reference and use. Often in a financial investigation, persons interviewed become trial witnesses. The record of the financial interview as prepared by the investigator can be used to refresh the witness's memory and assist the witness in the identification process relative to a financial document.

The complexity and investigative importance of an interview determines the best method to record it. In situations where no information is secured, a limited report or record of interview is acceptable. However, in situations where "case critical questions" are answered, or denials are made by an important witness, a more formal record becomes necessary. The only constraint in the recordation process is the requirement for accuracy and completeness by the investigator preparing the written summary.

When an investigator plays the role of an interviewer, he or she must be accurate, fair, and just. The prosecuting attorney relies on the investigator's written notes taken during an interview. The investigator's portrayal of the interview process should accurately and completely reflect the witness's testimony.

Informal Notes

The "informal notes" taken by investigators during the course of the interview, in conjunction with their recollections, provide the basis for the written record. Informal notes should contain sufficient detail to permit investigators to refresh their memories as to what transpired during the interview. Any method of recording the details is sufficient if it shows the date, time, place, persons present, and what occurred. The following is an example of the informal notes taken by Special Agent John Jones during an interview with Richard Smith. Special Agents Jones and Adams interviewed Smith concerning a financial transaction (the purchase of a car) he had with the suspect, Jim Dealer.

Re: Jim Dealer   *John Jones, IRS*
Talked with Richard Smith   *Mary Adams, DEA*
123 A Street   *July 25, 2018*
         10 A.M. - 10:47 A.M.

Dealer called Smith about truck Smith advertised. Dealer came to see truck about ½ hour after call. Test drove truck around block, then paid $25,000 in cash, in $100 bills, for truck.
2015 truck, serial #1173945

Memorandum

A second way to record interviews is to "formalize" the investigator's informal notes into a "memorandum of interview." A memorandum should be prepared when details of an interview are too numerous to be fully and properly related through informal notes. It should state what occurred during the interview and show the date, time, place, and persons present. If the person interviewed was advised of his or her constitutional rights during the interview, this fact should also be noted in the memorandum. The final typed memorandum should be prepared as soon as possible, and promptly signed and dated by the investigators present during the interview. The actual date of preparation should be shown at the bottom of the memorandum. If it becomes necessary to correct or supplement a memorandum after it has been finalized, the supplemental memorandum should clearly state the date and reason for such action, and the previous memorandum should be attached.

Handwritten notes made during an interview and used as the basis for a more detailed memorandum may be subject to inspection by a court and should be retained in the case file. Investigators should confine memorandums to the facts developed in the interviews and should avoid opinions, conclusions, and extraneous matters.

When deciding whether or not to use a memorandum as a means of recording interview notes, an investigator should consider the following advantages and disadvantages.

Advantages and Disadvantages of the Memorandum

Advantages	Disadvantages
Informal	Does not contain the exact words of the interviewee
Contains all pertinent testimony obtained in the interview	Since information was not mechanically recorded, there is a a chance for some information to be forgotten
Memorandums can be prepared by topic and, therefore, are easy to follow	
Does not require an oath or affirmation	

An example of a memorandum appears on the following page.

Example of Memorandum of Interview

In re: James Dealer
115 South Street
Miami, Florida

Present: Richard Smith, Witness
Special Agent, Mary Adams
Special Agent, John Jones

Place: Office of Richard Smith
117 Elm Street
North Miami, Florida

Date: July 25, 2018

Time: 10:00 A.M. to 10:47 A.M.

1. S/A Adams and I made a field call to a travel agency located at 117 Elm Street, the known employer of Richard Smith. Records obtained from State vehicle registration files reveal that Smith transferred the title of a truck (serial number 1173945) to Dealer in May 2017.
2. After proper introduction and identification (by displaying our credentials and badges), I asked Mr. Smith if he would answer a few questions about the sale of his truck. Mr. Smith agreed and, when asked, stated the following:

    a. He advertised his truck for sale in a newspaper at $25,000.
    b. Dealer responded to the ad and bought the truck by paying $25,000 in currency, composed of one hundred dollar bills.
    c. The sale was completed on May 29, 2017, when the currency was exchanged for the truck and registration paperwork.

3. Mr. Smith further stated that he would agree to reducing the information to a written affidavit and swear to its accuracy.
4. I suggested that we meet again tomorrow at his home to prepare the affidavit. Mr. Smith agreed.
5. This interview concluded at 10:47 A.M. when we left Mrs. Smith's office.

I (prepared/dictated) this memorandum on July 26, 2018, after refreshing my memory from notes made during and immediately after the interview with Richard Smith.

John Jones
Special Agent

I certify that this memorandum has recorded in it a summary of all pertinent matters discussed with Richard and immediately after the interview with Richard Smith.

Mary Adams
Witness

Question and Answer Statement

A question and answer statement is a complete transcript of the questions, answers, and statements made by each participant during an interview. It may be prepared from a stenographer's notes or from a mechanical recording device. The source used to prepare the transcript should be preserved and associated with the case file as it may be needed in court to establish what was said.

A question and answer statement should contain:

- When and where the testimony was obtained

- The name and address of the person giving the testimony

- The matter the testimony relates to, including the purpose of the interview

- The name and title of the investigator asking questions and the name and title of the person giving answers

- The names and titles of all persons present during the testimony and the reason for each person being present, if not obvious

- The consent of the person being interviewed to use a tape recorder if a mechanical recording is being made

- Information given to the person being interviewed concerning his or her rights to counsel and against self-incrimination, if appropriate

- Administration of an oath if given

- Questions and answers establishing that the statement was made freely and voluntarily, without duress, and that no promises or commitments were made by the investigators

- Signatures of the investigators who conducted the interview and the person being interviewed

- Signature and the certification of the person transcribing the statement, showing the soured of the original information used

- Information that the person being interviewed was given the opportunity to examine the statement, correct any errors, and sign it

Question and Answer Statement Format

    Testimony of (name, address) given at (location including address) at (time) on (date) about (subject of investigation and their address).

    Present at this interview are (names and titles of all persons present).

    Questions were asked by (name and title of person asking the questions) and answers given by (person being interviewed).

    This interview is being recorded, as agreed upon, by means of (method of recording).

1. Q. You were requested to appear at (location) to answer questions concerning (subject matter). (If appropriate, advise the person being interviewed of his or her rights to counsel, etc.).

2. Q. Please stand and raise your right hand. Do you (person being interviewed) solemnly swear that the answers you are about to give to the questions asked will be the truth, so help you God?

3. Q. Did you sell a truck that you owned to Mr. Jim Dealer?
   A. (answer)

4. Q. How much did he pay you for the truck?
   A. (answer)

NOTE: The interview is brought to a close with the following questions?

120. Q. Have I, or has any other investigator or officer, threatened or intimidated you in any manner?
   A. (answer)

121. Q. Have I, or any other investigator or officer, offered you any rewards, promises, or immunity, in return for this statement?
   A. (answer)

122. Q. Have you given this statement freely and voluntarily?
   A. (answer)

123. Q. Is there anything further you care to add for the record?
   A. (answer)

    After this statement has been transcribed, you will be given an opportunity to read it, correct any errors, and sign it.

    NOTE: When transcribing the statement include the following:

    I have carefully read the foregoing statement consisting of page 1 to (last page number), inclusive, which is a correct transcript of my answers to questions asked me on (date of statement) at (location where statement was given), relative to (subject of investigation and their address). I hereby certify that the foregoing answers are true and correct, that I have made the corrections shown, have placed my initials opposite each correction, and that I have initialed each page of the statement.

(signature of person giving statement)

Subscribed and sworn to before me at (time), on (date) at (present location).

(signature and title of investigator)
(signature and title of witnessing investigator)

I (name of person transcribing statement), do hereby certify that I took the foregoing statement of (person giving statement) from (method of recording) and personally transcribed it and have initialed each page.

(signature and title of transcriber)

Normally, people will review and sign a question and answer statement after it has been put in its final form. Sometimes, for various reasons, the person may change his or her position and refuse to sign the statement. When an investigator is faced with such a refusal, he or she should request that the statement be read and verified for correctness. In such situations, the following can be inserted at the end of the statement.

This statement was read by (name) on (date) who stated that it was true and correct, but refused to be placed under oath or to sign it.

Just as there are advantages and disadvantages to using a memorandum as a recording device, so there are for the use of a question and answer statement.

Advantages and Disadvantages of the Question and Answer Statement

Advantages	Disadvantages
Reflects both questions and answers	Usually contains unnecessary material
Questions are generally asked in a logical sequence	Is often very long and involved
Is difficult to dispute with claims of misunderstanding	It is unedited; therefore, it picks up incorrect grammar, etc.
Is preferred when the issues are complicated	Tape recorder will pick up outside noises which can disrupt recording
Is useful when the person testifying under oath is illiterate or below average intelligence	Unable to make voice distinction
	Mechanical failure (if tape recorder used)
Can be used to challenge or discredit a witness	Can be viewed as intimidating by deponent; therefore, witnesses are often not willing to participate

Affidavit

An affidavit is a written declaration of facts made voluntarily and confirmed by oath or affirmation. The text of an affidavit may be prepared extemporaneously or composed by agreement between the affiant, the person making the statement, and the investigator. An affidavit can be either typed or handwritten, and prepared either by the affiant or investigator. There are certain advantages to allowing the affiant to compose and write an affidavit. These advantages are:

- The affidavit will be in the affiant's own words.
- The affidavit will be more credible because it is in the affiant's own handwriting. It would be difficult for the affiant to later deny the affidavit was his or hers.

One advantage to having the investigator prepare the affidavit is that the investigator will ensure that only relevant information will be covered and that the information will appear in an orderly fashion. In cases where the affiant is unable to either read or write, a witness other than the affiant or the investigator must read the affidavit to the affiant before he or she signs it. The affidavit must also be signed by both the investigator and witness.

No particular form of affidavit is required by common law. It is customary that affidavits have a caption or title, the judicial district in which given, the signature of the affiant, and the jurat. A jurat is the certification on an affidavit declaring when, where, and before whom it was sworn.

The affidavit is one of the most commonly used forms of recording testimony. It can be used during trial to impeach a witness, refresh memory, or it can be introduced as evidence. An affidavit should not contain hearsay or information about which the witness has no direct knowledge. If the person being interviewed was advised of his or her constitutional rights, this should be included in the affidavit.

A sample affidavit is found on the next page.

Sample Affidavit

United States of America
Southern Judicial District of Florida

I, <u>Richard L. Smith</u>   state that:
I reside at <u>123 A Street, Miami, Florida</u>   .
I am currently employed as a travel agent at Miami Travel, located at 117 Elm Street, Miami, Florida. On May 28, 2018, I placed a newspaper advertisement in the Miami Herald classified ads offering my 2017 truck for sale. I listed the asking price as $25,000. On May 29, I received a phone call from a man who said that he read the ad and would like to see my truck. He stated that he would like to look at it that afternoon. I gave him my address, and he came over about 30 minutes later. I gave him the keys, and we took a ride around the block. He said that he would buy the truck for $25,000. He opened the trunk of the car he was driving and pulled out a briefcase. We went into my house where he took $25,000 in one hundred dollar bills from the briefcase to pay for the truck. I was surprised at being paid in currency, but the man stated that he wanted the truck today and knew that it would take time for a check to clear the bank, so he brought cash. I gave him the ownership papers for the truck. I said thanks for buying the truck and gave him my business card requesting that he give me a call if he needed any travel planning. He gave me his business card and said he was in the import-export business. Jim went to his car and made a telephone call and a couple of minutes later two guys arrived and one drove Jim's car while Jim drove the truck away. I have not seen or heard from Jim since that day. On today's date, I gave Special Agent Jones a copy of the truck registration, serial number 1173945, that I sold to Jim Dealer on May 29, 2018, and the business card I received from Jim Dealer on that same date. I have received a receipt for both of these items from Special Agent Jones.

I have read the foregoing statement consisting of <u>1</u>   page(s) and have signed it. I fully understand this statement and it is true, accurate, and complete to the best of my knowledge and belief.

I made this statement freely and voluntarily without any threats or rewards, or promises of reward having been made to me in return for it.

Richard L. Smith
(Signature of affiant)
Subscribed and sworn to me before this <u>29</u>[th]
day of <u>July</u>   , <u>2018</u>.
at <u>Miami, Florida</u>

John Jones
(Signature)
Special Agent
(Title)

Mary Adams
(Signature of witness, if any)

The affidavit, like the memorandum and the question and answer statement, has advantages and disadvantages to its use. Prior to using an affidavit, the items listed below should be considered.

Advantages and Disadvantages of an Affidavit

Advantages	Disadvantages
Preserves probable testimony	Does not reflect questions asked
Frequently used in requiring testimony from:	May contain non-related information if prepared by affiant
Hostile witnesses	May not contain all pertinent information when prepared by affiant
Witnesses who have changed allegiance	May not be well written or clear if prepared by affiant
May be used as grounds to impeach witness	
Usually is easier to write than other types	
Valuable in developing an investigation	
May be written or typed and prepared on the spot	
May be concise and brief	

Sworn Statement

A sworn statement is, in a general sense, a declaration of matters of fact. It may be prepared in any form and should be signed and dated by the person preparing it. A sworn statement has the same judicial bearing as an affidavit. The investigator taking the statement administers an oath prior to the witness signing the statement. The following is an example of an oath that can be administered.

Do you (name of person giving statement) solemnly swear that everything contained in this statement is true and correct?

Mechanical Recordings

A mechanical recording device may be used to record statements when a stenographer is not readily available if all parties to the conversation consent. A recording device also may be used in conjunction with a stenographer, when necessary, again provided that all parties consent. When mechanical recording devices are used, the following guidelines are suggested:

- Identify, on tape, the individuals engaged in the conversation, any other persons present, and the time, date, and location.

- Immediately after the original has been made, make a copy of the tape for use in transcribing the conversation. If the recording was made during an undercover operation, seal and store the original after a transcribed copy has been made.

- Keep a written record of the tape's custodians and storage arrangements from the time it was recorded to the time it is submitted as evidence.

- When tape recordings are going to be used in taking a confession, advise the suspect of his or her rights and have the suspect state at the start of the tape recording that he or she is aware that a recording is being made.

- Off the record discussions between the investigator and the suspect should not be permitted during a recorded interview and should be kept to a minimum during a recorded interview with anyone else.

Form Letter

A form letter can be used to request information of a similar nature from several third parties. Following is an example of a form letter.

Sample Form Letter

Prosecuting Attorney's Office
Glynn County
300 South Main Street, 4th Floor
Brunswick, GA 31523
Telephone: (912) 555-5982
June 4, 2018

Ms. Michelle Tallmadge
1111 B Street
Glynco, GA 31520

Dear Ms. Tallmadge:

This office is conducting an investigation concerning Rosemary Westbury for the years 2016, 2017, and 2018. Ms. Westbury is a corporate officer of Massey TB, Inc. She is also the trustee for Massey TB Trust. We have reviewed the bank records of Massey TB, Inc. and Massey TB Trust. We found several checks made payable to you. Please answer the questions below which relate to the checks we found. We have included copies of the checks for your review.

Should you have any questions, please call investigator Dennis S. Paul at the telephone number listed above.

1. Did you receive check numbers 1521, 1571, 1681, 1952, 1991?
2. Did you endorse these checks?
3. Please explain why these checks were deposited into Massey TB Trust's bank account.
4. We would like to talk to you about these checks. Please call us, or provide your daytime telephone number so we can schedule an appointment.

Sincerely,

Dennis S. Paul

Grand Jury Transcript

A complete grand jury transcript will contain the questions, answers, and statements made by each participant before the grand jury. This transcript can be used as basis for a charge of perjury if the witness gives false information before the grand jury.

THE ART OF INTERVIEWING

Through practice, an investigator can improve his or her interview skills. But, equally important is practicing the art of critical self-analysis when dealing with others. This starts by stripping away the prejudices and other self-imposed barriers to impartiality that surface when communicating with people. It continues by learning to converse in different styles of language. Interviewing a college graduate and a fifth grade drop-out require different communication skills. How something is said is just as important as what is said. Everyone communicates through speech patterns and non-spoken behavior patterns. Witnesses sense the presence of the investigator's questions, not only with their ears, but by watching his or her gestures, making or avoiding eye contact, and feeling the stress in the room.

The interview process should flow naturally. The investigator should enter into the interview with general questions in mind. After the first question is asked, the investigator assumes a new role as the listener. Contingent upon what is heard, the investigator leads the interview toward the next question and then listens. This asking and listening process, controlled by the investigator, continues until the objectives of the interview have been achieved.

A successful interviewer has empathy for others. No one likes the thought of appearing foolish. Many witnesses are actually victims of fraudulent actions committed against them by the subject of the investigation and are embarrassed about being victimized. For example, businesses victimized by insiders are often reluctant to let the public know that they were vulnerable to fraud. A business may have more than money at stake. It becomes a matter of confidence and prestige in the public or industry's eye. An investigator who can become sensitive to a witness's situation quickly improves his or her interviewing techniques.

SUMMARY

The goal of an investigator is to conduct each interview in such a manner as to gather all available information and documents pertaining to the investigation and then make a permanent record of each witness's testimony for further reference.

The planning phase of the interview process is the foundation of an interview. Poor planning will have the same effect on an interview as a weak foundation has on a building. Proper planning enhances the probability of a successful interview. A successful interview can create a cooperative witness who can breathe life into financial records. It could also provide additional leads for the investigator to solve the case.

Once the investigator has decided on who, when, where, and how to interview the witness, the investigator should prepare a topical outline of the questions to be asked. Just as planning is the foundation of the interview process, the opening of an interview sets its tone. The body of the interview is the fact finding part of the process. The closing summarizes the key facts and provides an opportunity for the witness and the investigator to agree with the summation.

The medium used to record an interview should be reflective of the significance of the witness and the information and records provided by the witness.

22

Interviewing is a skill that can be developed and improved upon through practice. Few skills are as important to the financial investigator as the ability to talk to people and successfully gather information from them.

QUESTIONS AND EXERCISES

Answer the following questions and then check your responses with those provided following the questions and exercises.

1. How does an interview differ from an interrogation?

2. How do questions asked in a financial interview differ from those asked in other types of investigative interviews?

3. What are some things an investigator should consider when planning financial interviews during the course of an investigation?

4. Identify and describe the three methods of questioning that can be used in a financial interview.

5. Why is the introduction critical to a successful interview?

6. How can an investigator gain the cooperation of a hesitant witness?

7. Explain the following statement:
   The interview process is more than just asking questions and writing down responses.

8. What is wrong with the following question?
   He didn't have anyone with him when he came into the bank did he, but if he did, do you remember if the person was male or female and can you give a description of the person?

9. What is the last question an investigator should ask during an interview?

10. You are preparing to record an interview and you can't decide which method of recordation to use. You are torn between the memorandum and the question and answer statement. Describe the pros and cons of each.

11. What advantages are there to having a witness compose and write his or her own affidavit?

KEY (CORRECT ANSWERS)

1. A financial interview is conducted to obtain information and documentation from a witness. A financial interrogation is conducted for a different purpose. Its purpose is to elicit confessions or admissions of culpability from suspects or hostile witnesses.

2. Many investigative interviews focus on the recollection of witnesses. Questions such as, "Do you remember seeing any suspicious cars in the neighborhood?" or "What color jacket was he wearing?" are asked. Financial interviews go beyond recollection questions and deal with the specific details of financial transactions and the movement of money.

3. When planning interviews, an investigator should consider the following:

   - Who should I interview?
   - In what order should I interview the witnesses?
   - What type of witness is this person going to be?
   - Should I contact the suspect?
   - When should I contact the suspect?
   - What method of questioning should I use?

4. There are three general methods of questioning an investigator can use during a financial interview:

   - The chronological method
   - Questioning according to documents
   - Questioning according to transactions or events

   With the chronological method of questioning, a witness is questioned about the events in the order that they occurred, from beginning to end. With questioning according to documents, a particular document (financial statement, canceled check, tax return) is the focus of the interview. When questioning according to transaction or event, questions focus on a particular situation.

5. The introduction is critical as it sets the tone for the whole interview. Its primary objective is to put the witness at ease and get him or her to agree to answer questions.

6. To get hesitant witnesses to agree to cooperate, an investigator must avoid coming across as a threat. He or she should try to lead witnesses to believe that they will benefit from cooperating with the investigator.

7. An investigator must actively participate in the interview process. He or she must constantly analyze responses, and continually check for inconsistencies, inaccuracies, and incompleteness. Also, investigators must attend to what witnesses do during an interview. The visual and non-verbal aspects of an interview are very important.

8. The sentence is negatively phrased, and so long and complex that no one is going to understand it. Investigators should avoid asking complex and negatively phrased questions. All questions should be simple, to the point, and positively phrased.

9. The final question an investigator should ask is: "Is there anything else that you would like to say?" It gives the witness one final chance to say anything that he or she wishes.

10. The major advantage of the question and answer statement is that it contains all of the questions asked and answers provided during an interview. Of course, this could be viewed as a disadvantage also. The statement will be long, unedited, and could contain unnecessary material. On the other hand, the memorandum is more informal and it contains all pertinent testimony obtained during the interview. However, the testimony is recorded as the investigator recalls after refreshing his or her memory through informal notes. The memorandum does not contain the exact words of the witness. Both the memorandum and question and answer statement are good methods for recording an interview. The choice the investigator makes should be based on the complexity and investigative importance of the interview.

11. By allowing the affiant to create the affidavit, the investigator ensures that the affidavit will be in the affiant's own words and the credibility of the affidavit will increase because it is in the affiant's own handwriting. It would be difficult for the affiant to later deny the affidavit was his or hers.

FINANCIAL SOURCES OF INFORMATION

This section addresses where to look for information that may ultimately be used as evidence against, or, on the other hand, in support of a suspect. As a financial investigation begins, questions concerning a suspect's finances are plentiful. Does the suspect own the home in which she lives or does she rent? If she owns the home, how much did she pay for it and how did she pay for it? If she rents, how much does she pay, and is she the one who pays or does some second party pay the rent? Does she have a criminal record? Does she own the car she drives? How did she pay for the trip to China she took last year? It all seems pretty simple—just ask her! Well, sometimes, if you have a cooperative suspect, it is that simple. But how cooperative would you be if you had the authorities investigating your actions—especially if you had something to hide?

This chapter begins with a discussion on selecting suspects to target for an investigation. The decision to target a suspect is not made lightly as both the suspect and the investigative team can be affected by a poor decision. The remainder of the chapter identifies some of the many sources of information of interest to an investigator. For the investigator, the important thing to keep in mind is that most financial transactions, whether lawful or unlawful, are recorded and can be recreated if the investigator can piece together the correct "paper trail". The sources listed in this chapter provide a foundation for the initiation of that paper trail.

- Discuss what factors influence the selection of a suspect to target in an investigation.
- Identify appropriate sources to obtain specific information.
- Analyze financial records for leads.

No matter how many computers, police cars, or Swat teams law enforcement may possess, not one criminal will be put behind bars unless the most precious of all commodities is available—information. Discovering, understanding, analyzing, and using information is one of the keys to successful law enforcement. When an investigator initiates an investigation, his or her knowledge of information sources is invaluable. This chapter provides you with many sources of information of interest to the financial investigator. These are selected sources and by no means should the listings provided be considered exhaustive. Remember, information is everywhere. The key is to focus on information that will resolve the allegation.

INITIAL CONSIDERATIONS

Before listing and describing various sources of information, we will explore some of the things that are considered when an investigation is initiated. What should be considered before targeting a suspect for investigation? How should an investigator deal with a suspect as a source of information? What happens when a suspect refuses to cooperate? Each of these issues will be address below.

Selecting Who to Target for Investigation

The role of a financial investigator is to gather evidence to support, or in the alternative, dispel allegations of financial criminal activity. Where to look and what to look for are two integral questions facing every investigator. In theory, neither question is difficult to answer—merely look everywhere for everything. But a problem surfaces when reality is thrown into the equation. Investigators cannot spend their whole careers working on only one investigation.

Account Transactions

Account transactions are financial events that directly affect the movement of money through a bank account. In this context, "directly affect" means deposits to, or withdrawals from, an account. Account transactions occur in checking, savings, and credit union accounts. Records of account transactions are maintained through the use of the following documents:
- Signature card
- Bank statements
- Deposit tickets/items
- Checks/withdrawal items
- Credit and debit memorandums

Signature Cards—Opening an Account

The first document prepared and maintained in a bank's system of recordkeeping is the signature card. Every financial institution requires that a customer (individuals, trusts, business organizations, etc.) fill out a signature card when opening an account. It indicates who owns the account and may require that the account owner(s) supply his or her address, occupation, employer, date/place of birth, and social security number. When a business organization opens an account, corporate resolutions, and partnership and trust agreements, if applicable, often are included as part of the background information requested by the bank. This type of information is kept with the signature card.

For the investigator, the signature card provides valuable leads to other witnesses or unknown co-conspirators. Since the card contains the signature of the account owner(s), it can serve as a sample of the owner's handwriting.

Bank Statements—Record of Transactions

Banks periodically reconcile the financial activity in each account. A record of this reconciliation is prepared and retained by the institution and a copy is sent to the account's owner. Details of all financial activity affecting the account for the period in question are shown on a bank statement. A portion of Anthony Benidect's bank statement is shown on the next page. Mr. Benedict is a suspect in a drug trafficking investigation.

The financial investigator should retrieve all bank statements related to the time frame under investigative consideration, keeping in mind that some criminal activities are well underway prior to detection; therefore, bank statements must be retrieved for a period of time prior to the detection of criminal activity. Through bank statement analysis, the investigator will be able to reconstruct the financial transactions that occurred during the period of criminal activity, and identify sources of information or investigative leads to the movement of money. These sources or leads may include:
- Unusually high monthly balances in comparison to known sources of income
- Unusually large deposits, deposits in round numbers, or deposits in repeated amounts which are not attributable to legitimate sources of income
- The timing of deposits. This is particularly important when dates of illegal payments are known.
- Checks written in unusually large amounts (in relation to the suspect's known practices)
- A lack of account activity. This may indicate transactions in currency or the existence of other unknown bank accounts

Checking Account Summary National Bank of the Nation

Customer Service-Operations Center
P.O. Box 001, Washington, D.C. 20009

National Bank of the Nation

Anthony Benidect
1229 Springtide Pl, NW
Washington, D.C. 20001

Statement Period
03/20/17-04/20/17

If you have questions about your account, please call 202-555-1111 or toll free 800-222-9999

Checking summary for account 097405813			
Beginning balance	1.532.46	Minimum Balance	1,040.33
3 Deposit(s) totaling	10,041.94+	Average Balance	4,304.59
Interest this period	0.00+		
8 Deduction(s) totaling	1,246.60-		
Other deductions	0.00-		
Service charges this period	0.00-		
Ending balance	10,327.80		

Description of Account Transactions		Date	Amount	Balance
Beginning balance				$1,532.46
Cash withdrawal	Trans. #4552			
Landmark 1	Alexandria, VA	03/22	100.00-	1,432.46
Check 546		03/23	67.25-	1,365.21
Check 547		03/27	234.63-	1,130.58
Purchase				
Mobil	Herndon VA	03/28	15.25-	1,115.33
Cash withdrawal	Trans #0849			
West Village	Washington, DC	03/30	75.00-	1,040.33
Deposit		04/01	1,645.97+	2,686.30
Check 548		04/01	623.34-	2,062.96
Deposit		04/02	6,50.00+	8,812.96
Check 550		04/05	118.23-	8,694.73
549		04/12	12.90-	8,681.83
Deposit		04/15	1,645.97+	10,327.80
			Ending Balance	$10,327.80

Deposit Slips/Deposit Items

From the bank's point of view, the deposit function is the most important of all of the banking transactions. The majority of loans and investments made by the institution come from the depositors' dollars. When deposits cease, the institution ceases.

From the investigator's point of view, seeing a suspicious deposit on a bank statement does not in and of itself provide enough detail of the financial transaction. If a deposit appears to be suspicious, the investigator will want to examine the corresponding deposit slip. Upon reviewing Mr. Benidect's previously shown bank statement, the investigator wants to further examine the deposit made on April 2, 2017. That deposit slip is shown below, and it reveals that the deposit was comprised of $4,500 in currency and a check for $2,250.

```
        DEPOSIT TICKET             CURRENCY   4,500—
                              CASH                           15-099
        Anthony Benidect            COIN                      540
     1229 Springtide Place, NW  LIST CHECKS SINGLY 2,250—
        Washington, DC 20001

  Date April 2, 2017           TOTAL FROM OTHER SIDE  —  —
  DEPOSITS MAY NOT BE AVAILABLE FOR IMMEDIATE WITHDRAWAL   TOTAL   6,750—      USE OTHER SIDE FOR
                                                                              ADDITIONAL LISTING
                                LESS CASH RECEIVED    —  —
    SIGN HERE FOR CASH RECEIVED (IF REQUIRED)   NET DEPOSIT  6,750—

  National Bank of the Nation

  ⑇054000991⑇ 097405813⑇      9987
```

Upon reviewing the deposit slip, the investigator has to wonder where Anthony Benidect got $4,500 in cash and who wrote the check that was deposited. Bank statements and deposit slips do not speak for themselves; they need to be interpreted by "financial witnesses"—the currency, checks, and other items that comprise the deposit. By retrieving and examining the items of deposit, the investigator may find additional leads to follow.

The original documents involved in a deposit are not retained by the bank. Currency is returned to circulation, checks go back to the bank of origin, and deposits made via an electronic transfer show up as mere bookkeeping entries. However, copies of each deposited item, except currency, are made. The bank organizes and maintains these copies on microfilm. By reviewing these records, the investigator may be able to locate other witnesses.

To successfully gather information from bank deposits, the investigator needs an understanding of the bank's system of maintenance, organization, and retrieval of deposit information. An overview of the system is shown on the next page and discussed below.

Transaction Entry Point

A deposit enters the banking system through a transaction entry point. There are three different types of transaction entry points:

- **Teller.** A teller receives deposits directly from the customer, or through the mail or automatic teller machine.

- **Cash Services Department.** High volume deposit customers such as major retail establishments, grocery stores, or governmental units make their deposits to the bank via armored cars or delivery services. The Cash Services Department handles these types of deposits.

- **Other Internal Departments of the Bank.** Deposit transactions can occur through intra-account activities (transfer of funds from a savings account into the same customer's checking account) or electronic transfers between financial institutions. Additionally, with the advent of direct deposit, businesses and companies can make deposit transactions into bank accounts from their own bookkeeping departments. Such services are handled by different departments inside the financial institution.

The transaction entry point is vital in the investigative process. It's even more than vital because at the point of deposit two undeniable events occur: money is moved from somewhere by someone and a permanent record is made.

During the early stages of a financial investigation, books and records usually reveal nothing out of the ordinary and bank statements often seem inconclusive of any wrongdoing. The information collected by the investigator is sketchy and denials by the suspect are frequent:
"I don't even know that guy."
"My firm never did business with that company."
However, through deposit analysis, the investigator often finds:

- A photograph of the person who "didn't even know the guy" depositing currency into the "guy's" savings account. Financial institutions have security cameras that record teller window transactions.
- Checks from "that firm" going into "that company's" checking account.

Banking Operations

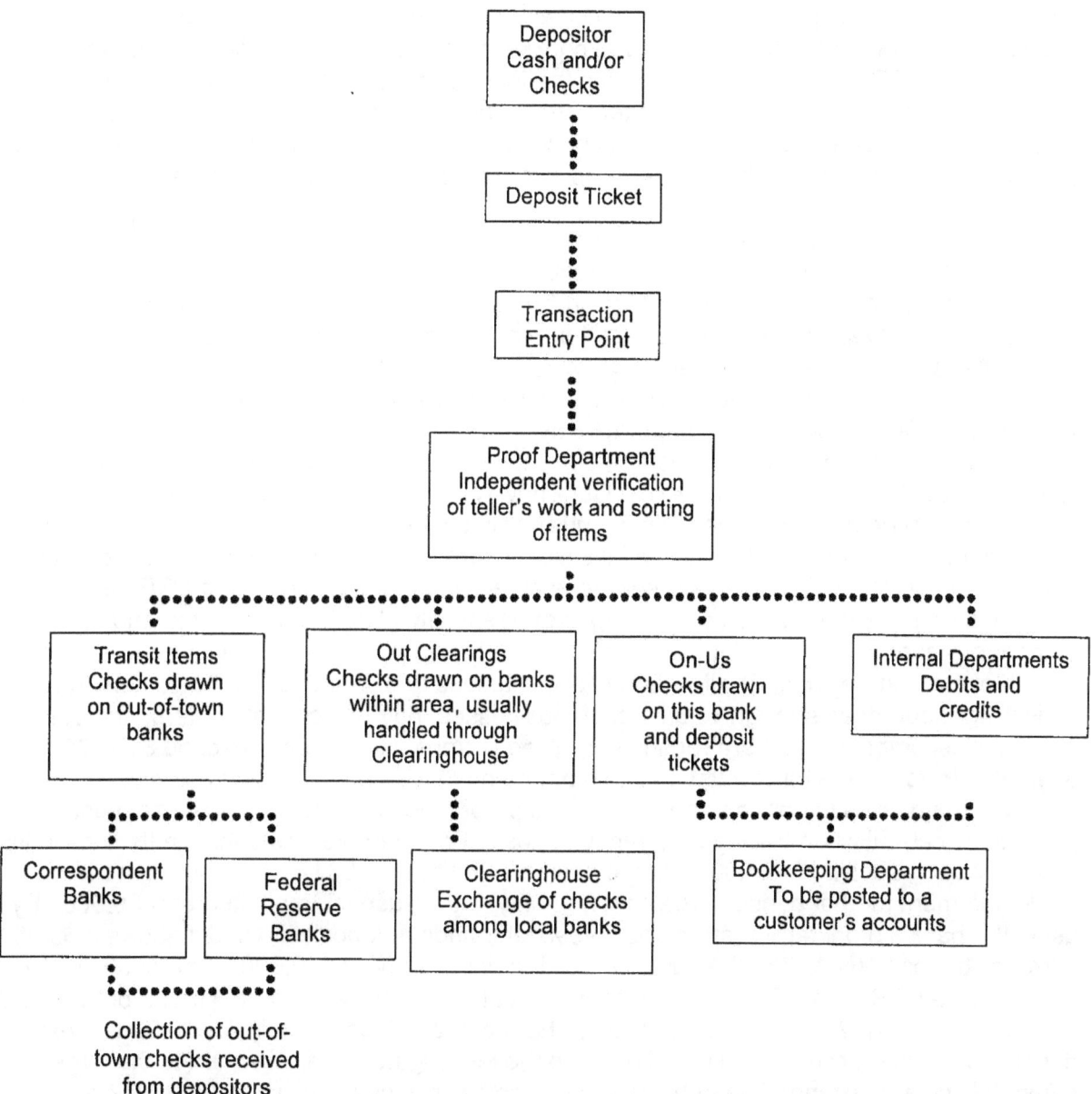

In certain investigations, the transaction entry point can be critical to the investigation's success. In a counterfeiting investigation, for example, intervention by law enforcement at the point of entry is crucial. The same holds true for situations involving buy money (narcotics cases) or marked bills (extortion or blackmail cases). Investigators, perpetrators, and the currency in question must meet simultaneously at the transaction point of entry, in order to successfully defeat the criminal act. The importance of this is highlighted by the fact that all currency, once inside the banking system, is treated alike. Once past the point of entry, it is extremely difficult, if not entirely impossible, to reconstruct the source of the currency. Accordingly, in these situations the financial institution should be requested to separate and segregate the currency in question before it enters any further into the banking system.

The Proof Department

From the transaction entry point, deposits go to the Proof Department. Here, checks are encrypted with the bank's own numerical codes—proof numbers. Proof numbers establish the "location keys" for the bank's retrieval and bookkeeping system. Magnetic ink character recognition (MICR) encoding also occurs in the Proof Department. An MICR number enables a check to be read by high speed computers during the processing and clearing procedure. A portion of the MICR number is placed on checks when they are initially printed. After a check is deposited, the remainder of the MICR number is placed on the check in the bank of deposit's Proof Department.

In addition to being encoded, the check is microfilmed. In the microfilming process, all checks shown on one deposit slip are microfilmed consecutively before proceeding to the next group of deposited items. The order of microfilming is generally determined by the transaction entry point. For example, all of Teller No. 1's transactions are microfilmed and then all of Teller No. 2's transactions are microfilmed, etc.

Currency is not microfilmed. Once it is inside the bank, it is counted and, after the count has been verified, it goes its own separate way. Title 31 U.S.C. §5313 states that financial institutions are required to file a report on currency transactions. One such report is the Department of the Treasury Form 4789, Currency Transaction Report (CTR), the first page of which is shown on the next page. When currency in excess of $10,000 is deposited, the CTR identifies the depositor by address, social security number, and date of birth, and the actual owner of the currency if he or she is someone other than the depositor. The CTR also records the total amount of the transaction, the types of bills involved in the transaction, and various other information.

Government regulations allow financial institutions to exempt certain customers from the CTR filing requirements. High volume cash businesses, payroll account holders, and other commercial companies that are routinely involved in transactions which exceed $10,000 may be exempt. However, the bank must maintain a record of these exempted customers.

When an investigator searches the bank's proof tapes (microfilm), he or she must be particularly careful when tracing a currency deposit. For example, investigative findings indicate that a suspect received $18,000 in illegal payments on May 1, 2017. A review of the target's bank statement for that period reveals that on May 1, the suspect deposited only $9,000. By using the bank's proof tape system, the investigator finds a deposit slip and it shows a $9,000 currency deposit. (Note that the suspect kept the deposit under $10,000 so he or she would not have to file a CTR form.) The investigator has located half of the illegal payment, but where did the other $9,000 go? A continued search of the proof tape locates a similar $9,000 currency deposit to another account which, unknown to the investigator, is also owned to the target. Often, this type of extended search will uncover split currency deposits and/or multiple transactions.

Form 4789
(Rev. September 1991)
Department of the Treasury
Internal Revenue Service

Currency Transaction Report

▶ File a separate report for each transaction. ▶ Please type or print.
▶ For Paperwork Reduction Act Notice, see page 3.
(Complete all applicable parts—See instructions)

OMB No. 1545-0183
Expires: 9-30-94

1 Check appropriate boxes if: a ☐ amends prior report, b ☐ exemption limit exceeded, c ☐ suspicious transaction.

Part I — Identity of individual who conducted this transaction with the financial institution

2 If more than one individual is involved, see instructions and check here . . . . ▶ ☐

3 Reason items 4-15 below are not fully completed (check all applicable boxes): a ☐ Armored car service (name) ▶ ....
 b ☐ Mail deposit/shipment   c ☐ Night deposit or ATM transaction   d ☐ Multiple transactions (see instructions)

4 Last name	5 First name	6 Middle initial	7 Social security number
8 Address (number, street, and apt. or suite no.)		9 Occupation, profession, or business	
10 City	11 State	12 ZIP code	13 Country (if not U.S.)	14 Date of birth (see instructions)

15 Method used to verify identity: a Describe identification ▶ ....
 b Issued by ▶   c Number ▶

Part II — Person (see General Instructions) on whose behalf this transaction was conducted

16 If this transaction was conducted on behalf of more than one person, see instructions and check here . . . . ▶ ☐

17 This person is an: ☐ individual or ☐ organization 18 If trust, escrow, brokerage, or other 3rd party account, see instructions and check here . ▶ ☐

19 Individual's last name or Organization's name	20 First name	21 Middle initial	22 Social security number

23 Alien identification: a Describe identification ▶ .... Employer identification number
 b Issued by ▶   c Number ▶

| 24 Address (number, street, and apt. or suite no.) | | 25 Occupation, profession, or business | |
| 26 City | 27 State | 28 ZIP code | 29 Country (if not U.S.) | 30 Date of birth (see instructions) |

Part III — Types of accounts and numbers affected by transaction (If more than one of the same type, use additional spaces provided below)

31 s ☐ Savings ▶ .... T ☐ Securities ▶ .... N ☐ CD/Money market ▶ ....
 C ☐ Checking ▶ .... L ☐ Loan ▶ .... O ☐ Other (specify) ▶ ....

Part IV — Type of transaction. Check applicable boxes to describe transaction

32 E ☐ Currency exchange (currency for currency)

33 CASH IN: F ☐ CD/Money market purchased 34 CASH OUT: R ☐ CD/Money market redeemed
 D ☐ Deposit   H ☐ For wire transfer   C ☐ Check cashed   U ☐ From wire transfer
 G ☐ Security purchased A ☐ Receipt from abroad   T ☐ Security redeemed B ☐ Shipment abroad
 P ☐ Check purchased K ☐ Other (specify) ▶   W ☐ Withdrawal   Y ☐ Other (specify) ▶

35 Total amount of currency transaction (in U.S. dollar equivalent) (always round up) 36 Amount in item 35 in U.S. $100 bills or higher 37 Date of transaction (see instructions)

Cash in $ .... .00   Cash in $ .... .00
Cash out $ .... .00   Cash out $ .... .00 ☐ Unknown

38 If other than U.S. currency is involved, please furnish the following information: a Exchange made ☐ for or ☐ from U.S. currency
 b Country .... c Amount of currency (in U.S. dollar equivalent) $ .... .00
 b Country .... c Amount of currency (in U.S. dollar equivalent) $ .... .00

39 If a negotiable instrument or wire transfer was involved in this transaction, please furnish the following information and check this box (see instructions) . ▶ ☐
 a Number of negotiable instruments involved .... c Total amount of all negotiable instruments and all wire transfers
 b Number of wire transfers involved   (in U.S. dollar equivalent) ▶ $ .... .00

Part V — Financial institution where transaction took place

40 a ☐ Bank (enter code number from instructions here) ▶
 b ☐ Savings and loan association c ☐ Credit union d ☐ Securities broker/dealer e ☐ Other (specify) ▶

41 Name of financial institution	42 Address where the transaction occurred (see instructions)	43 Employer identification number
44 City	45 State	46 ZIP code	47 MICR number	Social security number

48 If this is a multiple transaction, please indicate: a Number of transactions ▶   c ZIP codes ▶
       b Number of branches ▶

Sign Here ▶

49 Signature (preparer)	50 Title	51 Date
52 Type or print preparer's name	53 Approving official (signature)	54 Date	55 Telephone number

Cat. No. 42004W

From the Proof Department, deposited items take different routes through the bank of deposit's system. The path that an item takes is dependent upon the bank of origin's (bank upon which the item is drawn) relationship to the bank of deposit. Let's look at the four paths an item of deposit may take by looking at four items deposited into Bank A. The four types of items and their paths are shown and described on the following pages.

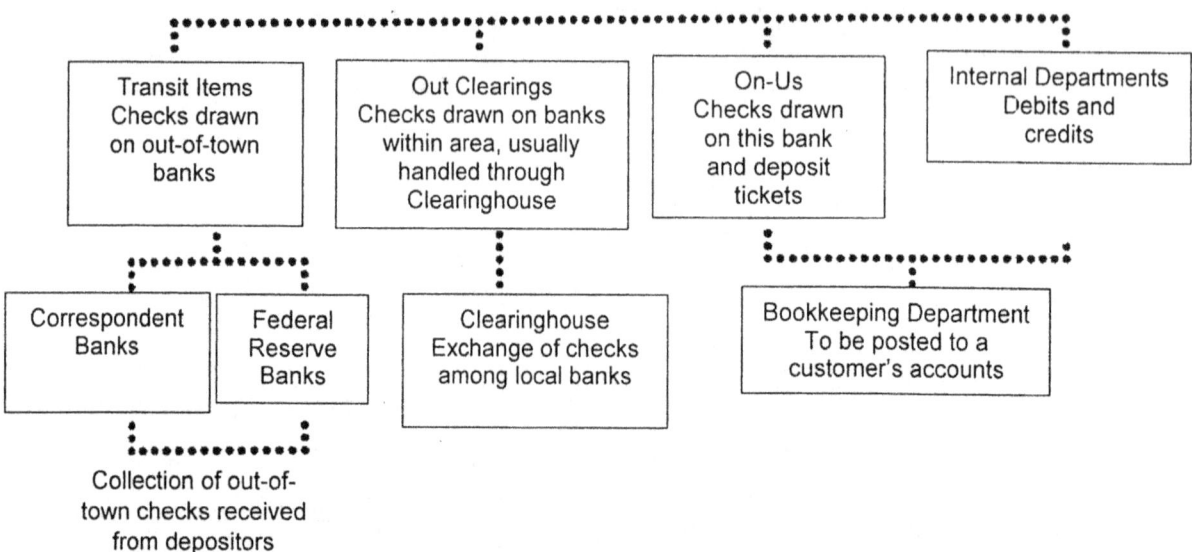

- **Transit Items.** The first of our four items deposited into Bank A is a transit item. Transit items are checks and other items (money orders and traveler's checks) drawn on financial institutions other than the bank of deposit. In the case of a check, the bank of deposit ships the check back to the bank of origin. The bank of origin, in turn, normally sends the check back to the customer by including it in his or her bank statement. This happens after the bank of deposit sends the check to an intermediary bank that was established to assist in the clearing process.

  Certain banks act as clearinghouses for transit items. These banks, known as correspondent and clearinghouse banks, receive items from banks all over the country and process them back to the bank of origin located in their particular area. Major banks in metropolitan areas act as correspondent banks. Also, the Federal Reserve Bank is a clearinghouse bank.

  Actually, there are 12 Federal Reserve Banks (and some have branch banks) located throughout the country. The role of each is to monitor the commercial and savings banks in its region to ensure that they follow Federal Reserve Board regulations. Each Federal Reserve Bank is a separate corporation, its stock owned by commercial banks that are members of the Federal Reserve System. The Federal Reserve System is made up of all nationally chartered banks and any state chartered bank that is accepted for membership.

  Transit items are provided with proof numbers and microfilmed by each bank they pass through during their return trip to the bank of origin. This establishes a retrieval "audit trail" for each item.

- **Out Clearings.** The second item deposited into Bank A is an out clearing item. An out clearing item is an item drawn on a bank in the same geographic area as the bank of deposit. These items are handled in the same way as transit items and, like transit items, they are given proof numbers and microfilmed by each bank they pass through on their return trip to the bank of origin.

- **On-us Items.** The third item deposited in Bank A is an on-us item. An on-us item is a check draw on the bank of deposit. Certain on-us items require special handling during the clearing process and are sent to a particular internal department for final processing. All on-us items eventually flow into the bookkeeping department.

- **Items from a Bank's Internal Departments.** The fourth item that Bank A deals with is an item from one of its internal deposits. This item might be a transfer between intrabank accounts, loan proceeds, a certificate of deposit, or an electronic transfer into an account.

Checks/Withdrawal Items

Funds normally are withdrawn from a bank account through the issuance of a check. Withdrawal slips and automatic teller machines are also used to withdraw funds. The face of a check contains information that is of interest to an investigator. It shows the bank of origin, date and amount of the check, name of the payee (the entity to whom the check was made payable), and the authorized signature of the owner of the account on which the check is drawn. The following information also appears on the face of a check:

- **American Banker's Association (ABA) Transit Number and Federal Reserve Routing Code.** Have you ever noticed the number on the upper right side of a check that looks something like a fraction? It provides several pieces of information. The numerator contains the ABA transit number; the denominator is the bank of origin's check routing symbol.

  An ABA transit number is a two-part code assigned to banks and savings institutions by the American Banker's Association. The first part shows a two- or three-digit number that corresponds to the city, state, or territory where the bank of origin is located. The second part of the ABA transit number identifies the bank itself. The ABA transit number on the check shown below tells an investigator that the bank is located in Washington, DC and that "099" is the code for the National Bank of the Nation.

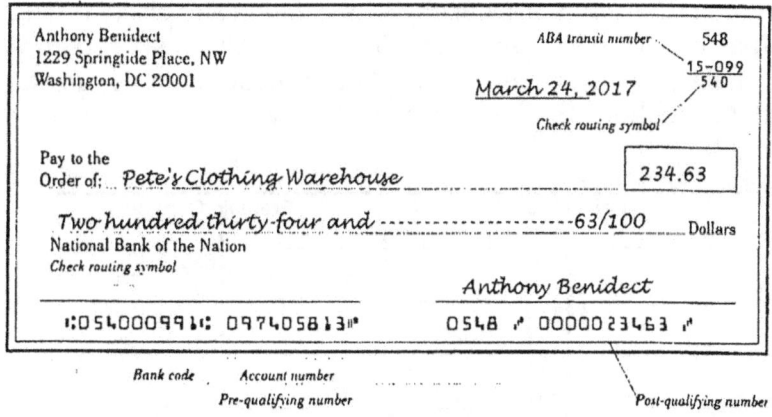

The bank of origin's check routing symbol is a three- or four-digit number that provides the following three pieces of information:

- The bank of origin's Federal Reserve district
- The Federal Reserve facility through which the check is collected
- The fund's availability assigned to the check. Funds availability is either immediate or deferred. If "0" is the last digit, immediate availability is indicated. A digit of 1 through 9 indicates a deferred payment.

- **Pre-Qualifying Numbers.** The portion of the MICR number that comes printed on a check. The pre-qualifying number indicates bank of origin information (paying bank's number and check routing symbol), customer account number, and the check's number.

- **Post-Qualifying Number.** The portion of the MICR number entered by the bank of deposit's Proof Department. It shows the dollar amount of the check.

When investigators request a copy of a check, they should ask for copies of both sides because the back side of a check also contains valuable information. For one thing, it will show who endorsed the check. If the check was issued to an individual, it should contain that person's signature; if it was issued to a business organization, it will probably contain a stamped endorsement. The back of a check will also contain information related to the movement of money. Proof numbers from all of the banks that the check passed through will be available.

When a payee receives a check, he or she may either deposit it or cash it. If the check is deposited, it follows the clearing process previously discussed. Checks that are cashed are recognizable by teller stamps or "cashed" codes that are encoded or stamped on the face of the check itself. These codes can lead an investigator to the teller who cashed the check and who, therefore, needs to be interviewed about the specific transaction. A teller's stamp or "cashed" code also can be a possible link between a specific teller and the suspect. Many times a suspect will go to the same teller and develop a relationship with that person. Conversations between these people may reveal leads to the crime. Whether knowingly or unknowingly, the teller may possess valuable information.

From an investigator's standpoint, checks are of equal or greater importance than deposits. Checks establish a strong financial link that cannot be overcome by verbal denials. Checks may identify other bank accounts, credit cards, the purchase or location of major assets, and loan transactions which directly impact on financial investigations. A $25 check for a utility hookup may identify a $250,000 hidden condo.

Checks can be organized to reveal patterns of financial activity through an investigative technique known as check spread analysis. To perform check spread analysis, the investigator lists a suspect's checks by payee. A sample check spread analysis, using checks obtained from our suspect, Mr. Anthony Benidect, is show below.

Check by Payee Analysis

Date	Virginia Electric	Date	Franklin Gardens
1/23	$101.79	1/3	$650
2/21	$121.32	2/2	$650
3/21	$92.56	3/1	$650
4/25	$87.87		
5/21	$59.12	5/2	$650
6/27	$63.45	6/2	$650
7/22	$79l73	7/1	$650
8/20	$98.92	8/3	$650
9/23	$92.83	9/2	$650
10/21	$64.55	10/	$650
11/24	$58.52		
12/28	$87.62	12/2	$650

In the sample check analysis, the investigator listed all of Mr. Benidect's checks payable to the Virginia Electric Company for one calendar year. From this list, the investigator is able to determine that Mr. Benidect paid his electric bill every month. The investigator then listed all checks payable to "Franklin Garden Apartments," the complex where Mr. Benidect rents an apartment. The investigator finds that checks for rental payments are missing for the months of April and November. The investigator will want to find out how Mr. Benidect paid his rent for those months. The absence of a check may indicate a currency payment which can lead to possible undisclosed sources of illegal income.

Credit and Debit Memos—Special Transactions

Any transaction that affects an account but does not involved a deposit ticket or check withdrawal requires special handling. A record of these "unusual transactions" is listed on the customer's bank statement through memorandum entries. These entries are shown to report the movement of money that takes place without going through the normal transaction points of entry or withdrawals through checks. Credit memos or "CM" indicate an increase in the account funds, a flow of funds into the account. A debit memo or "DM" indicates a decrease in the account funds, a flow of funds out of the account.

Credit and Debit Memos

CM (+)	DM (-)
Interest earned	Interest payment
Loan proceeds	Loan payment
Wire transfer in	Wire transfer out
Special collection of funds	Check printing fees
Transfer between accounts	Transfer between accounts
Electronic deposit	Electronic withdrawal

Non-Account Transactions

Non-account transactions are financial transactions that occur at a financial institution but do not flow through an account. Examples of non-account transactions include loans; purchase or negotiation of cashier's checks, money orders, traveler's checks, and currency transactions such as exchanging currency for currency and cashing third-party checks. For investigative purposes, wire transfers, entries into a safe-deposit box, and the purchase or sale of securities are also considered non-account transactions.

Loans

Loan applications, loan repayment ledgers, and loan correspondence files are usually maintained by financial institutions. A loan application usually requires a financial statement completed by the individual requesting a loan. It represents a good "financial lead document" for the investigator. If an investigator is looking to identify a suspect's assets and accounts, he or she should turn to any available loan applications, since the suspect, eager to impress the bank with his or her solvency, will identify assets and other accounts more candidly on that document than in an investigative interview. Furthermore, loan applications most often contain a statement that the applicant is aware, by signing the document, that it is a federal crime to knowingly make false statements when applying for a loan.

The loan repayment schedule and correspondence files can be used by the investigator to detect:

- **Repayment Methods.** Lump sum, accelerated, or unusual repayments can be traced through the bank's proof system.
- **Final Disposition of Loan Proceeds.** The disposition may be within the bank (on-us items) or elsewhere. Either situation is traceable through the bank's recordkeeping system.
- **Loan Collateral.** The security pledged for the loan, if any, may be an unknown asset.
- **Downpayment.** The loan proceeds may have been used to finance an asset, the downpayment for which came from illegal funds.
- **Credit Checks and Internal Memoranda.** The investigations done by the credit department to determine the risk for the bank may lead the investigator to additional assets, loans, bank accounts, etc.

In any case, loan information leads to other people and other assets. For example, loan proceeds may have been deposited into hidden accounts or these accounts may have been used to repay a loan. Loan documents may have been co-signed by a previously unknown associate or the suspect may have taken a loan out for someone else. Loan repayments could be traced to previously unknown accounts or associates. Tracing the ultimate disposition of the loan proceeds and the ultimate source of the loan repayments is a vital technique for the trained investigator.

Cashier's Checks, Certified Checks, Traveler's Checks, and Money Orders.

These financial instruments require special handling by a bank because they involve various departments inside the bank. Cashier's checks are checks drawn by the bank on its own funds and are issued by an authorized officer of the bank. The bank employee will ask the customer to designate a remitter (person purchasing the check) and a payee in order to fill in these lines on the check. A certified check is a check where the bank guarantees that there are sufficient funds on deposit for that particular check. A money order is a negotiable instrument that serves as a substitute for a check. The money order is issued for a specific amount of payment and the customer fills in the name of the purchaser and payee. The bank employee imprints only the amount of payment. A traveler's check is an internationally redeemable draft. It is purchased in various denominations, such as $20.00, $50.00, and $100.00, and is only valid with the holder's own endorsement against his or her original signature.

Investigative analysis of the bank checks described above follow the "proof process" if they were deposited into or purchased by withdrawal from a known account. If these documents were purchased with currency or checks drawn on an unknown account, locating them is significantly more difficult. In most situations, retrieval requires a hand search of each bank check written, which is a very labor-intensive process. In the alternative, interviewing bank employees in an attempt to pinpoint the transaction date and the amount may prove more successful. If the suspect goes to the same bank and uses the same bank officer or teller to complete his or her bank transactions, these people may be able to assist in narrowing the search for the retrieval of the bank checks at issue.

Currency Transactions—Currency Exchanges and the Cashing of Third-Party Checks

Documenting the movement of money involved in a pure currency exchange is difficult. Currency-for-currency exchange transactions generally leave no paper trail inside the bank system unless the amount exceeds the $10,000 and then a CTR must be filed. The best source of information is the testimonial recollections of bank personnel.

A third-party check is a check that the payee endorses to another party. It can be traced by the bank's "proof system" if the third party is a legitimate entity. Financial institutions routinely require two forms of identification to cash a check, but if the check is made payable to a fictitious third party and is cashed using false identification, the proof system is unworkable. When this situation occurs, the only alternative is to contact the entity who originated the check.

Wire Transfers—Electronic Transfers

There is nothing mysterious about a wire transfer. Records detailing both ends of the transaction should be available either from the bank of origin or destination, or both. Out-of-the-country (off shore) wire transfers can create a retrieval problem depending on the country involved. Various "haven countries" are known to offer a legal tender and/or economic climate for laundering money or hiding illegally gotten profits. These are often located in the Caribbean and other areas, and restrict dissemination of this type of financial information. When money is moved by a wire transfer and neither the source of the funds nor the date of the transfer is known, retrieval of any identifying information is very difficult.

Safe-Deposit Boxes

Financial institutions rent or lease storage facilities in secured areas of the bank to its customers. The safe-deposit box rental agreement indicates the date the box was first rented and the identity of the renter; however, bank records will not reveal the contents of the box. An entry log maintained by the bank shows the date and times of visits to the box and also reports the identity of the visitor. This information may have significant investigatory importance. For example, records of entry into a safe-deposit box can corroborate testimony relating to the receipt of illegal currency or the proceeds from illegal activities.

Bank Credit Cards

Since many banks offer credit cards to their customers, charge slips and repayment information relating to these cards might be available. The financial investigator may find leads to purchases of jewelry, cars, furs, etc. through these records.

Questions About Bank Records

Before discussing other types of financial institutions as sources of information, the following two items concerning the retrieval of financial records should be addressed.

How Easy It is for an Investigator to Obtain Financial Records from a Financial Institution

The most knowledgeable source of financial information are the suspects targeted for investigation. Just as they have the answers to questions relating to guilt or innocence, they also have custody of financial records of importance to the investigator. Suspects are the customers of banks, the applicants for loans, and the purchasers of the securities. Therefore, they possess the original records relating to the money movement. By asking for these records, the investigator can gain access to this otherwise restricted information.

Financial institutions restrict access to records of money movement. The Bank Secrecy Act and the Right to Financial Privacy Provisions of Federal law restrict open dissemination of financial information to law enforcement. Accordingly, without the individual customer's permission, banks are forbidden to provide financial records to anyone, except when they are legally compelled to do so. Banks are also required to notify the customer of any request unless legally told not to. Such legal compulsion can take the form of subpoenas, summonses, or court orders.

While financial institutions cannot provide documents or access to information in the customer's account, except in accordance with the law, they can notify the government of the existence of relevant information in those records. The law states, "Nothing in this chapter shall preclude any financial institution, or any officer, employee, or agent of a financial institution from notifying a government authority that such institution or officer, employee, or agent has information which may be relevant to a possible violation of any statute or regulation.

In other words, if a financial institution has information or a belief that information exists relating to a violation of a Federal statute or regulation, they can contact the government (or agency charged with responsibility for compliance) and tell them that such information exists. It is up to the Federal agency to go through the hoops to get the proper authority for dissemination of the records.

How Long is a Financial Institution Required to Maintain Customer Records?

The Bank Secrecy Act requires financial institutions to keep certain records of customer transactions. United States Treasury Regulations implementing the Bank Secrecy Act provide, in part, that an original, microfilm, or other copy or reproduction of most checking account deposits and savings accounts records must be retained for 5 years. The records must include the following:

- Signature card
- Statements, ledger cards, or other records disclosing all deposits and withdrawals
- Copies of both sides of customer checks, bank draft money orders, and cashier's checks drawn on the bank or issued and payable by it

In addition, banks must retain, for a 2-year period, all records necessary to:

- Reconstruct a customer's checking account. These records must include copies of customers' deposit tickets.
- Trace and supply a description of a check deposited to a customer's checking account.

The requirements listed above apply only to checks and deposits in excess of $100. Most banks, however, find it cheaper to microfilm all such records including checks and deposits of less than $100 rather than sort their records. The Bank Secrecy Act also requires financial institutions to retain a record of any extension of credit over $5,000, as well as every transfer of more than $10,000 outside the United States.

BROKERAGE FIRMS AS A SOURCE OF INFORMATION

To analyze stock accounts, an investigator must possess a knowledge of the different types of brokerage transactions and terminology related to the field. There are two basic types of brokerage markets: securities and commodities. The securities market involves buying and selling of stocks and bonds. The commodities market involves buying and selling of produced goods, such as grain, livestock, gold, or timber. Both markets operate under similar structures, but the terminologies may differ somewhat.

Fundamentals of Securities

People who own stock own part of the corporation issuing the stock. A person's ownership is represented by the number of shares that he or she owns. The shares are a claim on the corporation's assets and earnings. A bond is any interest bearing or discounted government or corporate security that obligates the issuer to pay the bondholder a specified sum of money, usually at specific intervals, and to repay the amount of the loan at maturity.

Stocks

When a corporation is formed, capital stock may be issued. Capital stock is stock that is authorized by the company's charter and represents ownership of the corporation. Each stockholder is entitled to a stock certificate showing ownership of a specified number of shares of stock in the corporation. There are two principal classes of stock, common and preferred. Common stock are units of ownership that allow the owner to receive dividends on his or her holdings. A dividend is a distribution of earnings. Preferred stock is so called because of the preferences granted to its owners. One preference concerns dividends. If a corporation declares dividends, the preferred stockholders will receive their dividend before common stockholders. Preferred stock does not ordinarily carry voting rights. If a corporation is authorized to issue only one class of stock, it is common stock that is authorized. The number of shares authorized by a company's charter can be changed by formal approval of the stockholders.

Shares issued and subsequently reacquired by the corporation through purchase or donation are referred to as treasury stock. Treasury stock cannot be voted, and it pays or accrues no dividends. The number of shares of stock that a corporation has outstanding will always equal the number of shares issued, less the number of shares of treasury stock.

If a stockholder desires to buy more stock, it is not necessary to obtain the permission of the corporation. The stockholder acquires it privately or by purchase in the open market. Conversely, if a stockholder desires to sell shares, he or she cannot demand that the corporation buy back the stock. Instead, the stockholder is free to seek a buyer for the stock either in the open market or by private sale.

After the sale terms have been agreed upon, the mechanics are simple. The seller signs his or her name on the back of the stock certificate and delivers it to the buyer or the buyer's broker. A record of all outstanding stock certificates is kept by the corporation or by its duly appointed transfer agent, usually a commercial bank appointed by the corporation. The transfer agent records the names and addresses of the stockholders and the number of shares owned by each. After determining that an old stock certificate is in proper form for transfer, the transfer agent issues a new certificate to the new owner. Most companies have a registrar whose duty is to double check the actions of the transfer agent to prevent improper issue of stock or fraudulent transfer.

Dividends

A corporation may pay a dividend in cash, stock, or property. When cash dividends are paid, the company or its dividend disbursing agent (usually a bank) sends checks to all stockholders whose names appear on the books of the company. When cash dividends are distributed, they are paid in terms of so much per share.

Some companies, in order to conserve cash, pay a dividend in their own stock. A stock dividend is usually stated as a percentage of the outstanding shares, up to a maximum of 25 percent.

When a corporation pays a property dividend, it is usually in the form of stock of another corporation which has been acquired for investment or some other purpose.

Bonds

When a corporation or governmental unit wishes to borrow money for some period, usually for more than 5 years, it will sell a bond issue. Each bond is generally of $1,000 denomination and the certificate issued serves as evidence of a loan from the bondholder to the corporation or governmental unit. A bond pays a stated rate of interest and matures on a stated date. On that date, a fixed sum of money will be repaid to the bondholder. Bondholders do not have corporate ownership privileges as stockholders do.

There are several different types of bonds. Some are described below.

- **Corporate Bond.** A corporate bond is issued by private corporations such as railroads public utilities, and industrial corporations. They are registered bonds, that is, they are bonds registered in the name of the holder on the books of the issuer or the issuer's registrar and can be transferred to another owner only when endorsed by the registered owner.

- **Municipal Bond.** A municipal bond is an obligation of a state, county, municipality, or any agency thereof. By statute, all municipal bonds issued after July 1, 1983 are registered. The interest accrued on a municipal bond is free from Federal taxes.

- **U.S. Government Obligations:**

    Treasury Bills. T-Bills are short-term securities with maturities of one year or less (13 weeks, 26 weeks, and 52 weeks). They do not pay a fixed rate of interest, and they are issued, and subsequently traded, at a discount from face value. No certificate is issued; the purchase and payment are strictly accounting entries. T-Bills are issued in minimum denominations of $10,000 with $5,000 increments.

    Treasury Notes. T-Notes are intermediate securities with maturities from one to ten years and are issued in denominations ranging from $1,000 to $1 million, or more. They carry a fixed interest rate and are issued and traded at face value or at a percentage of their face value.

- **Treasury Bonds.** T-Bonds are long-term bonds with maturities of 10 years or longer (usually 25-40 years). They carry a fixed interest rate and are issued and traded as a percentage of their face value. Minimum denomination is $1,000.

Not only are there different types of bonds, there are also the following classifications:

- **Registered Bond.** The name of the owner of a registered bond appears on the bond certificate. The owner's name is also recorded on the proper corporate records (usually maintained by a registrar and/or transfer agent). Interest on the bond is paid by check directly to the registered holder. While a registered bond possesses limited negotiability, it has the advantage of protecting the owner in the event of its loss.

- **Coupon Bond.** A coupon bond has coupons attached to the bond certificate, one coupon for each interest payment due during the life of the bond. The interest is payable to whoever turns in the coupon, whether or not that person initially bought the bond. The holder of the coupons is the bond's legal owner, hence the term "bearer bond."

- **Registered Coupon Bond.** With a registered coupon bond, the name of the owner appears on records maintained by a registrar and/or transfer agent. The interest coupons attached to the bond certificate do not contain the name of the owner and are payable to the bearer. Registered coupon bonds are registered for the principal only, not for interest.

Organized Securities Exchanges

Securities exchanges or stock exchanges neither buy nor sell securities themselves. An exchange functions as a central marketplace and provides facilities for executing orders. Member brokers representing buyers and sellers carry out these transactions.

The two major exchanges are the New York Stock Exchange (NYSE) and the American Stock Exchange (AMEX), both located in New York City. While there are approximately a dozen additional regional exchanges (Midwest, Pacific Coast, Philadelphia-Baltimore-Washington, etc.), the NYSE and AMEX together handle more than 90 percent of the trading done through organized exchanges.

If a security is to be traded on an exchange, the issue must be approved for listing by that exchange. Securities traded on the NYSE or AMEX may also be listed and traded on a regional exchange; however, no security is listed on both NYSE and AMEX.

Over-the-Counter Market

The over-the-counter securities market handles most of the securities transactions that take place in the United States. In fact, its operations are so extensive that the easiest way to describe it is to indicate what it does not do in securities transactions. The over-the-counter market does not handle the purchase or sale of securities that are listed on securities exchanges, but it handles everything else in the way of securities transactions.

Thus, securities not listed on a securities exchange are "unlisted," that is, traded over-the-counter.

Many different types of securities are traded over-the-counter. They include the following:

- Bank stocks
- Insurance company stocks
- U.S. government securities
- Municipal bonds
- Open-end investment company shares (mutual funds)
- Most corporate bonds
- Stocks of a large number of industrial and utility corporations, including nearly all new issues
- Securities of many foreign corporations

The over-the-counter market is not located in any one central place. Rather, it consists of thousands of securities houses located in hundreds of different cities and towns all over the United States. These securities houses are called brokers or dealers and are engaged in buying and selling securities, usually for their own account.

Ownership of Securities

There are two principal ways securities are held, in the name of the account holder or in street name. In the first instance, the securities owned simply reflect the name of the customer who maintains the account. When securities are held in a street name, they are registered in the name of the broker.

Fundamentals of Commodities

Where the stock market is involved with the buying and selling of shares in corporations, the commodities market is generally involved with buying and selling commonly accepted quantities of marketable materials. Things sold on the commodities market include soy beans, wheat, corn, pork bellies, rice, gold, silver, and many more too numerous to mention. In the commodities market, the basic instrument of exchange is called the futures contract. A futures contract is a legally binding commitment to make delivery (sell) or take delivery (buy) of a given quantity and quality of a commodity to a contracted price and date. Virtually every type of marketable item is sold on the commodities market.

Organized Commodity Exchanges

In general, futures contracts are bought and sold on commodities exchanges. Commodities exchanges are similar to stock exchanges in that they function as central marketplaces and provide facilities for executing buy and sell orders. Two major commodities exchanges are the Chicago Board of Trade and the Chicago Mercantile Exchange. Other U.S. commodities exchanges are located in New York, Minneapolis, and Kansas City. The exchanges do not enter into the trading of contracts or establishment of contract prices.

Actual trading of futures contracts is done "on the floor" of the exchange by exchange members. There are specific rules governing the trading of futures. All contracts are standardized regarding sized, date, and delivery terms. Basically, the price of the contract is the sole variable, and this is negotiated at the exchange. Buying or selling a futures contract does not mean that an investor necessarily accepts or makes delivery of the actual commodity (although legally obligated to do so). The primary means of fulfilling one's obligation under the contract is to enter into an offsetting contract. This legally cancels the outstanding obligation.

Available Documentation

A broker is an agent who handles the public's orders to buy and sell securities and commodities, usually for a commission. A broker may be a corporation, partnership, or individual and is often a member of a stock exchange or a member of the stock exchange securities firm. A registered representative, also known as a securities salesperson, account executive, or just plain broker, personally places customers' orders and maintains their accounts. While commonly referred to as a broker, a registered representative is usually an employee of a brokerage firm rather than a member.

The broker or brokerage firm can furnish virtually all source documents relating to securities and/or commodities account activity. The principal documents available are:

- **An application for an account.** This document is prepared by the customer when opening of an account. It includes personal data and some financial information such as bank reference, credit checks performed, etc.

- **Customer account cards.** This card is kept in the broker's personal files for reference. The broker records all transactions conducted for the customer on this card. A sample card is shown below.

Client		Anthony Benidect		Account number		40-3801	
Home Address		1229 Springtide Place, NW Washington, DC 20001		Home telephone		(202) 555-7896	
Business address		94 West Avenue Sterling, VA 22170		Business telephone		(703) 555-3654	
Investment objective		Growth					
Special interests		None					
		Bought			Sold		Approximate
Description	Date	#Share	Price	Date	#Share	Price	Profit	Loss
Kingman	6/4	10	$22^5/_8$	6/20	10	$17¼$		$54
Kingman	6/17	12	$23¼$					
Kingman	8/1	20	$17^1/_8$					
Dane Ind.	10/2	40	$16^3/_8$	10/16	40	$23½$	$280	
Kingman	10/4	6	$19^7/_8$					
Bremer Co.	11/7	22	$20¾$					

- **Signature card.** A signature card shows who has authority to conduct transactions o the account.

- **Securities receipts.** These receipts are issued to a customer when he or she delivers securities to the broker for sale.

- **Cash receipts.** These receipts are issued to a customer when he or she delivers currency to the broker.

- **Confirmation slips.** Confirmation slips are issued to a customer to show the type of transaction (buy or sell) and the amount involved in the transaction.

- **Securities delivered receipt.** This receipt is signed by the customer when a securities purchase is actually delivered to the customer.

- **Brokerage account statement.** The brokerage account statement is usually issued on a monthly basis and provides information on all transactions conducted during the period. It lists all purchases and sales, the name of the security, the number of units, the amount per unit, the total amount of the transaction, the account balance, payments received from the customer, disbursements to the customer (usually with the check number issued), and the customer's position (securities that are held by the brokerage firm for the customer). A sample statement is shown below.

Roberts and Company Incorporated

Member New York Stock Exchange-American Stock Exchange
14851 Street, NW, Washington, DC 20006
(202) 555-4500

Entry Date	Bought or Received	Sold or Delivered	Description	Price or Entry Description	Amount Debited	Amount Credited
02/12	100		Overton Airlines	Sec Rec		
02/12		100	Overton Airlines	9 5/8		$936.30
02/14		100	Polk Corp.	41 5/8		$4,098.60
02/15			Funds	Cash Dsb	$5,034.50	
02/15		100	Weber Corp.	36 7/8		$3,624.60
02/15	100		Weber Corp.	Sec Rec		
02/15	100		Dare, Inc.	Sec Rec		
02/23		100	Dare, Inc.	84 ¾		$8,412.50
02/28			Closing Balance			$12,037.10
			Position None			
Mr. Anthony Benidect 1229 Springtide Place, NW Washington, DC 20001			02/28/17 Period Ending	40-3801 Account Number	1 Page	

When a subject purchases stock, he or she usually has the option of taking "delivery" of the certificates from the broker or leaving them in the broker's custody for possible future sale. A person active in trading usually keeps all stock with his or her broker. If the customer takes delivery of the certificates, the number of shares would be noted in the "sold or delivered" column, and the "date" column would show the date of delivery. The same holds true if a customer delivers stock certificates to the broker for sale, except the number of shares would be placed in the "bought or received" column.

OTHER FINANCIAL INSTITUTIONS

Banks and brokerage firms are not the only financial institutions where financial transactions occur. Let's take a look at two other types of financial institutions and see what information they can provide to the financial investigator.

Western Union

A financial transaction conducted with a Western Union money order creates the following three documents:

- The original application prepared by the purchaser or sender
- The original request for payment prepared by the recipient of the funds
- The bank draft drawn by Western Union payable to the person receiving the money

The canceled drafts, after clearing through banking channels, are united with the original telegram applications and sent to the St. Louis, Missouri office for storage under the jurisdiction of the money order auditor. These records (except for money orders over $1,000) are destroyed after three years.

Casinos

Casino operations maintain extensive financial information concerning the movement of money. Their records represent a blend of information—bank account statements, credit card and loan applications, and hotel/room service documentation. Since the casino industry is government regulated, currency movements in excess of $10,000 (purchase of chips or redemption of winnings) musts be reported to the U.S. Treasury Department via a Currency Transaction Report by Casinos, Form 8362. A sample Form 8362 is found below.

SUMMARY

This chapter describes the types of financial information available from banks, brokerage houses, casinos, and Western Union. The key is to know what information is available and how to interpret it. Seemingly insignificant details, such as charges for interest on a bank statement, have resulted in resolving major financial crimes. Securities held in a "street name" have led to the discovery of information that has put criminals behind bars. High rollers at "the tables" have been defeated by financial documents revealing their activities. Tracing financial records to and through financial institutions is much more than a mere paper chase. Whether it is a check, a wire transfer, a deposit, a sale of a stock or bond, a purchase of a marketable security, the movement of money and the paper trail which it leaves behind is, for the financial investigator, "where the action is" and the road map of criminal activity.

QUESTIONS AND EXERCISES

Answer the following questions, then check your responses with those provided at the end.

1. What information does the following check provide?

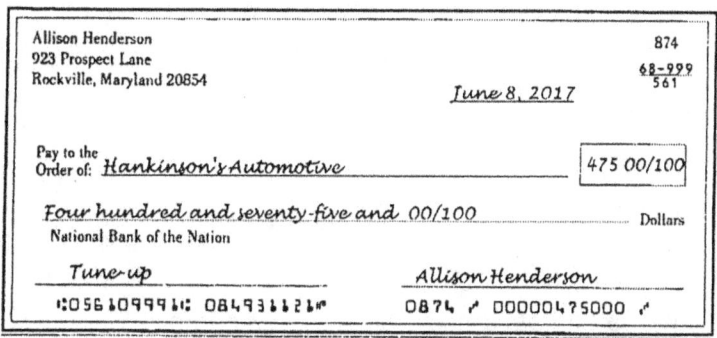

2. Why is check spread analysis a useful investigative tool?

3. What information surrounding a safe deposit box is useful in a financial investigation?

4. For a checking account, what records are banks required to retain for 5 years?

5. Why is it difficult to trace a currency-for-currency transaction?

6. What must an investigator do to gain access to a suspect's bank records?

7. What are "haven countries" and what role do they play ii financial investigations?

8. Why is a loan application a good source of financial information?

9. What financial information is available from the following:
   a. Western Union

   b. A casino

10. Distinguish between the following:
    a. Securities and commodities

b. Stock and bond

c. Common stock and preferred stock

d. Transfer agent and registrar

e. Corporate bond and municipal bond

f. Treasury bill and treasury bond

g. Securities held in owner's name and securities held in street name

11. Analyze the following three bank statements and identify four things an investigator will want to follow up on.

Checking Account Summary **Conewango Bank**
Account Number 65432198

David Davids
8 Mockingbird Lane
Herndon, Virginia 22070

Statement Period
05/01/17-05/31/17

Beginning Balance			$2,145.98
Transaction	**Date**	**Amount**	**Balance**
Check 176	05/02	745.00-	1,400.98
Deposit	05/02	1,534.56+	2,935.54
Check 177	05/09	57.23-	2,878.31
Check 178	05/13	152.61-	2,725.70
Deposit	05/15	1,534.56+	4,260.26
Check 179	05/22	19.56-	4,240.70
Check 180	05/25	198.21-	4,042.49
Check 181	05/28	234.34-	3,808.15
Ending Balance			$3,808.15

Checking Account Summary — Conewango Bank

Account Number 65432198

David Davids
8 Mockingbird Lane
Herndon, Virginia 22070

Statement Period
06/01/17-06/30/17

Beginning Balance			$3,808.15
Transaction	**Date**	**Amount**	**Balance**
Check 182	06/02	745.00-	3,063.15
Deposit	06/02	1,534.56+	4,597.71
Check 183	06/06	2,000.00-	2,597.71
Deposit	06/10	5,000.00+	7,597.71
Deposit	06/15	1,534.56+	9,132.27
Check 184	06/20	22.03-	9,110.24
Check 185	06/23	189.13-	8,921.11
Check 186	06/29	429.84-	8,491.27
Ending Balance			$8,491.27

Checking Account Summary — Conewango Bank

Account Number 65432198

David Davids
8 Mockingbird Lane
Herndon, Virginia 22070

Statement Period
07/01/17-07/31/17

Beginning Balance			$8,491.27
Transaction	**Date**	**Amount**	**Balance**
Deposit	07/01	1,534.56+	10,025.83
Check 187	07/04	5,000.00-	5,025.83
Check 188	07/14	54.11-	4,971.72
Check 189	07/14	156.21-	4,815.51
Deposit	07/15	1,534.56+	6,350.07
Check 190	07/20	22.46-	6,327.61
Check 191	07/28	141.69-	6,185.92
Check 192	07/30	533.37-	5,652.55
Ending Balance			$5,652.55

a.

b.

c.

d.

12. Why would you be suspicious if you located the following deposit slips?

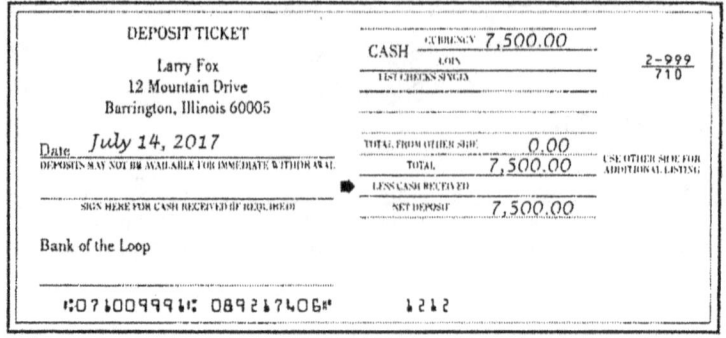

13. Interpret the following brokerage account statement.

Henry and Sons, Inc.   Member New York Stock Exchange-Washington Stock Exchange
920 H Street, NW, Washington, DC 20006
(202) 555-9700

Entry Date	Bought or Received	Sold or Delivered	Description	Price or Entry Description	Amount Debited	Amount Credited
07/18	250		Lakewood, Inc.	5½	$1,375.00	
07/22	1000		K Engines	Sec Rec		
07/22		100	Lakewood, Inc.	6		$600.00
07/22	100		Smith, Inc.	$17^3/_8$	$1,737.50	
07/24		50	Lakewood, Inc.	$6^7/_8$		$1,031.25
07/30	200		Warren Inc.	10	$2,000.00	
07/31			Closing Balance Position None		$5,112.50	$1,631.25
Nancy Garrity 25 Chelsea Lane, N.E. Washington, DC 20007			07/31/17 Period Ending	72-8072 Account Number	1 Page	

KEY (CORRECT ANSWERS)

1. The check provides the following information:
   - Owner of the account is Allison Henderson. She lives in Rockville, Maryland at 923 Prospect Lane.
   - The payee is Hankinson's Automotive. Apparently, Allison took her car in for a tune-up and paid for it on June 8, 2017.
   - Allison's checking account number is 0849311121
   - The first part of the ABA transit number, "68," tells us that the Capital Bank and Trust is located in Virginia.
   - The second part of the ABA transit number tells us that the code for the Capital Bank and Trust is "999."
   - The number "561" is the check routing symbol. The "5" means that the Capital Bank and Trust is located in the fifth Federal Reserve district (Richmond). The "6" corresponds to the Federal Reserve facility that collected the check, and the "1" indicates a deferred payment.

2. Check spread analysis is a useful investigative tool because it reveals a suspect's pattern of financial activity. A break in the pattern is cause for further investigation; for example, if a usual monthly payment (mortgage, rent, phone, electric, etc.) is absent, the investigator will want to see how the suspect made the payment.

3. A safe deposit box rental agreement and entry log are available. The rental agreement will show who rented the box and on what date. The entry log shows the date and times of visits to the box and who made them. Bank records do not reveal the contents of the box.

4. Banks are required to retain the following records for 5 years:
   - The signature card filled out when the account was opened.
   - Bank statements disclosing all deposits and withdrawals
   - Copies of both sides of customer checks

5. It is difficult to trace currency-for-currency transactions because they seldom leave a paper trail inside the bank unless the transaction is in excess of $10,000. Transactions of $10,000 or more must be recorded on a Currency Transaction Report.

6. An investigator can ask suspects for their bank records or for permission to get them from the bank. If a suspect is uncooperative, it becomes a bit more difficult for the investigator because the Bank Secrecy Act and the Right to Financial Privacy Provisions of Federal law cause banks to restrict access to a customer's records. However, banks can be legally compelled to provide records.

7. A haven country is a country that offers a legal and/or economic climate for laundering money or hiding illegally gotten profits. It is difficult for an investigator to gain access to information concerning money sent to a haven country via a wire transfer.

8. A loan application is a good source of financial information because a suspect, wanting to get the loan approved, will identify assets and other accounts to impress the person who reviews the application.

9. The documentation surrounding a Western Union money order will identify who purchased the money order, who received it, and the money order's worth.

    A casino can provide bank statements, loan applications, credit card applications, and other financial information. Casinos are also required to file reports on currency transactions in excess of $10,000.asinos are also required to file reports on currency transactions in excess of $10,000.

10. a. Securities are stocks and bonds whereas commodities are produced goods, such as grain, livestock, gold, or timber.

    b. A stock represents ownership in a corporation, that is, a claim against the corporation's assets and earnings. A bond is issued when a corporation or governmental unit wishes to borrow money for some period. Stockholders can sell their shares of stock at any time, and receive a profit or loss based on the relationship of the purchase price to the selling price. Bondholders can collect on their investment only at a specified time.

    c. Common stock are units of ownership that allow owners to receive dividends on their holdings and vote on matters affecting the corporation in which they own stock. If a stockholder owns preferred stock, he or she will be paid dividends before common stockholders; however, preferred stock does not ordinarily carry voting rights. If a corporation is authorized to issue only one class of stock, it is common stock that is authorized.

    d. Transfer agents keep a record of a corporation's outstanding stock certificates. A transfer agent is usually a commercial bank appointed by the corporation. A registrar double checks the actions of the transfer agent to prevent improper issue of stock or fraudulent transfer.

    e. A corporate bond is a registered bond issued by a private corporation. A municipal bond is an obligation of a state, county, municipality, or any agency thereof. All municipal bonds issued after July 1, 1983 are registered. The interest on a municipal bond is free from Federal taxes.

    f. Treasury bills are short-term securities with maturities of one year or less. They do not pay a fixed rate of interest and are issued and subsequently traded at a discount from face value. Treasury bills are issued in minimum denominations of $10,000, with $5,000 increments. Treasury bonds are long-term bonds with maturities of 10 years or longer. They carry a fixed interest rate and are issued and traded as a percentage of their face value. Their minimum denomination is $1,000.

    g. Securities held in the name of the account holder simply reflect the name of the customer who maintains the account. Securities held in a street name are registered in the name of the owner's broker.

11. An investigator will probably want to pursue the following:
    a. Check 183, written for $2,000
    b. Check 187, written for $5,000. Both Checks 183 and 184 are significantly higher than the next highest payment ($745).
    c. The $5,000 deposit on June 10. All other deposits to be account are the same amount and deposited at the same time in each month.
    d. No check was written in the amount of $745 in July. Mr. Davids has plenty of money to make the payment. Maybe he forgot. Maybe he paid in cash.

12. Both of the deposit slips show that currency was deposited. The total amount deposited equals $13,500. Had all of the currency been deposited into one account, the bank would have had to file a Currency Transaction Report (CTR). Since the deposits are into two different accounts owned by the same person, it looks like that person may have split the deposit to avoid having to have a CTR filed.

13. The brokerage account statement reveals that Nancy Garrity bought, sold, and received stock during July 2017. She made a $256.25 profit on her Lakewood, Inc. stock. Unless other account statements are available for analysis, an investigator cannot determine if Nancy's brokerage activities for July 2017 are unusual.

INVESTIGATIVE REFERENCES

Appendix

This appendix contains a listing of selected sources of business information and government records available to the financial investigator.

Business Records

Abstract and Title Company Records
- Maps and tract books.

- Escrow index of purchasers and sellers of real estate (primary source of information)

- Escrow files (number obtained from index)

- Escrow file containing escrow instructions, agreements, and settlements

- Abstracts and title policies

- Special purpose newspapers published for use by attorneys, real estate brokers, insurance companies, and financial institutions. These newspapers contain complete reports on transfers of properties, locations of properties transferred, amounts of mortgages, and releases of mortgages.

Agriculture Records
- County veterinarians

- Commission merchants

- Insurance companies (insure shipments)

- Transportation companies

- Storage companies

- County and state fair boards

- County farm agents

- State cattle control boards (some states maintain records of all cattle brought in and taken out of state)

Automobile Manufacturer and Agency Record
- Franchise agreements

- Financial statements of dealers

- New car sales and deliveries (used car purchases, trade-ins, and sales)
- Service department (mileage, order, and delivery signature to indicate presence in area)

Bonding Company Records
- Investigative and other records on persons and firms bonded

- Financial statements and date

- Address of person on bond

Specialized Commercial Credit Organizations
- United Beverage Bureau

- National Fuel Credit Association
- Jewelers Board of Trade

- Lumbermen's Credit Association
- Produce Reporter Company
- Packer Produce Mercantile Agency
- Paper and Allied Trade Mercantile Agency
- Lyon Furniture Mercantile Agency
- American Monument Association

Credit Reporting Agencies

The Fair Credit Reporting Act of 1971 restricts the availability of information from credit reporting agencies to governmental investigative agencies. Credit reports may only be furnished:

—In response to the order of a court having the jurisdiction to issue such an order;
—Upon written request of the consumer; or
—To a person who has a legitimate business need for the information in regard to a business transaction involving the consumer, including but not limited to credit, insurance, and employment purposes.

There is no specific exception provided in the act that will allow law enforcement agencies to obtain credit reports for investigative purposes. The act provides criminal penalties for obtaining information under false pretenses and for unauthorized disclosures by officers or employees of consumer reporting agencies.

The identifying information which is available under the act is limited to a consumer's name, address, former addresses, place(s) of employment, and former place(s) of employment.

If identifying information is needed for investigative purposes the following credit reporting agencies can be checked:
- Local credit rating and collection agencies
- Local office of National Association of Retail Credit Men
—Insurance applicants

—American Service Bureau

—Hooper Holmes Agency

—Retail Credit Company
- Mortgage Loans
—Loan exchange (clearing house loan information)

—Retailer's Commercial Agency (performs credit investigations for credit cards, banking, and mortgages)

- Transportation
—TRINC (furnishes statistics on the trucking industry).
—Motor Carrier Directory (lists motor carriers with revenues totaling $50,000 or more).

- Manufacturers
—The "Census File of Manufacturers" contains a census of manufacturing plants in the United States.

- Marketing Services
  — Dun and Bradstreet, Inc.

  — Market Service Bureau

  — Middle Market Director (business guide of firms with a net worth between $500,00 and $1,000,000)

  — Million Dollar Directory (business guide firms with a net worth of $1,000,000 or more)

  — Metal Working Directory (marketing director of metal working plants in the United States)

  — Vendor Account Services (used by retail stores in processing accounts payable, buying, and merchandise control)
- International

  — International Credit Reports (a division of Dun and Bradstreet which furnishes credit reports on overseas credit)

  — International Market Guides (Middle and South America only)

  — Continental Europe (lists European businesses in 39 countries)

  — Guide to Key British Enterprises (lists prominent firms throughout the United Kingdom)

  — Synopsis of Dun-Mexico

  — Synopsis of Dun-Brazil

  — Reference book- Argentina

  — Bradstreet Register

International Mercantile Claims Division

Department Store Records
- Charge accounts

- Credit files

Detective Agency Records
- Investigative files
  — Civil

  — Criminal

  — Commercial

  — Industrial

- Character checks

- Fraud and blackmail investigations

- Divorce evidence

- Missing persons search

- Security patrols and guards

- Undercover agents

- Shadow work

- Lie detector tests

- Personnel screening and fingerprinting

- Service checking

- Restaurants

- Public transportation

- Stores

Distributors' Records
- Wholesale toiletry (cash rebates are paid by toiletry manufacturers). Details of available contracts which pay rebates to wholesale toiletry distributors are contained in publications issued by the Toiletry Merchandisers Association, Inc., 230 Park Avenue, New York, N.Y. 10017, and the Druggist Service Council, Inc., 1290 Avenue of the Americas, New York., N.Y. 10019
- Gambling equipment
- Wire service
- Factory, farm, home, office equipment, etc.

Drug Store Records
- Prescription records (name, address, date, and physician issuing prescription)

Fraternal, Veterans, Labor, Social, and Political Organization Records
- Membership and attendance records
- Dues, contributions, and payments
- Locations and history of members

Hospital Records
- Entry and release dates
- Payments made

Hotel Records
- Identity of guest
- Payments made by guest
- Credit record
- Forwarding address
- Reservations for travel (transportation companies and other hotels)
- Telephone calls made to and from room
- Freight shipments and luggage (in and out)

Insurance Company Records (Life, accident, fire, burglary, automobile, and annuity policies)
- Applications (background and financial information, insurance carried with other companies)
- Fur and jewelry floaters (appraised value and description)
- Customers' ledger cards
- Policy and mortgage loan accounts
- Dividend payment records
- Cash value and other net worth data
- Correspondence files
- Payment records on termination, losses, or refunds on cancellations
- Payments to doctors, lawyers, appraisers, and photographers hired directly by the insurance company to act for the company or as an independent expert

Laundry and Dry Cleaning Records
- Marks and tags (marks are sometimes invisible and are

brought out by use of ultraviolet rays)

•Files of laundry marks
—Local or State police departments

—National Institute of Dry Cleaning, Inc., Washington, D.C.

Lenders Exchange or Consumer Loan Exchange

An organization known as the Consumer Loan Exchange or Lenders Exchange exists in all of the large cities in the United States, as well as in some of the smaller cities. It is a nonprofit organization supported by and for its members. Most the lending institutions are members of the exchange. It can supply information concerning open and closed loan accounts with member companies, and is a good source of general background information. These organizations are not listed in directories or telephone books. Their location in a city may be obtained through local lending agencies.

National Charge Plan Records

National agencies, such as American Express, Diners Club, and Carte Blanche, which provide credit cards for use in charging travel, entertainment, goods and services, can determine whether an individual or business has an account from their central index files. If details of the account are needed, information requests should indicate whether only copies of the monthly statements or copies of both the statements and charge slips are desired, name, social security number, the time period to be covered, the subject's address, and the name and address of the subject's employer or business. Requests should be directed to:

American Express Company, 770 Broadway, New York, N.Y. 10003, and Diners Club/Carte Blanche, Adjustment Department, 180 Inverness Drive West, Englewood, CO 80111.

Newspaper Records (from a newspaper's morgue)
•Relatives, associates, and friends

•Previous places of employment (employee or company publications)

•Police and FBI files

•Schools (yearbooks, school papers, etc.)

•License bureaus (drivers, chauffeurs, taxis, etc.)

•Military departments

•Fraternal organizations

•Church groups

•Race tracks

•Nightclub or sidewalk photographers and photography studios

Public Utility Company Records

- Present and previous address of subscriber

- Payments made for service and "major" purchases

Publications

- *Who's Who in America* and various States

- Tax services

- City directories

- *Billboard* (amusements, coin-machines, burlesque, drive-ins, fairs, state, radio, TV, magic, music machines, circuses, rinks, vending machines, movies, letter lists, and obituaries)

- *Variety* (literature, radio, TV, music, state, movies, obituaries, etc.)

- *American Racing Manual* (published by Triangle Publications, Inc., 10 Lake Drive, P.O. Box 1015 Highstown, New Jersey 08520). Records showing amounts paid to owners of winning horses by each race track in the United States, Canada, and Mexico

- Professional, trade, and agriculture directories and magazines

- *Moody's Investors Service Inc.*

- *Standard and Poor's Corporation*

Real Estate Agency or Savings and Loan Association Records

- Property transactions

- Financial statements

- Payments made and received (settlement sheets)

- Credit files

- Loan applications. These do not contain quite the same information as loan applications given to a bank. A savings and loan association depends primarily upon real estate security rather than upon other assets and liabilities of a borrower.

Telephone Company Records

- Local directories, library of "out of city" directories

- Message unit detail sheets (in some areas) which list numbers called by a particular telephone

- Investigative reports on telephones used for illegal purposes

- Payments for service

- Toll calls. Because of the existence of more than one long distance carrier, toll records of a local phone company may be an incomplete listing of such calls. There may be a second telephone bill from another company, such as GT&E or MCI.

Transportation Company Records

- Passenger lists, reservations
- Destinations
- Fares paid
- Freight carrier-shippers, destinations, and storage points
- Departure and arrival times

Government Records
State Police (Central Records Section)

- Criminal cases
- Criminal intelligence
- Inflammable liquid installations
- Firearms registrations
- Investigations conducted for other departments
- Traffic arrests and motor vehicle accident investigations
- Noncriminal and criminal fingerprint records
- "Rogues gallery"
- Investigation of aviation rules and non-carrier civilian aircraft accidents
- Police training school files

City Police

- Criminal identification
  — Records of arrests, accidents, and general information
  — Alphabetical indexes of every complainant or suspect
  — "Aided" cards (citizen assistance)
  — Gun permits or applications and registrations
  — Lost or stolen articles Pawn shop files
  — Towed or repossessed autos
  — Ambulance files
  — Business information files
  — "Scofflaw files" (consistent violator of minor offense- primarily traffic)
- Other divisions
  — Criminal division files
  — Forgery squad (check squad)
  — Juvenile division
  — Morals or vice squad files
  — Narcotics bureau
  — Organized crime division
  — Police force personal history files
  — Public relations office (press file)
  — Traffic division files

Small Town Police

- Criminal index cards
- Criminal arrest cards

- Accident reports
- Complaint forms
- Offense reports

County Police (Sheriff)
- Criminal records

— Crimes involving bodily violence

— Crimes involving theft

— Crimes involving worthless checks

— Personal history sheets on people connected with the crimes

— Juvenile division records

— County business owners Traffic records

— Name, address, license plate number, driver's license number, arrest number, date and place of birth, sex, color, age, occupation, height, weight, complexion, color of hair, eyes, marks, and facts of arrest

National Sheriffs Association Directory
- List of State institutions and their superintendents

- State and Federal enforcement agencies and territorial jurisdictions
-
- Associate members of National Sheriffs Association

- County sheriffs

- Address of National Auto Theft Bureau

Other State and Local Law Enforcement and Quasi-Law Enforcement Organizations
- Specialized police organizations
- Public, semi-public, and private organizations
- The industrial security officer

- International Association of Chiefs of Police

- The monthly police administration review list of police publications

State and Local Court Records

Typically, there are three levels of courts within the State system. There is a Trial Court, where most litigation begins, an Appellate Court, which is the first level of appeal, and Court of Final Appeal. Sometimes you will find a court below the Trial Court which works much like the magistrate does in the Federal system.

Most litigation, such as divorce or breach of contract, takes place in the State and local system. Documents submitted to the court in connection with a divorce are particularly helpful in financial investigations. It is not unusual for detailed asset and liability information to be present in a divorce file.

Probate records describing estates and distribution of estates are also found in the State and local court system. These may be particularly helpful in negating nontaxable sources of cash.

Anytime a person is involved in a civil action, whether it be for breach of contract or some type of negligence action, a wealth of background information on the individual is usually provided to the opposing party through the court. A record of this information will be kept in the case files of the court and is available to an investigator.

Federal Government Records

Bureau of Alcohol, Tobacco, and Firearms (ATF)
• Distillers, brewers, and persons or firms who manufacture or handle alcohol, as a sideline or main product

• Inventory or retail liquor dealers and names of suppliers as well as amounts of liquor purchased by brand

• Names and records of known bootleggers

• Names of subjects of investigations by ATF

• Processors, manufacturers, and wholesalers of tobacco products

• List of all Federal firearms license holders, including manufacturers, importers, and dealers

• List of all Federal explosives license holders, including manufacturers, importers and dealers

• For weapons manufactured or imported after 1986, capability of tracing any firearm from manufacturer or importer to retailer

Bureau of the Public Debt
• U.S. savings bonds purchased and redeemed

• Requests for information must be addressed to:
Bureau of the Public Debt
Division of Transactions and Rulings
200 Third Street
Parkersburg, West Virginia 26101

Federal Aviation Agency (FAA)
This agency maintains records which reflect the chain of ownership of all civil aircraft in the United States. These records include documents relative to their manufacture and sale (sales contracts, bills of sale, mortgages, liens, transfers, inspections, and modifications). They also maintain licensing and medical information on pilots.

Federal Aviation Administration Civil Aviation Security Division AAC- 90, P.O. Box 25082 Oklahoma City, Oklahoma 73125

Department of Agriculture
• Licensed meat packers and food canners

• Inspections made under Pure Food and Drug Act

- Transactions with individuals and businesses (subsidies and adjustments)

Department of Defense
The Department of Defense maintains data concerning pay, dependents, allotment accounts, deposits, withholding statements (Forms W-2), and any other financial information relative to military personnel. This information is available at one the following offices, depending upon the branch of the Armed Forces to which the individual was or is presently attached:

United States Army Finance Center
Indianapolis, Indiana 46249
Request must include the complete name and Army serial number

Air Force Finance Center RPTP

Denver, Colorado 80279
Director, Bureau of Supplies and Accounts Department of the Navy 13th and Euclid Streets Cleveland, Ohio 44115

Department of State
- Import and export licenses
- Foreign information
- Passport records (date and place of birth required). Recent data may be obtained from the local district court.

Drug Enforcement Administration (DEA)
- Licensed handlers of narcotics
- Criminal records of users, pushers, and suppliers of narcotics

Federal Bureau of Investigation (FBI)
- Criminal records and fingerprints
- Anonymous Letter Index
- National Stolen Property Index (stolen Government property, including military property)
- Nonrestricted information pertaining to criminal offenses and subversive activities
- National Fraudulent Check Index

U.S. Customs Service
- Record of importers and exporters
- Record of custom house brokers
- Record of custom house truckers (cartage licenses)
- List of suspects
- Records of persons who transport or cause to be transported currency of more than $10,000, or certain monetary instruments at one time into or out of the United States

U.S. Secret Service

- Records pertaining to counterfeit, forgery, and United States' security violation cases

- Records pertaining to anonymous letters and background files on persons who write "crank" letters

- Secret Service's central files in Washington, D.C., contain an estimated 100,000 handwriting specimens of known forgers. An electronic information retrieval system facilitates comparison of questioned handwriting with the specimens on file for identification purposes.

U.S. Postal Service

- Mail watch or cover

- Current or forwarding addresses of subjects and third parties

- Photostats of postal money orders. Requests for such records must be addressed to:
Money Order Division
Postal Data Center
P.O. Box 14965
St. Louis, Missouri 63182

- Addresses of post office box holders. These requests should be made only when efforts to obtain the information from other sources are unsuccessful. Information can be obtained from the Inspector-in-Charge or Postal Inspector. Check with the local post office to learn the identity of the inspector who can furnish the information.

Immigration and Naturalization Service (INS)

- Records of all immigrants and aliens

- Deportation proceedings

- Passenger manifests and declarations (ship, date, and point of entry required)

- Naturalization records (names of witnesses to naturalization proceedings and people who know the suspect)

- Lists of passengers and crews on vessels from foreign ports

- Financial statements of aliens and persons sponsoring their entry

Interstate Commerce Commission (ICC)

The ICC has information concerning individuals who are or have been officers of transportation firms engaged in interstate commerce. This information includes the officer's employment and financial affiliations.

In addition to the record information available from the ICC, most safety inspectors of the ICC are good sources of "reference" information because they have personal knowledge of supervisory employees of the various carriers in their region.

IRS National Computer Center

The National Computer Center is located in Martinsburg, West Virginia and it maintains the Master File, a tax record of all known taxpayers. The Master File is designed to accumulate all data pertaining to the tax liabilities of all taxpayers, regardless of location. The Master File is separated into several categories. Two of the categories are the Business Master File and the Individual Master File.

Securities and Exchange Commission (SEC)

- Records of corporate registrants of securities offered for public sale, which usually show:
— A description of registrant's properties and business

— A description of the significant provisions of the security to be offered for sale and its relationship to the registrant's other capital securities

— Information as to the management of the registrant

— Certified financial statements of the registrants

- Securities and Exchange Commission News Digest (a daily publication giving a brief summary of financial proposals files and the actions taken by the SEC)

- The SEC Bulletin is issued quarterly and contains information of official actions with respect to the preceding month. It also contains a supplement which lists the names of individuals reported as being wanted on charges of violations of the law in connection with securities transactions. It is available upon request at any of the SEC regional or branch offices in the following cities:

Atlanta, GA
Miami, FL
Boston, MA
New York, NY
Chicago, IL
Philadelphia, PA
Cleveland, OH
Salt Lake City, UT
Denver, CO
San Francisco, CA
Detroit, MI
Seattle, WA
Fort Worth, TX
St. Louis, MO
Los Angeles, CA
Washington, D.C.

- The SEC's Securities Violations Section maintains comprehensive files on individuals and firms who have been reported to the Commission as having violated Federal or State securities laws. The information pertains to official actions taken against such persons, including denials, refusals, suspensions, and revocations of registrations; injunctions, fraud orders, stop order, cease and desist orders; and arrests, indictments, convictions, sentences, and other official actions.

Social Security Administration

The Social Security Administration, headquartered in Baltimore, is responsible for the issuance of social security numbers. Records on social security paid by an individual or business are not available for review by the public.

If a social security number is known, it might lead to helpful information regarding the location in which the card was issued. Since many people apply for a social security number at a young age, this in turn can lead to locating the place of birth of an individual. There are nine digits in the social security number. With the exception of the 700 series, the first three digits reflect the state of issue. The last six digits are individual identifiers. The table on the next page contains a listing of the states of issue of the first three digits.

Initial Numbers	State of Issuance	Initial Numbers	State of Issuance
001 - 003	New Hampshire	449 - 467, 627 - 645	Texas
004 - 007	Maine	468 - 477	Minnesota
008 - 009	Vermont	478 - 485	Iowa
010 - 034	Massachusetts	486 - 500	Missouri
035 - 039	Rhode Island	501 - 502	North Dakota
040 - 049	Connecticut	503 - 504	South Dakota
050 - 134	New York	505 - 508	Nebraska
135 - 158	New Jersey	509 - 515	Kansas
159 - 211	Pennsylvania	516 - 517	Montana
212 - 220	Maryland	518 - 519	Idaho
221 - 222	Delaware	520	Wyoming
223 - 231	Virginia	521 - 524	Colorado
232 - 236	West Virginia	525, 585, 648 - 649 allocated, not in use	New Mexico
237 - 246, 232 with middle digits 30	North Carolina	526 - 527, 600 - 601	Arizona
247 - 251	South Carolina	528 - 529, 646 - 647 allocated, not in use	Utah
252 - 260	Georgia	530	Nevada
261 - 267, 589 - 595	Florida	531 - 539	Washington
268 - 302	Ohio	540 - 544	Oregon
303 - 317	Indiana	545 - 573, 602 - 626	California
318 - 361	Illinois	574	Alaska
362 - 386	Michigan	575 - 576	Hawaii
387 - 399	Wisconsin	577 - 579	Washington, DC
400 - 407	Kentucky	580 groups 01 - 18	Virgin Islands
408 - 415	Tennessee	580 (groups above 20) - 584, 596 - 599	Puerto Rico
416 - 424	Alabama	586	Guam, American Samoa, Northern Mariana Islands, Philippine Islands
425 - 428, 587 588 allocated, not in use	Mississippi	700 - 728	Railroad employees with special retirement act
429 - 432	Arkansas		
433 - 439	Louisiana		
440 - 448	Oklahoma		

Veterans Administration (VA)

•Records of loans, tuition payments, insurance payments, and nonrestrictive medical data related to disability pensions are available at regional offices. This information, including photostats, may be obtained by writing the appropriate regional office. All requests should include a statement covering the need and intended use of the information. The veteran should be identified clearly and, if available, the following information should be furnished:

—VA claim number

—Date of birth

—Branch of service

—Dates of enlistment and discharge

Federal Reserve Bank (FRB)

•Records of issue of United States Treasury Bonds

United States Coast Guard

•Records of persons serving on United States ships in any capacity

•Records of vessels equipped with permanently installed motors

•Records of vessels over 16 feet long equipped with detachable motors

Treasurer of the United States

Checks paid by the U.S. Treasury are processed through the Office of the Treasurer of the United States. Photostats of the canceled checks may be obtained by initiating a request through the U.S. government agency which authorized the check.

National Crime Information Center (NCIC)

The National Crime Information Center is a repository of data relating to crime and criminals gathered by local, State, and Federal law enforcement agencies. The NCIC's computer equipment is located at FBI Headquarters in Washington, D.C. The present equipment is capable of accommodating nearly 2 million records on criminal activities. In a matter of seconds, stored information can be retrieved through equipment in the telecommunications network. Connecting terminals are located throughout the country in police departments, sheriffs offices, State police facilities, and Federal law enforcement agencies. Dispatchers can respond quickly to requests. NCIC, as well as operating statewide systems, furnishes computerized data in a matter of seconds to all agencies participating in the centralized State systems. The goal of NCIC is to serve as a national index to fifty statewide computer systems and heavily populated metropolitan area systems.

NCIC Headquarters might be compared to a large automated "file cabinet" with each file having its own label or classification. Such a cabinet of data contains information concerning:

Stolen, missing, or recovered guns

Stolen articles

Wanted persons

Stolen/wanted vehicles

Stolen license plates

Stolen/wanted boats

Stolen/embezzled/missing securities

National Law Enforcement Telecommunications System (NLETS)
NLETS is a computerized communication network linking State and local enforcement agencies in all 50 States. It can provide information such as criminal history, driver's licenses, and vehicle registration.

El Paso Intelligence Center (EPIC)
EPIC is a multi-agency operation that collects, processes, and disseminates information on narcotics traffickers, gun smugglers, and alien smugglers in support of ongoing field investigations.

If a suspect is or has been engaged in any of the previously mentioned activities, it is possible that EPIC will have intelligence information on him or her. This information might include the name of the individual, his or her known activities, significant events, associations among individuals or activities, aircraft or vessels used by the subject, observations of both foreign and domestic movements of the subject, and his or her associates and their aircraft or vessels. EPIC also provides the name, agency, and telephone number of each investigator having expressed an interest in or having data regarding a subject. EPIC records often contain substantial *financial* information relative to the subject.

International Criminal Police Organization (Interpol)
Interpol is an international police agency with bureaus set up in member countries. In the United States, the National Central Bureau is under the direction and control of the Departments of Justice and Treasury.

The National Central Bureau can assist in such things as criminal history checks, license plate and driver's license checks, and the location of suspects, fugitives, and witnesses.

The Federal Courts
This system is basically a three step process. The first step is the U.S. District Court;, the second, the U.S. Court of Appeals; and the third, the U.S. Supreme Court. Since most court records are similar, we will

only deal with the U.S. District Court in this appendix.

•U.S. District Courts

There are U.S. District Courts in every State (the larger States have several) and in the District of Columbia, Guam, Puerto Rico, the Canal Zone, and the Virgin Islands.

The U.S. District Court has exclusive jurisdiction in bankruptcy, maritime and admiralty, patents, copyright penalties, fines under Federal law, and proceedings against consul and vice consuls of foreign states. In addition, it has jurisdiction when the United States or a national bank is a party, and in cases where the law specifically states that the U.S. District Court has original jurisdiction. The U.S. District Courts have concurrent jurisdictions with State courts on "Federal questions" when the dispute arises under the Constitution, laws, or treaties of the United States; disputes between citizens of different States; one U.S. citizen and one citizen of a foreign state; or a citizen and a foreign state.

The U.S. District Court has broad criminal jurisdiction over all offenses against the laws of the United States. When both Federal and State laws are violated by one committing a crime, the offender is subject to prosecution in both the Federal and State courts for the separate crimes.

The files of the clerk's office of a U.S. District Court are not as complex as those of a State court of original jurisdiction. For the investigator, **the most important records in the custody of a clerk of a U.S. District Court are the case records.** These records consist of the files (case papers), the minutes, and the dockets.

—The files consist of pleadings, processes, and written orders and judgments of the court, and such other papers as pertain directly to the case.

—The minutes record, in summary form, of what happened during the proceedings. In some courts, the minutes are an integral part of the file.

—The docket sheet on each case is a chronological summary, not only of what takes place in court, but also of the papers in the file. The docket sheet can be very valuable to an investigator who is looking for only one item in a huge file. In most U.S. District Courts there are separate sets of dockets for bankruptcy, and civil and criminal cases. Some clerks have found it to their advantage to keep a set of miscellaneous dockets, and most clerks keep the docket sheets for closed cases in a separate area.

The clerk of a district court will have a record of banking institutions that have been designated as depositories for money of estates in bankruptcy.

The United States District Courts have jurisdiction to naturalize aliens and maintain copies of the certificates of naturalization as well as a name index of the individuals naturalized. If an alien elects to change his or her name at naturalization, both the old an new name appears in the index. In addition, a copy of the subject's Application to File Petition for Naturalization appears in the court records. This form (N-400) contains considerable information about the alien being naturalized.

• Other Federal Courts

To handle particular types of cases, Congress has established special courts. They are described in the *Guide to Court Systems* as follows:

—Court of Claims—The U.S. Government permits certain claims to be brought against itself in the U.S. Court of Claims.

—U.S. Customs Court— When certain merchandise is imported into the United States, customs duties have to be paid to the U.S. Government. Customs collectors at various ports in the United States classify merchandise and appraise it. When an importer complains on the rate, or that the merchandise was improperly excluded, the U.S. Customs Court is the court to which the case must be brought. Appeals from the U.S. Customs Courts are taken to the Court of Customs and Patent Appeals. This court also reviews certain decisions of the Patent Office and the U.S. Tariff Commission.

This appendix contains information regarding the American Bankers Association prefix numbers of cities and states and a listing of Federal Reserve Districts.

Federal Reserve Districts
1 - Boston
2 - New York
3 - Philadelphia
4 - Cleveland
5 - Richmond
6 - Atlanta
7 - Chicago
8 - St. Louis
9 - Minneapolis
10 - Kansas City
11 - Dallas
12 - San Francisco

American Bankers Association Prefix Numbers

THE NUMERICAL SYSTEM
of The American Bankers Association
Index to Prefix Numbers of Cities and States
Numbers 1 to 49 inclusive are Prefixes for Cities
Numbers 50 to 99 inclusive are Prefixes for States
Numbers 50 to 58 are Eastern States
Number 59 is Hawaii
Numbers 60 to 69 are Southeastern States
Numbers 70 to 79 are Central States
Numbers 80 to 88 are Southwestern States
Number 89 is Alaska

Prefix Numbers of Cities in Numerical Order

1 New York, N.Y.	14 New Orleans, La.	26 Memphis, Tenn.	38 Savannah, Ga.
2 Chicago, Il.	15 Washington, D.C.	27 Omaha, Neb.	39 Oklahoma City, Ok.
3 Philadelphia, Pa.	16 Los Angeles, Ca.	28 Spokane, Wash.	40 Wichita, Kan.
4 St Louis, Mo.	17 Minneapolis, Minn.	29 Albany, N.Y.	41 Sioux City, Iowa
5 Boston, Mass.	18 Kansas City, Mo.	30 San Antonio, Tx.	42 Pueblo, Co.
6 Cleveland, Ohio	19 Seattle, Wash.	31 Salt Lake City, Ut	43 Lincoln, Neb.
7 Baltimore, Md.	20 Indianapolis, Ind.	32 Dallas, Tx.	44 Topeka, Kan.
8 Pittsburgh, Pa.	21 Louisville, Ky.	33 Des Moines, Iowa	45 Dubuque, Iowa
9 Detroit, Mich.	22 St. Paul, Minn.	34 Tacoma, Wash.	46 Galveston, Tx.
10 Buffalo, N.Y.	23 Denver, Colo.	35 Houston, Tx.	47 Cedar Rapids, Iowa
11 San Francisco, Ca.	24 Portland, Ore.	36 St. Joseph, Mo.	48 Waco, Tx.
12 Milwaukee, Wis.	25 Columbus, Ohio	37 Fort Worth, Tx.	49 Muskogee, Ok.
13 Cincinnati, Ohio			

Prefix Numbers of States in Numerical Order

50 New York	64 Georgia	77 North Dakota	89 Alaska
51 Connecticut	65 Maryland	78 South Dakota	90 California
52 Maine	66 North Carolina	79 Wisconsin	91 Arizona
53 Massachusetts	67 South Carolina	80 Missouri	92 Idaho
54 New Hampshire	68 Virginia	81 Arkansas	93 Montana
55 New Jersey	69 West Virginia	82 Colorado	94 Nevada
56 Ohio	70 Illinois	83 Kansas	95 New Mexico
57 Rhode Island	71 Indiana	84 Louisiana	96 Oregon
58 Vermont	72 Iowa	85 Mississippi	97 Utah
59 Hawaii	73 Kentucky	86 Oklahoma	98 Washington
60 Pennsylvania	74 Michigan	87 Tennessee	99 Wyoming
61 Alabama	75 Minnesota	88 Texas	101 Territories
62 Delaware	76 Nebraska		
63 Florida			

FINANCIAL INVESTIGATIVE TERMS

Glossary

This glossary contains terms presented in the text as well as terms which may be brought out in discussion.

Account
An accounting device used in recording the day-to-day changes in revenue, expense, asset, liability, and owner's equity items.

Account, nominal. Temporary account for an item appearing on an income statement and closed to a balance sheet account at the end of an accounting period.

Account, real. Account for an item appearing on a balance sheet.

Accounting
The system of recording and summarizing business and financial transactions in books and analyzing, verifying, and reporting the results.

Accounting, cost. The process of collecting material, labor, and overhead costs and attaching them to products.

Accounting Period
The period of time over which the transactions of a business are recorded and at the end of which a financial statement is prepared.

Account Payable
An obligation to pay an amount to a creditor.

Account Receivable
An amount that is owed to the business, usually by one of its customers, as a result of the ordinary extension of credit.

Account Transactions
Financial events that directly affect the movement of money through a bank account.

Accrual Basis of Accounting
Recording business revenues when they are earned, regardless of when they are collected, and recording expenses when they are incurred, regardless of when cash was disbursed.

Accrued Expenses
Expenses incurred but not yet paid for.

Accrued Income
Income earned but not yet received.

Adjusting Entry
Recording the correction of an error, accruals, write-offs, provisions for bad debts or depreciation, etc., expressed in the form of a simple journal entry.

Affiant
The person who prepares an affidavit.

Affidavit
A handwritten or typed declaration or statement of facts made voluntarily and confirmed by the oath or affirmation of the party making it before an officer having authority to administer such oath.

Alien Corporation
Corporation of another nationality operating in the United States.

Amortize
To write off a portion or all of the cost of an intangible asset.

Appraise
Cash or value established by systematic procedures that include physical examination, pricing, and often engineering estimates.

Asset
Property or resources owned by a business or individual.

Asset, current. An asset which is either currently in the form of cash or is expected to be converted into cash within a short period, usually one year.

Asset, fixed. Tangible property of relatively long life that generally is used in the production of goods and services.

Association Matrix
The graphic summary that results from link analysis.

Audit
A critical review of a business's accounting records.

Bad Debts
Accounts that are considered to be uncollectible.

Balance, Beginning
The amount in an account at the start of the accounting period.

Balance, New
The amount in an account at the end of the accounting period, it is the difference between the beginning balance plus increases and minus decreases.

Balance Sheet
A financial statement that reports the assets, liabilities, and equities of a company as of a specified time.

Balance Sheet consolidated. Aggregate accounts for the various categories of assets and liabilities of a corporate family (more than one corporation).

Bank Deposit Method
An indirect method of proving unknown sources of funds through an analysis of bank records and other financial transactions entered into by a suspect.

Bank Reconciliation
A comparison of the customer's records with the records of the bank, listing differences to bring balances into agreement.

Bank Statement
A document rendered by the bank to the depositor, usually monthly, which reflects deposits and checks which have cleared the bank.

Blackmail
A demand for money or other considerations under threat to do bodily harm, to injure property, to accuse of crime, or to expose disgraceful defects.

Bond

Any interest bearing or discounted government or corporate security that obligates the issuer to pay the bondholder a
specified sum of money, usually at specific
intervals, and to repay the amount of the loan at maturity.

Bond, corporate. A bond issued by a private corporation.

Bond, coupon. A bond that has coupons attached to the bond certificate, one coupon for each interest payment due during the life of the bond. The interest is payable to whoever turns in the coupon, whether or not that person initially bought the bond.

Bond, municipal. A bond issued by a state, county, municipality, or any agency thereof
Bond, registered. A bond where the name of the owner appears on the bond certificate. Interest on the bond is paid by check directly to the registered holder.

Bond, registered coupon. A bond where the name of the owner appears on records maintained by a registrar and/or transfer agent. The interest coupons attached to the bond certificate do not contain the name of the owner and are payable to the bearer. Registered coupon bonds are registered for the principal only, not for interest.

Bribery
When money, goods, services, information, or anything else of value is offered with the intent to influence the actions, opinions, or decisions of the taker.

Bylaws
The rules adopted by the stockholders setting forth the general method by which the corporate functions are to be carried on subject to the corporate charter.

Case Law
The practice of judges and lawyers looking into decisions from past cases to determine the state of law for the case they are currently handling.

Cash Basis of Accounting
Recording business revenues when cash is received and business expenses when cash is paid.

Cash Flow
The cash flow calculation attempts to measure the actual cash receipts and cash expenses of a firm.

Cashier's Check
A check drawn by a bank on its own funds and issued by an authorized officer of the bank.

Certified Check
A check where the bank guarantees that there are sufficient funds on deposit for that particular check.

Chart of Accounts
A listing, in sequentially numbered order, of a business's accounts.

Civil Law
That body of law that deals with conflicts and differences between individuals.

Closed Corporation
Corporation owned by a few stockholders, not available for investment by public.

Codification
The process of collecting and arranging laws by subject.

Collateral
Something of value pledged as security for a loan.

Common Law
The system of law that originated in England and was the body of law carried by the earliest English settlers to the American colonies.

Contingency
A possible future event or condition arising from causes unknown or at present undeterminable.

Contra Account
One of two or more accounts which partially or wholly offset each other. On financial statements, they may either be merged or appear together, for example, an account receivable from and payable to the same individual.

Cooperative
A corporation in which profits are distributed to shareholders in proportion to the amount of business each shareholder does with the company.

Counterfeiting
Copying or imitating an item without having been authorized to do so and passing the copy off for the genuine or original item.

Corporation
An artificial being or business entity created under state or federal law which is legally separate from the persons who own it.
Ownership is in the form of stock and the liability of the owners is limited to the amount of their investment in the company.

CR
Abbreviation of credit.

Credit Entry
An entry on the right-hand side of a T-account.

Creditor
One who lends money.

Criminal Law
That branch of law that deals with offenses of a public nature, that is, wrongs committed against the state.

Cartilage
The area inside the boundary of a person's residence or business location which has been marked off by man-made or naturally-occurring devices.

Debit Entry
An entry on the left-hand side of a T-account.

Debt
Current and non-current liabilities.

Defalcation
The embezzlement of money.

Depreciation
The expiration of an asset's "quality of usefulness."

Discount   Amount by which the face value of a financial investment exceeds the sales price.

Dividend
Portion of a company's profits distributed to stockholders.

Dividend, cash. Dividend paid in the form of cash.

Dividend, property. Dividend paid in the form of stock from another corporation.

Dividend, stock. Dividend paid in the form of shares of stock in the issuing corporation.

Domestic Corporation
A corporation doing business in the state from which it received its charter.

Double Entry Accounting
The type of accounting in which the two aspects of each financial event are recorded.

DR
Abbreviation of debit.

Draft
An order in writing directing the payment of money by one party (the drawee) to another party (the payee). A bank check is an example of a draft.

Electronics Fund Transfer
A transaction with a financial institution by means of a computer, telephone, or electronic instrument.

Elements of a Crime
Those constituent parts of a crime that must be proven to sustain a conviction.

Elements of a Crime
Those constituent parts of a crime that must be proven to sustain a conviction.

Embezzlement
When one entrusted with money or property appropriates it for his or her own use and benefit.

Entry, Closing
An entry reducing one account to zero and offset by an entry increasing another account by the same amount. It is one step in transferring the balance of an account to another account.

Equity, Owner's
Claims against assets by the owner(s).

Evidence
Anything that can make a person believe that a fact or proposition is true or false.

Evidence, circumstantial. Evidence relating to a series of facts other than those at issue that tend, by inference, to establish the fact at issue.

Evidence, direct. Evidence precise to the point at issue.

Evidence, documentary.

Evidence in the form of writings and documents.

Evidence, real. Evidence that is tangible.

Evidence, testimonial. Evidence given by word of mouth.

Exemplar
Non-testimonial identification evidence from a defendant, such as a blood or handwriting sample.

Expenditure
Payment for acquiring an asset or service.

Expenditures Method
An indirect method of determining unknown sources of funds by comparison of all known expenditures with all known receipts during a particular period of time.

Expense
Goods or services consumed in operating a business.

Expense, accrued. A liability account arising from expenses that are incurred prior to the related expenditure, for example, accrued wages.

Expense, prepaid. An expense recognized after a relevant expenditure, for example, future benefits.

Extortion
Illegally obtaining property from another by actual or threatened force, fear, or violence, or under cover of official right

Felony
A serious crime punishable by incarceration for a period exceeding one year, a fine, and the loss of certain civil rights.

Financial Condition
The results conveyed by presenting the assets, liabilities, and capital of an enterprise in the form of a balance sheet. Sometimes called financial position.

Financial Interviewing
The systematic questioning of persons who have knowledge of events, those involved, and evidence surrounding a case under investigation.

Fiscal Year
An accounting period of twelve successive calendar months.

Foreign Corporation
A corporation with a charter from another state. A California corporation doing business in Nevada is a foreign corporation in Nevada.

Forensic Science
The application of scientific techniques to legal matters.

Forgery
Passing a false or worthless instrument, such as a check or counterfeit security, with the intent to defraud or injure the recipient.

Forfeiture
A legal proceeding that the Government initiates against the proceeds of an illegal activity.

Fraud
Falsely representing a fact to another in order to induce that person to surrender something of value.

General Partner
A partner personally liable for partnership debts.

Goodwill
An intangible asset representing the difference between the purchase price and the value of the tangible assets purchased.

Grand Jury
A jury who hears evidence obtained by the prosecution and then decides whether or not a trial ought to occur.

Guarantor
One who promises to make good if another fails to pay or otherwise perform an assigned or contractual task.

Hearsay
Evidence that does not come from the personal knowledge of the declarant but from the repetition of what the declarant has heard others say.

Hybrid Method
Method of accounting which is a combination of the cash and accrual methods.

Immunity
An investigative tool used by the grand jury that allows a witness to provide testimony or documents without fear of prosecution.

Income Statement
A financial statement showing revenues earned by a business, the expenses incurred in conducting business, and the resulting net income or net loss.

Income, Net
Excess of total revenues over total expenses in a given period.

Indictment
A formal written complaint of criminal charges.

Indirect Methods
Ways of proving unknown or illegal sources of funds which rely upon circumstantial evidence.

Informant
A person who has specific knowledge of a criminal event and provides that information to a law enforcement officer.

Insider Trading
Using "inside" or advance information to trade in shares of publicly held corporations.

Intangible Asset
Any nonphysical asset, such as goodwill or a patent, which has no physical existence. Its value is dependent on the rights that possession confers upon the owner

Interest
Charge for the use of money.

Interrogation
Questioning of suspects and/or uncooperative witnesses for the purpose of obtaining testimony and evidence or proof of significant omissions.

Interview
A specialized form of face-to-face communication between people that is entered into for a specific task-related purpose associated with a particular subject matter.

Inventory
Goods being held for sale, and material and partly finished products, which upon completion, will be sold.

Investment Banker
A person or company in the business of marketing bonds and stocks for a corporation desiring to raise money

Invoice
Bill for goods delivered or services rendered.

Journal
A book of original entry in which transactions are initially recorded before being posted to a ledger.

Judicial Notice
When a court recognizes the existence and truth of certain facts.

Kickback
When a person who sells an item pays back a portion of the purchase price to the buyer or public official.

Lapping
The substitution of checks for cash received. A term used in embezzlement schemes.

Larceny
Wrongfully taking another person's money or property with the intent to appropriate, convert, or steal it.

Law
A formal means of social control intended to guide or direct human behavior toward ends that satisfy the common good.

Ledger
An accounting device used to summarize journal entries by specific accounts.

Lessee
The person or company possessing and using a leased item.

Lessor
The person or company holding legal title to a leased item.

Letter of Credit
A document issued by a bank authorizing designated banks to make payments on demand to a specified individual up to a stated total amount.

Liability
A debt owed.

Liability, current. Obligation that becomes due within a short time, usually one year.

Liability, long-term. Obligation with maturity dates more than one year after the balance sheet date.

Line of Credit
A commitment by a bank to a borrower to lend money at a stated interest rate for a stated period

Link Analysis
A technique for evaluating, integrating, and presenting complex information collected from various sources and putting them together to show patterns and meanings.

Liquidity
Ability to meet current obligations.

Loss, Net
Excess of total expenses over total revenue in a given period.

Mala In Se
Crimes that are said to be evil or immoral in and of themselves.

Mala Prohibita
Offenses that are made criminal by statute but in and of themselves are not necessarily immoral.

Maturity of Loan
The due date of a loan.

Memorandum
A written record of an interview embodying something that an investigator desires to fix in memory.

Moms Rea
A legal term meaning proof of criminal intent.

Misdemeanor
Crimes less serious than felonies that are punishable by incarceration for a period of less than one year and/or a fine.

Money Laundering
The process by which one conceals the existence, illegal source, or legal application of income and then disguises that income to make it appear legitimate.

Money Order
A negotiable instrument that serves as a substitute for a check.

Mutual Company
Type of corporation that has no stockholders, but is owned by its customers.

Net Worth
The excess of asset value over creditor claims; Assets Liabilities = Net Worth (Equity).

Net Worth Method
An indirect method of proving unknown sources of funds by comparing net worth at the beginning and end of specified period of time.

Note
A written promise to repay a loan.

Note Receivable
A debt that is evidenced by a note or other written acknowledgment.

Open Corporation
A corporation whose stock is available for investment by the public.

Partner
One of the owners of an unincorporated business.

Par Value
A specified amount printed on the face of a stock certificate.

Partnership
A company created when two or more individuals agree to do business together.

Percentage Method
An indirect method of proving unknown sources of funds by using percentages or ratios considered typical of a business under investigation.

Physical Inventory, Taking of
Counting all merchandise on hand, usually at the end of an accounting period.

Posting
Transfer of an entry from a journal to a ledger account.

Probable Cause
All the facts and circumstances within the knowledge of an investigator about a criminal activity that can be considered reasonable and trustworthy.

Proceeds
Whatever is received when an object is sold, exchanged, or otherwise disposed of.

Profit and Loss Account
A temporary account where revenue and expense accounts are transferred at the end of an accounting period.

Profit, Gross
Sales minus cost of goods sold.

Proof
The establishment of a fact by evidence.

Proprietor
The owner of an unincorporated business.

Proprietorship
A business owned by one person who is usually both the manager and the owner.

Prospectus
A summary of a corporation registration statement designed to inform a prospective purchaser of securities. It must contain a fairly extensive disclosure statement of essential facts pertinent to the security.

Question and Answer Statement
A complete transcript of the questions, answers, and statements made by each participant during an interview.

Questioned Document
A document that has been questioned in whole or in part in respect to its authenticity, identity, or origin.

Racketeering
Running an illegal business for personal profit.

Reasonable Doubt
The degree of certainty a person has in accomplishing or transacting the more important concerns in everyday life.

Registration Statement
A statement describing, in detail, the financial condition of a corporation, its business, and the reasons it proposes to offer an issue of stocks or bonds to the public.

Revenue
An increase in owner's equity arising from operations.

Search Warrant
A written order by a judge or magistrate, it describes the place to be searched as well as the items to be seized.

Security
A stock, bond, note, or other document that represents a share in a company or a debt owed by a company or government entity.

Shell Corporation
A corporation that has no assets or liabilities, simply a charter to do business.

Single-Entry Accounting
A system of accounting that makes no effort to balance accounts.

Silent Partner
A partner not liable for debts of the partnership beyond the amount of his or her investment in the partnership and who does not participate in management. Also known as a limited partner.

Stakeout
A common term for stationary surveillance.

Sting
A short-term undercover operation.

Stock
Ownership of a corporation represented by shares that are a claim on the corporation's assets and earnings.

Stock, capital. Stock that is authorized by a company's charter.

Stock, common. Units of ownership in a company that allow the owner to receive dividends on his or her holdings.

Stock, issued. The number of shares of stock actually sold or distributed by a corporation.

Stock, outstanding. Issued stock less treasury stock.

Stock, preferred. The class of stock entitled to preferential treatment with regard to dividends or with regard to the distribution of assets in the event of liquidation.

Stock, treasury. Shares of stock issued and subsequently reacquired by the corporation.

Stock Certificate
A document evidencing ownership in a corporation.

Stockholders
An owner of an incorporated business with the ownership being evidenced by stock certificates.

Stock Split
An exchange of the shares outstanding for two or more times their number.

Subpoena
A document that requires a witness to appear before a grand jury or requires the witness to produce records and documents for the grand jury.

Substantive Law
The body of law that creates, discovers, and defines the rights and obligations of each person in society.

Surplus, Capital
An increase in owner's equity not generated through the company's earnings.

Surveillance
The secretive and continuous observation of persons, places, and things to obtain information concerning the identity and activity of individuals suspected of violating criminal laws.

T-Account
An accounting device used for recording increases and decreases on either side of vertical line, with account title on the top.

Tax Evasion
Committing fraud in filing or paying taxes.

Torts
A terms used in civil law, it refers to the private wrongdoings between individuals.

Transaction
The exchange of goods and services.

Treasury Bill
A short-term security offered by the U.S. Government with maturities of 13 weeks, 36 weeks, and 52 weeks.

Treasury Bond
A long-term security offered by the U.S. Government with maturities of 10 years or longer.

Treasury Note
An intermediate-term security offered by the U.S. Government with maturities from one to ten years.

Trial Balance
A list of the account balances arranged in "balance sheet order" by debits and credits with adjustment columns for entries. Used as a basis summary for financial statements.

Undercover Operation
An investigative tool where law enforcement officers or private individuals assume an identity other than their own for the purpose of gathering information relating to criminal violations.

Underwriter
A person or firm guaranteeing and usually participating in the marketing of securities to the public. The guarantee states the dollar amount the underwriter guarantees that the corporation will receive from the sale.

Underwriting Syndicate
A group of underwriters formed for the purpose of guaranteeing the successful sale of a particular issue of securities.

Unit and Volume Method
An indirect method of proving unknown or illegal sources of funds by applying price or profit figures to the known quantity of business.

United States Code
A multi-volume publication of the text of statutes enacted by Congress.

Voucher System
A control system within a company for cash payment.

Worksheet
An accounting device used to organize accounting data.

GLOSSARY OF LEGAL, MEDICAL, SOCIAL WORK TERMS

TABLE OF CONTENTS

	Page
Abandonment ... Advocacy	1
Affidavit ... Annual Review of Dependency Cases	2
Anomie ... Battery	3
Best Interests of the Child ... Caretaker	4
Cartilage ... Child Abuse	5
Child Abuse and Neglect	6
Child Abuse Prevention and Treatment Act ... Child Health Visitor	7
Child in Need of Supervision ... Child Welfare League of America	8
Child Welfare Resource Information Exchange ... Circumstantial Evidence	9
Civil Proceeding ... Community Organization	10
Community Support Systems	11
Compliance ... Corporal Punishment	12
Cortex ... Custody	13
Custody Hearing ... Denver Model	14
Dependency ... Discipline	15
Dislocation ... Due Process	16
Duodenum ... Evidence	17
Exhibit ... Expungement	18
Extravasated Blood ... Family Dynamics	19
Family Dysfunction ... Family Violence	20
Federal Regulations ... Fracture	21
Frontal ... Helpline	22
Hematemesis ... Hypovitaminosis	23
Identification of Child Abuse and Neglect ... Incest	24
Incidence ... Infanticide	25
Institutional Child Abuse and Neglect ... Juvenile Judge	27
Labeling ... Legal Rights of Persons Identified in Reports	28
Lesion ... Local Authority	29
Long Bone ... Maternal Characteristics Scale	30
Maternal-Infant Bonding ... Model Child Protection Act	31
Mondale Act ... National Center for the Prevention and Treatment of Child Abuse and Neglect	32
National Center on Child Abuse and Neglect ... National Committee for the Prevention of Child Abuse	33
National Register ... Nurturance	34
Occipital ... Parent Effectiveness Training	35
Parental Stress Services ... Pathognomonic	36
Perinatal ... Pre-trial Diversion	37

TABLE OF CONTENTS
(Continued)

Prevention of Child Abuse and Neglect ... Probation	38
Program Coordination ... Public Defender	39
Public Law 93-247 ... Regional Resource Center	40
Registry ... Res Ipsa Loquitor	41
Retina ... Self-Incrimination	42
Sentencing ... Social Assessment	43
Social History ... Societal Child Abuse and Neglect	44
Special Child ... State Authority	45
Status Offense ... Subdural Hematoma	46
Subpoena ... Surrogate Parent	47
Suspected Child Abuse and Neglect ... Trauma	48
Trauma X ... Vascular	49
Venereal Disease ... Willful	50
Witness ... X-Rays	51
ACRONYMS	52

GLOSSARY OF

Legal, Medical, Social Work Terms

ABANDONMENT
Act of a parent or caretaker leaving a child without adequate supervision or provision for his/her needs for an excessive period of time. State laws vary in defining adequacy of supervision and the length of time a child may be left alone or in the care of another before abandonment is determined. The age of the child also is an important factor. In legal terminology, "abandonment cases" are suits calling for the termination of parental rights.

ABDOMINAL DISTENTION
Swelling of the stomach area. The distention may be caused by internal injury or obstruction or by malnutrition.

ABRASION
Wound in which an area of the body surface is scraped of skin or mucous membrane.

ABUSE (See CHILD ABUSE AND NEGLECT)

ABUSED CHILD (See INDICATORS OF CHILD ABUSE AND NEGLECT)

ABUSED PARENT
Parent who has been abused as a child and who therefore may be more likely to abuse his/her own child.

ABUSER, PASSIVE (See PASSIVE ABUSER)

ACADEMY OF CERTIFIED SOCIAL WORKERS (ACSW)
Professional category identifying experienced social workers. Eligibility is determined by written examination following two years' full-time or 3,000 hours part-time paid post-Master's degree experience and continuous National Association of Social Workers (NASW) membership.

ACTING OUT
1) Behavior of an abusive parent who may be unconsciously and indirectly expressing anger toward his/her own parents or other significant person.
2) Aggressive or sexual behavior explained by some psychoanalytic theorists as carrying out fantasies or expressing unconscious feelings and conflicts.
3) Children's play or play therapy activities used as a means of expressing hitherto repressed feelings.

ACUTE CARE CAPACITY
Capacity of a community to respond quickly and responsibly to a report of a child abuse or neglect. It involves receiving the report and providing a diagnostic assessment including both a medical assessment and an evaluation of family dynamics. It also involves rapid intervention, including immediate protection of the child when needed and referral for long term care or service to the child and his/her family.

ADJUDICATION HEARING
Court hearing in which it is decided whether or not charges against a parent or caretaker are substantiated by admissible evidence. Also known as jurisdictional or evidentiary hearing.

ADMISSIBLE EVIDENCE
Evidence which may be legally and properly used in court. (See also EVIDENCE, EVIDENTIARY STANDARDS, EXPERT TESTIMONY)

ADVOCACY
Interventive strategy in which a helping person assumes an active role in assisting or supporting a specific child and/or family or a cause on behalf of children and/or families. This could involve finding and facilitating services for specific cases or developing new

services or promoting program coordination. The advocate uses his/her power to meet client needs or to promote causes.

AFFIDAVIT
Written statement signed in the presence of a Notary Public who "swears in" the signer. The contents of the affidavit are stated under penalty of perjury. Affidavits are frequently used in the initiation of juvenile court cases and are, at times, presented to the court as evidence.

AGAINST MEDICAL ADVICE (AMA)
Going against the orders of a physician. In cases of child abuse or neglect, this usually means the removal of a child from a hospital without the physician's consent.

AID TO FAMILIES WITH DEPENDENT CHILDREN (AFDC) (See SOCIAL SECURITY ACT)

ALLEGATION
An assertion, declaration, or statement of a party to a legal action, which sets out what he or she expects to prove. In a child abuse or neglect case, the allegation forms the basis of the petition or accusation containing charges of specific acts of maltreatment which the petitioner hopes to prove at the trial.

ALOPECIA
Absence of hair from skin areas where it normally appears; baldness.

AMERICAN ACADEMY OF PEDIATRICS (AAP)
P.O. Box 1034
Evanston, Illinois 60204
AAP is the pan-American association of physicians certified in the care of infants, children, and adolescents. It was founded in 1930 for the primary purpose of ensuring "the attainment of all children of the Americas of their full potential for physical, emotional, and social health." Services and activities of AAP include standards-setting for pediatric residencies, scholarships, continuing education, standards-setting for child health care, community health services, consultation, publications, and research.

AMERICAN HUMANE ASSOCIATION, CHILDREN'S DIVISION (AHA)
5351 S. Roslyn St.
Englewood, Colorado 80110
National association of individuals and agencies working to prevent neglect, abuse, and exploitation of children. Its objectives are to inform the public of the problem, to promote understanding of its causes, to advise on the identification and protection of abused and neglected children, and to assist in organizing new and improving existing child protection programs and services. Some of the programs and services of CDAHA include research, consultation and surveys, legislative guidance, staff development training and workshops, and publications. AHA includes an Animal Division in addition to the Children's Division.

AMERICAN PUBLIC WELFARE ASSOCIATION (APWA)
1125 Fifteenth St. N.W. Suite 300
Washington, D.C. 20005
APWA was founded in 1930 and has, from its inception, been a voluntary membership organization composed of individuals and agencies interested in issues of public welfare. National in scope, its dual purpose is to: 1) exert a positive influence on the shaping of national social policy, and 2) promote professional development of persons working in the area of public welfare. APWA sponsors an extensive program of policy analysis and research, testimony and consultation, publications, conferences, and workshops. It works for policies which are more equitable, less complex, and easier to administer in order that public welfare personnel can respond efficiently and effectively to the needs of persons they serve.

ANNUAL REVIEW OF DEPENDENCY CASES
Annual or other periodic reviews of dependency cases to determine whether continued

child placement or court supervision of a child is necessary. Increasingly required by state law, such reviews by the court also provide some judicial supervision of probation or casework services.

ANOMIE
A state of anomie is characterized by attitudes of aimlessness, futility, and lack of motivation and results from the breakdown or failure of standards, rules, norms, and values that ordinarily bind people together in some socially organized way.

ANOREXIA
Lack or loss of appetite for food.

APATHY-FUTILITY SYNDROME
Immature personality type often associated with child neglect and characterized by an inability to feel and to find any significant meaning in life. This syndrome, often arising from early deprivations in childhood, is frequently perpetuated from generation to generation within a family system. (Polansky)

APPEAL
Resort to a higher court in an attempt to have a decision or ruling of the lower court corrected or reversed because of some claimed error or injustice. Appeals follow several different formats. Occasionally, appeals will result in a rehearing of the entire case. Usually, however, appeals are limited to consideration of questions of whether the lower court judge correctly applied the law to the facts of the case.

ASSESSMENT
1) Determination of the validity of a reported case of suspected child abuse or neglect through investigatory interviews with persons involved. This could include interviews with the family, the child, school, and neighbors, as well as with other professionals and paraprofessionals having direct contact with the child or family.
2) Determination of the treatment potential and treatment plan for confirmed cases.

ASSAULT
Intentional or reckless threat of physical injury to a person. Aggravated assault is committed with the intention of carrying out the threat or other crimes. Simple assault is committed without the intention of carrying out the threat or if the attempt at injury is not completed. (See also BATTERY, SEXUAL ASSAULT)

ATROPHY
Wasting away of flesh, tissue, cell, or organ.

AVITAMINOSIS
Condition due to complete lack of one or more essential vitamins. (See also HYPOVITAMINOSIS)

BATTERED CHILD SYNDROME
Term introduced in 1962 by C. Henry Kempe, M.D., in the *Journal of the American Medical Association* in an article describing a combination of physical and other signs indicating that a child's internal and/or external injuries result from acts committed by a parent or caretaker. In some states, the battered child syndrome has been judicially recognized as an accepted medical diagnosis. Frequently this term is misused or misunderstood as the only type of child abuse and neglect. (See also CHILD ABUSE AND NEGLECT)

BATTERED WOMEN
Women who are victims of non-accidental physical and/or psychological injury inflected by a spouse or mate. There seems to be a relationship between child abuse and battered women, with both often occurring in the same family. (See also SPOUSE ABUSE)

BATTERY
Offensive contact or physical violence with a person without his/her consent, and which may or may not be preceded by a threat of assault. Because a minor cannot legally give consent, any such contact or violence against a child is considered battery. The action may be aggravated, meaning intentional, or it may be simple, meaning that the action was not intentional or did not cause

severe harm. Assault is occasionally used to mean attempted battery. (See also ASSAULT)

BEST INTERESTS OF THE CHILD
Standard for deciding among alternative plans for abused or neglected children. This is also known as the least detrimental alternative principle. Usually it is assumed that it is in the child's best interest and least detrimental if the child remains in the home, provided that the parents can respond to treatment. However, the parents' potential for treatment may be difficult to assess and it may not be known whether the necessary resources are available. A few authorities believe that except where the child's life is in danger, it is always in the child's best interest to remain in the home. This view reflects the position that in evaluating the least detrimental alternative and the child's best interest, the child's psychological as well as physical well-being must be considered. In developing a plan, the best interest of the child may not be served because of parents' legal rights or because agency policy and practice focuses on foster care. The best interest of the child and least detrimental alternative principles were articulated as a reaction to the overuse of child placement in cases of abuse and neglect. Whereas "best interest of the child" suggests that some placement may be justified, "least detrimental alternative" is stronger in suggesting that any placement or alternative can have some negative consequences and should be monitored.

BEYOND A REASONABLE DOUBT (See EVIDENTIARY STANDARDS)

BONDING
The psychological attachment of mother to child which develops during and immediately following childbirth. Bonding, which appears to be crucial to the development of a health parent/child relationship, may be studied during and immediately following delivery to help identify potential families-at-risk. Bonding is normally a natural occurrence but it may be disrupted by separation of mother and baby or by situational or psychological factors causing the mother to reject the baby at birth.

BRUISE (See INTRADERMAL HEMORRHAGE)

BURDEN OF PROOF
The duty, usually falling on the state as petitioner in a child maltreatment case, of producing evidence at a trial so as to establish the truth of the allegations against the parent. At the commencement of a trial, it is always up to the petitioner to first present evidence which proves their case. (See also EVIDENCE, EVIDENTIARY STANDARDS)

BURN
Wound resulting from the application of too much heat. Burns are classified by the degree of damage caused.
    1st degree: Scorching or painful redness of the skin.
    2nd degree: Formation of blisters.
    3rd degree: Destruction of outer layers of the skin.

BURN OUT (See staff burn out.)

CALCIFICATION
Formation of bone. The amount of calcium deposited can indicate via X-ray the degree of healing of a broken bone or the location of previous fractures which have healed prior to the X-ray.

CALLUS
New bone formed during the healing process of a fracture.

CALVARIUM
Dome-like portion of the skull.

CARETAKER
A person responsible for a child's health or welfare, including the child's parent, guardian, or other person within the child's own home; or a person responsible for a child's health or welfare in a relative's home, foster care home, or residential institution. A caretaker is responsible for meeting a child's

basic physical and psychological needs and for providing protection and supervision.

CARTILAGE
The hard connective tissue that is not bone but, in the unborn and growing child, may be the forerunner of bone before calcium is deposited in it.

CASE MANAGEMENT
Coordination of the multiplicity of services required by a child abuse and neglect client. Some of these services may be purchased from an agency other than the mandated agency. In general, the role of the case manager is not the provision of direct services but the monitoring of those services to assure that they are relevant to the client, delivered in a useful way, and appropriately used by the client. To do this, a case manager assumes the following responsibilities.
1) Ascertains that all mandated reports have been properly filed.
2) Informs all professionals involved with the family that
reports of suspected child abuse or neglect have been made.
3) Keeps all involved workers apprised of new information.
4) Calls and chairs the intial case conference for assessment, disposition, and treatment plans; conference may include parents, physician, probation worker, police, public health nurse, private therapist, parent aide, protective service and welfare workers, or others.
5) Coordinates interagency follow-up.
6) Calls further case conferences as needed. (See also PURCHASE OF SERVICE)

CASEWORK
A method of social work intervention which helps an individual or family improve their functioning in society by changing both internal attitudes and feelings and external circumstances directly affecting the individual or family. This contrasts with community organization and other methods of social work intervention which focuses on changing institutions or society. Social casework relies on a relationship between the worker and client as the primary tool for effecting change.

CATEGORICAL AID
Government financial assistance given to individuals who are aged or disabled or to families with dependent children. The eligibility requirements and financial assistance vary for different categories of persons, according to the guidelines of the Social Security Act. (See also SOCIAL SECURITY ACT)

CENTRAL REGISTER
Records of child abuse reports collected centrally from various agencies under state law or voluntary agreement. Agencies receiving reports of suspected abuse check with the central register to determine whether prior reports have been received by other agencies concerning the same child or parents. The purposes of central registers may be to alert authorities to families with a prior history of abuse, to assist agencies in planning for abusive families, and to provide data for statistical analysis of child abuse. Due to variance in state laws for reporting child abuse and neglect, there are diverse methods of compiling these records and of access to them. Although access to register records is usually restricted, critics warn of confidentiality problems and the importance of expunging unverified reports. (See also EXPUNGEMENT)

CHILD
A person, also known as minor, from birth to legal age of maturity for whom a parent and/or caretaker, foster parent, public or private home, institution, or agency is legally responsible. The 1974 Child Abuse Prevention and Treatment Act defines a child as a person under 18. In some states, a person of any age with a developmental disability is defined as a child.

CHILD ABUSE (See CHILD ABUSE AND NEGLECT)

CHILD ABUSE AND NEGLECT (CAN)
All-inclusive term, as defined in the Child Abuse Prevention and Treatment Act, for "the physical or mental injury, sexual abuse, negligent treatment or maltreatment of a child under the age of eighteen by a person who is responsible for the child's welfare. There is agreement that some parental care and supervision is essential, there is disagreement as to how much is necessary for a minimally acceptable environment.

Child Abuse refers specifically to an act of commission by a parent or caretaker which is not accidental and harms or threatens to harm a child's physical or mental health or welfare. All 50 States have a child abuse reporting law with varying definitions of child abuse and varying provisions as to who must and may report, penalties for not reporting, and required agency action following the report. Factors such as the age of the child and the severity of injury are important in determining abuse.

Physical Abuse
Child abuse which results in physical injury, including fractures, burns, bruises, welts, cuts, and/or internal injuries. Physical abuse often occurs in the name of discipline or punishment, and ranges from a slap of the hand to use of objects such as straps, belts, kitchen utensils, pipes, etc. (See also BATTERED CHILD SYNDROME)

Psychological/Emotional Abuse
Child abuse which results in impaired psychological growth and development. Frequently occurs as verbal abuse or excessive demands on a child's performance and results in a negative self-image on the part of the child and disturbed child behavior. May occur with or without physical abuse.

Sexual Abuse
Child abuse which results in any act of a sexual nature upon or with a child. Most states define any sexual involvement of a parent or caretaker with a child as a sexual act and therefore abuse. The most common form is incest between fathers and daughters.

Verbal Abuse
A particular form of psychological/emotional abuse characterized by constant verbal harassment and denigration of a child. Many persons abused as children report feeling more permanently damaged by verbal abuse than by isolated or repeated experiences of physical abuse.

Child Neglect refers to an act of omission, specifically the failure of a parent or other person legally responsible for a child's welfare to provide for the child's basic needs and proper level of care with respect to food, clothing, shelter, hygiene, medical attention, or supervision. Most states have neglect and/or dependency statutes; however, not all states require the reporting of neglect. While there is agreement that some parental care and supervision is essential, there is disagreement as to how much is necessary for a minimally acceptable environment. Severe neglect sometimes occurs because a parent is apathetic, impulse-ridden, mentally retarded, depressed, or psychotic.

Educational Neglect
Failure to provide for a child's cognitive development. This may include failure to conform to state legal requirements regarding school attendance.

Medical Neglect
Failure to seek medical or dental treatment for a health problem or condition which, if untreated, could become severe enough to represent a danger to the child. Except among religious sects prohibiting medical treatment, medical neglect is usually only one part of a larger family problem.

Moral Neglect
Failure to give a child adequate guidance in developing positive social values, such as parents who allow or teach their children to steal.

Physical Neglect
Failure to provide for a child's basic survival needs, such as food, clothing, shelter, and supervision, to the extent that the failure represents a hazard to the child's health or safety. Determining neglect for lack of supervision depends upon the child's age and competence, the amount of unsupervised time, the time of day when the child is unsupervised, and the degree of parental planning for the unsupervised period. For a particular kind of physical neglect involving failure to feed a baby or small child sufficiently, see FAILURE TO THRIVE SYNDROME.

Psychological /Emotional Neglect
Failure to provide the psychological nurturance necessary for a child's psychological growth and development. It is usually very difficult to prove the cause and effect relationship between the parent's unresponsiveness and lack of nurturance and the child's symptoms, and many states do not include psychological or emotional neglect in their reporting laws.

CHILD ABUSE PREVENTION AND TREATMENT ACT (PUBLIC LAW 93-247)

Act introduced and promoted in Congress by then U.S. Senator Walter Mondale and signed into law on January 31, 1974. The act established the National Center on Child Abuse and Neglect in the HEW Children's Bureau and authorized annual appropriations of between $15 million and $25 million through Fiscal Year 1977, but it is anticipated that Congress will extend the act for several years. Actual appropriations have been less than authorized. The purpose of the National Center is to conduct and compile research, provide an information clearinghouse, compile and publish training materials, provide technical assistance, investigate national incidence, and fund demonstration projects related to prevention, identification, and treatment of child abuse and neglect. In the 1974 act, not more than 20% of the appropriated funds may be used for direct assistance to states, which must be in compliance with specific legislative requirements including, among others, reporting and investigation of suspected neglect as well as abuse, provision of multidisciplinary programs, and appointment of a *guardian ad litem* to represent the child in all judicial proceedings. The act emphasizes multidisciplinary approaches. It also provides for funding for parent self-help projects.

Many persons do not understand that this act is primarily to support research and demonstration projects. Much larger amounts of funding for the ongoing provisions of child abuse and neglect services are provided to states through Title IV-B and Title XX of the Social Security Act.

CHILD DEVELOPMENT
Pattern of sequential stages of interrelated physical, psychological, and social development in the process of maturation from infancy and total dependence to adulthood and relative independence. Parents need to understand the level of maturity consistent with each stage of development and should not expect a child to display a level of maturity of which the child is incapable at a particular stage. Abusive or neglectful parents frequently impair a child's healthy growth and development because they do not understand child development or are otherwise unable to meet the child's physical, social, and psychological needs at a given stage or stages of development.

CHILD HEALTH VISITOR
Professional or paraprofessional who visits a home shortly after the birth of a baby and periodically thereafter to identify current and potential child health and development and family stress problems and to facilitate use of needed community services. While currently operating in many European countries, child health visitor programs are rare in the U.S. because they are perceived as contrary to the right to privacy and parental rights. A universal mandatory child health visitor program has, however, been recommended by several

authorities as the most effective way to assure children's rights and prevent child abuse and neglect. Also known as Home Health Visitor.

CHILD IN NEED OF SUPERVISION
Juvenile who has committed a delinquent act and has been found by a children's court judge to require further court supervision, such as 1) probation, or 2) the transfer of custody of the child to a relative or public or private welfare agency for a period of time, usually not to exceed one year. Also known as Person in Need of Supervision (PINS) or Minor in Need of Supervision (MINS).

CHILD NEGLECT (See CHILD ABUSE AND NEGLECT)

CHILD PORNOGRAPHY
The obscene or pornographic photography, filming, or depiction of children for commercial purposes. Recent campaigns have begun to increase public awareness of this problem. Also as a result of public pressure against these materials, the federal government and some states are currently implementing special legislation to outlaw the sale and interstate transportation of pornographic materials that portray children engaged in explicit sexual acts.

CHILD PROSTITUTION
Legislation prohibiting the use of children as prostitutes is currently being implemented by the federal government and many states. The use of or participation by children in sexual acts with adults for reward or financial gain when no force is present.

CHILD PROTECTIVE SERVICES or CHILD PROTECTION SERVICES (CPS)
A specialized child welfare service, usually part of a county department of public welfare, legally responsible in most states for investigating suspected cases of child abuse and neglect and intervening in confirmed cases. Qualifications of CPS workers vary, with some counties employing CPS workers without prior human services training and others requiring at least a , Bachelor's degree in social work. With over 3,000 counties in the U.S., there are many kinds of CPS programs of varying quality. Common to most is the problem of insufficient staff overburdened with excessive caseloads. This plus the pressure of CPS work creates stress for many CPS staff. (See also STAFF BURNOUT, STAFF FLIGHT, and STAFF SATISFACTION)

CHILD WELFARE AGENCY
A public or voluntary agency providing service to children in their own homes and/or in day care, and which may be licensed to place children in foster homes, group homes, or institutions or into permanent adoptive homes. The number of children served annually by child welfare agencies in the U.S. is estimated to be over one million, the majority being served by public agencies. Payments for foster care represent well over half the total of child welfare agencies' expenditures.

Child welfare agencies which meet certain standards, including Standards for Protective Services, are accredited by the Child Welfare League of America. It is estimated that the majority of social workers employed by these accredited agencies hold a Master's degree. In public child welfare agencies, Master's degree social workers are a minority, with specific educational requirements varying from state to state. However, unlike many other fields of social work which share responsibility with other professions, child welfare is a domain for which social work has been accorded major responsibility. Believing that child protection is a public child welfare agency responsibility, few private agencies provide it.

CHILD WELFARE LEAGUE OF AMERICA (CWLA)
67 Irving Place
New York,
N.Y. 10003
Founded in 1920, the Child Welfare League of America is a privately supported, non-sectarian organization which is dedicated to the improvement of care and services for

deprived, neglected, and dependent children and their families. Its program is directed toward helping agencies and communities in the U.S. and Canada to provide essential social services to promote the well-being of children. CWLA is an advocate for children and families, a clearinghouse and forum for knowledge and experience of persons in the field, and a coordinating facility through which all concerned with child welfare can share their efforts. Programs of the League and its membership of over 300 affiliated public and private agencies include: accreditation of agencies, adoption services, conferences, consultation, training, library/information services, publications, personnel services, public affairs and legislative programs, standards development, and surveys.

CHILD WELFARE RESOURCE INFORMATION EXCHANGE
A project of the Children's Bureau of the Administration for Children, Youth and Families, HEW. It is a source for materials on exemplary programs, curricula, technologies, and methods which ahve brought more effective and efficient services to children. Its purpose is to improve the delivery of child welfare services by identifying successful programs, methods, research, and materials, and by assisting agencies in adapting them for their own use. The Exchange disseminates information it has gathered through abstracts, a bimonthly bulletin, regional workshops, and colloquia.

CHILDHOOD LEVEL OF LIVING SCALE (CLL)
Instrument used to measure the level of physical and emotional/cognitive care a child is receiving in his/her home. Rated are adequacy of food, clothing, furniture, etc., as well as evidence of affection, type of discipline, and cultural stimulation. The scale is designed to be used as a guide to assessing nurturance levels rather than as objective evidence of neglect.

CHILDREN-AT-RISK
May refer to the possibility that children in the custody of a state or county will get lost in a series of placements or for other reasons not be returned to their natural homes when these homes are no longer threatening to the children's welfare. May also refer to children in potentially abusive institutions, but usually refer to children in families-at-risk. (See also FAMILIES-AT-RISK)

CHILDREN'S DEFENSE FUND (CDF) 1520 New Hampshire Ave., N.W. Washington, D.C. 20036
A non-profit organization founded in 1973. Staff includes researchers, lawyers, and others dedicated to long-range and systematic advocacy on behalf of children. CDF works at federal, state, and local levels to reform policies and practices which harmfully affect large numbers of children. Activities include investigation and public information, litigation, monitoring of federal agencies, and technical assistance to local organizations. Program priorities are to assure the rights of children to proper education, adequate health care, comprehensive child care and family support services, fair and humane treatment in the juvenile justice system, and the avoidance of institutionalization.

CHILDREN'S RIGHTS
Rights of children as individuals to the protections provided in the Constitution as well as to the care and protection necessary for normal growth and development. Children's rights are actually exercised through adult representatives and advocates. The extent to which children's rights are protected varies according to the individual state laws providing for the identification and treatment of child abuse and neglect. An unresolved issue is the conflict between children's rights and parents' rights or rights to privacy. (See also PARENTS' RIGHTS)

CHIP FRACTURE (See FRACTURE)

CIRCUMSTANTIAL EVIDENCE (See EVIDENCE)

CIVIL PROCEEDING
Any lawsuit other than criminal prosecutions. Juvenile and family court cases are civil proceedings. Also called a civil action.

CLEAR AND CONVINCING EVIDENCE
(See EVIDENTIARY STANDARDS)

CLOTTING FACTOR
Material in the blood that causes it to coagulate. Deficiencies in clotting factors can cause profuse internal or external bleeding and/or bruising, as in the disease hemophilia. Bruises or bleeding caused by such a disease may be mistaken as resulting from abuse.

COLON
The large intestine.

COMMINUTED FRACTURE (See FRACTURE)

COMMISSION, ACTS OF
Overt acts by a parent or caretaker toward a child resulting in physical or mental injury, including but not limited to beatings, excessive disciplining, or exploitation. (See also CHILD ABUSE AND NEGLECT)

COMMISSIONER (See HEARING OFFICER)

COMMUNITY AWARENESS
A community's level of understanding of child abuse and neglect. Ideally, this should include knowledge about the extent and nature of the problem and how to use the local resources. In reality, community awareness tends to focus on reporting rather than treatment and prevention.

COMMUNITY COUNCIL FOR CHILD ABUSE AND NEGLECT
Community group, including both professionals and citizens, which attempts to develop and coordinate resources and/or legislation for the prevention, identification, and treatment of child abuse and neglect. It is often the name given to the program coordination component of the community team (see COMMUNITY TEAM).

COMMUNITY EDUCATION
Developed for public audiences, this type of local level education provides understanding about a problem or issue of community and/or societal relevance, and information about appropriate community resources and services available to deal with the problem or issue. Sponsored by a professional agency or citizens' group, community education is usually provided through an ongoing speaker's bureau, through periodic lecture and discussion meetings open to the general public or offered to special groups, and/or through the local media and other publicity devices.

With reference to child abuse and neglect, it is important to combine community education with public awareness. Generally, public awareness is geared only to reporting child abuse and neglect, and may communicate a punitive image toward parents who abuse or neglect their children without communicating an understanding of the problem.

COMMUNITY NEGLECT
Failure of a community to provide adequate support and social services for families and children, or lack of community control over illegal or discriminatory activities with respect to families and children.

COMMUNITY ORGANIZATION
A social work method of achieving change in human service organizations or service delivery and utilization through social planning and/or social action. This kind of intervention rests explicitly or implicitly on understanding the nature of the community or service system which is the target of change and on organizing members of the community or system to participate in the change process. Professional community organizers assist, but do not direct, community groups in developing community organization strategies of confrontation, collaboration, coalition,

etc. Since child abuse and neglect is a multi-disciplinary, multiagency problem, community organization for coordination of services is imperative.

COMMUNITY SUPPORT SYSTEMS

Community resources such as schools, public health services, day care centers, welfare advocacy, whose utilization can aid in preventing family dysfunction and child abuse and neglect, and aid in treating identified cases of abuse and neglect.

COMMUNITY TEAM

Often used incorrectly to refer to a multidisciplinary professional group which only diagnoses and plans treatment for specific cases of child abuse and neglect. More accurately, a community team separates the diagnosis and treatment functions and provides a third component for education, training, and public relations. The community tream also includes a community task force or council, including citizens as well as professionals from various disciplines, which coordinates the three community team components and advocates for resources and legislation. Citizens on the community team also monitor the professionals and agency participants. For effective child abuse and neglect management, a community team should be established for every geographic area of 400,000 to 500,000 population, and should consist of the following components:

Identification/Diagnostic Team Component
The identification/diagnostic team component has primary responsibility for diagnosing actual cases of child abuse and neglect among those which are reported or otherwise come to their attention, providing acute care or crisis intervention for the child in immediate danger, and developing long-term treatment recommendations. This team should be multidisciplinary and should probably include a public health nurse, pediatrician, psychologist or psychiatrist, lawyer, law enforcement person, case aides, and a number of child protective services workers. The protective services workers on the diagnostic team undergo unusual physical and emotional fatigue, and they should have a two or three week break from this activity every several months. However, to further relieve this stress, the diagnostic team, and not the protective services workers alone, should make and be accountable for all decisions. To function effectively, this team must establish protocol, define roles of each team member, establish policies and procedures, and establish a network of coordination with acute care service agencies.

Long Term Treatment Component
The long term treatment component has responsibility to review treatment needs and progress of specific cases periodically, to establish treatment goals, to coordinate existing treatment services, and to develop new treatment programs. This component should include supervisors and workers from supportive and advocacy services as well as from adult, children, and family treatment programs. The community team must assure provision and use of this component.

Education, Training, and Public Relations Component
The education, training, and public relations component has responsibility for community and professional awareness and education. Professional education includes implementation and/or evaluation of ongoing training programs for professionals and paraprofessionals.

The interrelationship among these various components is diagrammed below:

A - Identification and Diagnosis B - Long-Term Treatment C - Education, Training, Public Relations	1 - Case Coordination 2 - Professional Training and Recruitment 3 - Public and Professional ducation, Professional Training 4 - Program Coordination

COMPLIANCE
1) The behavior of children who readily yield to demands in an attempt to please abusive or neglectful parents or caretakers.
2) A state child abuse and neglect law which conforms to requirements outlined in the Child Abuse Prevention and Treatment Act and further HEW regulations, and which therefore permits funding under this act for child abuse and neglect activities in the state. (See also CHILD ABUSE PREVENTION AND TREATMENT ACT)

COMPLAINT
1) An oral statement, usually made to the police, charging criminal, abusive, or neglectful conduct.
2) A district attorney's document which starts a criminal prosecution.
3) A petitioner's document which starts a civil proceeding. In juvenile or family court, the complaint is usually called a petition.
4) In some states, term used for a report of suspected abuse or neglect.

COMPOUND FRACTURE (See FRACTURE)

COMPREHENSIVE EMERGENCY SERVICES(CES)
A community system of coordinated services available on a 24-hour basis to meet emergency needs of children and/or families in crisis. Components of a CES system can include 24-hour protective services, homemaker services, crisis nurseries, family shelters, emergency foster care, outreach, and follow-up services.

CONCILIATION COURT (See COURTS)

CONCUSSION
An injury of a soft structure resulting from violent shaking or jarring; usually refers to a brain concussion.

CONFIDENTIALITY
Professional practice of not sharing with others information entrusted by a client or patient. Sometimes communications from parent to physician or social worker are made with this expectation but are later used in court, and many physicians and social workers are torn between legal vs. professional obligations. Confidentiality which is protected by statute is known as privileged communications. Confidentiality need not obstruct information sharing with a multidisciplinary team provided that the client is advised of the sharing and the team has articulated its own policy and guidelines on confidentiality. (See also PRIVILEGED COMMUNICATIONS)

CONGENITAL
Refers to any physical condition present at birth, regardless of its cause.

CONJUNCTIVA
Transparent lining covering the white of the eye and eyelids. Bleeding beneath the conjunctiva can occur spontaneously or from accidental or non-accidental injury.

CONTRAINDICATION
Reason for not giving a particular drug or prescribing a particular treatment, as it may do more harm than good.

CONTUSION
A wound producing injury to soft tissue without a break in the skin, causing bleeding into surrounding tissues.

CORPORAL PUNISHMENT
Physical punishment inflicted directly upon the body. Some abusive parents mistakenly believe that corporal punishment is the only way to discipline children, and some child development specialists believe that almost all parents must occasionally resort to corporal punishment to discipline or train children. Other professionals believe that corporal punishment is never advisable. In a Supreme Court ruling (Ingraham vs. Wright, April 19, 1977), corporal punishment in the schools was upheld. The Supreme Court ruled that the cruel and unusual punishment clause of the Eighth Amendment does not apply to corporal punishment in the schools. (See also DISCIPLINE).

CORTEX
Outer layer of an organ or other body structure.

COURTS
Places where judicial proceedings occur. There is an array of courts involved with child abuse and neglect cases, partly because different states divide responsibility for certain proceedings among different courts, and also because tradition has established a variety of names for courts which perform similar functions. Child abuse reports can result in proceedings in any of the following courts:

Criminal Court
Usually divided into superior court, which handles felony cases, and municipal court, which handles misdemeanors and the beginning stages of most felony cases.

Domestic Relations Court
A civil court in which divorces and divorce custody hearings are held.

Family Court
A civil court which, in some states, combines the functions of domestic relations, juvenile, and probate courts. Establishment of family courts is often urged to reform the presently wasteful and poorly-coordinated civil court system. Under some proposals, family courts would also deal with criminal cases involving family relations, thus improving coordination in child abuse litigation.

Court of Conciliation
A branch of domestic relations courts in some states, usually staffed by counselors and social workers rather than by lawyers or judges, and designed to explore and promote reconciliation in divorce cases.

Juvenile Court
Juvenile court, which has jurisdiction over minors, usually handles cases of suspected delinquency as well as cases of suspected abuse or neglect. In many states, terminations of parental rights occur in juvenile court proceedings, but that is generally the limit of juvenile court's power over adults.

Probate Court
Probate court may handle cases of guardianship and adoption in addition to estates of deceased persons.

CRANIUM
The skull.

CRIMINAL PROSECUTION
The process involving the filing of charges of a crime, followed by arraignment and trial of the defendant. Criminal prosecution may result in fines, imprisonment, and/or probation. Criminal defendants are entitled to acquittal unless charges against them are proven beyond a reasonable doubt. Technical rules of evidence exclude many kinds of proof in criminal trials, even though that proof might be admissible in civil proceedings. Criminal defendants are entitled to a jury trial; in many civil proceedings concerning children, there is no right to a jury trial.

CRISIS INTERVENTION
Action to relieve a specific stressful situation or series of problems which are immediately threatening to a child's health and/or welfare. This involves alleviation of parental stress through provision of emergency services in the home and/or removal of the child from the home. (See also EMERGENCY SERVICES and COMPREHENSIVE EMERGENCY SERVICES)

CRISIS NURSERY
Facility offering short-term relief of several hours to several days' duration to parents temporarily unable or unwilling to care for their children. The primary purpose are child protection, stabilization of the home, and prevention of child abuse and neglect.

CUSTODY
The right to care and control of a child and the duty to provide food, clothing, shelter, ordinary medical care, education, and discipline for a child. Permanent legal custody

may be taken from a parent or given up by a parent by a court action (see TERMINATION OF PARENTAL RIGHTS). Temporary custody of a child may be granted for a limited time only, usually pending further action or review by the court. Temporary custody may be granted for a period of months or, in the case of protective or emergency custody, for a period of hours or several days.

Emergency Custody
The ability of a law enforcement officer, pursuant to the criminal code, to take temporary custody of a child who is in immediate danger and place him/her in the control of child protective services. A custody hearing must usually be held within 48 hours of such action. Also known as police custody.

Protective Custody
Emergency measure taken to detain a child, often in a hospital, until a written detention request can be filed. In some states, telephone communication with a judge is required to authorize protective custody. In other states, police, social workers, or doctors have statutory authority to detain minors who are in imminent danger. (See also DETENTION)

CUSTODY HEARING
Hearing, usually held in children's court, to determine who has the rights of legal custody of a minor. It may involve one parent against the other or the parents vs. a social service agency.

CYCLE OF CHILD ABUSE OR NEGLECT
(See
WORLD OF ABNORMAL REARING)

DAUGHTERS UNITED
Organization name sometimes used for self-help groups of daughters who have been sexually abused. Daughters United is one component of a model Child Sexual Abuse Treatment Program in Santa Clara County, California. (See also PARENTS UNITED)

DAY CARE
A structured, supervised place for children to go more or less regularly while parents work or attend school. Experts believe that family stress can be relieved by more extensive provision of day care services, and day care providers are increasingly concerned with identification and prevention of child abuse and neglect.

DAY TREATMENT
1) Program providing treatment as well as structured supervision for children with identified behavioral problems, including abused and neglected children, while they remain in their own, foster, or group homes. Day treatment services usually include counseling with families or caretakers with whom the children reside.
2) Treatment and structured activities for parents or entire families in a treatment setting from which they return to their own homes evenings and weekends.

DELINQUENCY
Behavior of a minor which would, in the case of an adult, constitute criminal conduct. In some states, delinquency also includes "waywardness" or disobedient behavior on the part of the child. In contrast to dependency cases, where the parent(s) rather than the minor is assumed responsible, delinquency cases assume that the minor has some responsibility for his/her behavior.

DENVER MODEL
A multidisciplinary hospital-community coalition which originated in Denver, Colorado, and which has become a model replicated by many other programs. The following diagram outlines the components:

TIME	PLACE	FUNCTION
24 hours	Community	Child is identified as suspected abuse or neglect.
	Hospital	Child is admitted to hospital.
	Hospital	Telephone report is made to protective services.
	Community	Home is evaluated by protective services.
72 hours	Both	Dispositional conference is held.
	Community	Court is involved if needed.
2 weeks	Both	Implement dispositional plan.
6-9 months	Community	Maintain case.
	Both	Long-term Treatment program is followed.
	Both	Child is returned home when home has been made safe.

DEPENDENCY

A child's need for care and supervision from a parent or caretaker. Often a legal term referring to cases of children whose natural parent(s) cannot or will not properly care for them or supervise them so that the state must assume this responsibility. Many states distinguish findings of dependency, for which the juvenile is assumed to have little or no responsibility, from findings of delinquency, in which the juvenile is deemed to be at least partially responsible for his/her behavior.

DETENTION

The temporary confinement of a person by a public authority. In a case of child abuse or neglect, a child may be detained pending a trial when a detention hearing indicates that it is unsafe for the child to remain in his/her own home. This is often called protective custody or emergency custody. The child may be detained in a foster home, group home, hospital, or other facility.

DETENTION HEARING

A court hearing held to determine whether a child should be kept away from his/her parents until a full trial of neglect, abuse, or delinquency allegations can take place. Detention hearings must usually be held within 24 hours of the filing of a detention request. (See also CUSTODY)

DETENTION REQUEST

A document filed by a probation officer, social worker, or prosecutor with the clerk of a juvenile or family court, asking that a detention hearing be held, and that a child be detained until the detention hearing has taken place. Detention requests must usually be filed within 48 hours of the time protective custody of the child begins. (See also CUSTODY)

DIAGNOSTIC TEAM (See COMMUNITY TEAM)

DIAPHYSIS

The shaft of a long bone.

DIFFERENTIAL DIAGNOSIS

The determination of which of two or more diseases or conditions a patient may be suffering from by systematically comparing and contrasting the clinical findings.

DIRECT EVIDENCE (See EVIDENCE)

DIRECT SERVICE PROVIDERS

Those groups and individuals who directly interact with clients and patients in the delivery of health, education, and welfare services, or those agencies which employs them. It includes, among others, policemen, social workers, physicians, psychiatrists, and clinical psychologists who see clients or patients.

DISCIPLINE

1) A branch of knowledge or learning or a particular profession, such as law, medicine, or social work.
2) Training that develops self-control, self-sufficiency, orderly conduct. Discipline is

often confused with punishment, particularly by abusive parents who resort to corporal punishment. Although interpretations of both "discipline" and "punishment" tend to be vague and often overlapping, there is some consensus that discipline has positive connotations and punishment is considered negatively. Some general comparisons between the terms are:

a) Discipline can occur before, during, and/or after an event; punishment occurs only after an event.
b) Discipline is based on respect for a child and his/her capabilities; punishment is based on behavior or events precipitating behavior.
c) Discipline implies that there is an authority figure; punishment implies power and dominance vs. submissiveness.
d) The purpose of discipline is educational and rational; the purpose of punishment is to inflict pain, often in an attempt to vent frustration or anger.
e) Discipline focuses on deterring future behavior by encouraging development of internal controls; punishment is a method of external control which may or may not alter future behavior.
f) Discipline can lead to extrapolation and generalized learning patterns; punishment may relate only to a specific event.
g) Discipline can strengthen interpersonal bonds and recognizes individual means and worth; punishment usually causes deterioration of relationships and is usually a dehumanizing experience.
h) Both discipline and punishment behavior patterns may be transmitted to the next generation.

According to legal definitions applying to most schools and school districts, to accomplish the purposes of education, a schoolteacher stands in the place of a parent and may exercise powers of control, restraint, discipline, and correction as necessary, provided that the discipline is reasonable. The Supreme Court has ruled that under certain circumstances, the schools may also employ corporal punishment. (See also CORPORAL PUNISHMENT)

DISLOCATION
The displacement of a bone, usually disrupting a joint, which may accompany a fracture or may occur alone.

DISPOSITION
The order of a juvenile or family court issued at a dispositional hearing which determines whether a minor, already found to be a dependent or delinquent child, should continue in or return to the parental home, and under what kind of supervision, or whether the minor should be placed out-of-home, and in what kind of setting: a relative's home, foster home, or institution. Disposition in a civil case parallels sentencing in a criminal case.

DISPOSITIONAL CONFERENCE
A conference, preferably multidisciplinary, in which the child, parent, family, and home diagnostic assessments are evaluated and decisions are made as to court involvement, steps needed to protect the child, and type of long-term treatment. This conference should be held within the first 72 hours after hospital admission or reporting of the case.

DISPOSITIONAL HEARING (See DISPOSITION)

DISTAL
Far; farther from any point of reference. Opposite of proximal.

DOMESTIC RELATIONS COURT (See COURTS)

DUE PROCESS
The rights of persons involved in legal proceedings to be treated with fairness. These rights include the right to adequate notice in advance of hearings, the right to notice of allegations of misconduct, the right to assis-

tance of a lawyer, the right to confront and cross-examine witnesses, and the right to refuse to give self-incriminating testimony. In child abuse or neglect cases, courts are granting more and more due process to parents in recognition of the fact that loss of parental rights, temporarily or permanently, is as serious as loss of liberty. However, jury trials and presumptions of innocence are still afforded in very few juvenile or family court cases.

DUODENUM
The first portion of the small intestine which connects it to the stomach.

EARLY AND PERIODIC SCREENING, DIAGNOSIS, AND TREATMENT (EPSDT)
Program enacted in 1967 under Medicaid (Title 19 of the Social Security Act), with early detection of potentially crippling or disabling conditions among poor children as its goal. The establishment of EPSDT was a result of studies indicating that physical and mental defects were high among poor children and that early detection of the problems and prompt receipt of health care could reduce the consequences and the need for remedial services in later life. Although a recent study by the Children's Defense Fund has indicated that existing health systems are not adequate to facilitate the goals of EPSDT, the program has uncovered many previously undetected or untreated health problems among those children whom it has been able to reach.

EARLY INTERVENTION
Programs and services focusing on prevention by relieving family stress before child abuse and neglect occur; for example, help-lines, Head Start, home health visitors, EPSDT, crisis nurseries.

ECCHYMOSIS (See INTRADERMAL HEMORRHAGE)

EDEMA
Swelling caused by an excessive amount of fluid in body tissue. It often follows a bump or bruise but may also be caused by allergy, malnutrition, or disease.

EMERGENCY CUSTODY (See CUSTODY)

EMERGENCY SERVICES
The focus of these services is protection of a child and prevention of further maltreatment through availability of a reporting mechanism on a 24-hour basis and immediate intervention. This intervention could include hospitalization of the child, assistance in the home including homemakers, or removal of the child from the home to a shelter or foster home. (See also COMPREHENSIVE EMERGENCY SERVICES)

EMOTIONAL ABUSE (See CHILD ABUSE AND NEGLECT)

EMOTIONAL NEGLECT (See CHILD ABUSE AND NEGLECT)

ENCOPRESIS
Involuntary passage of feces.

ENURESIS
Involuntary passage of urine.

EPIPHYSIS
Growth center near the end of a long bone.

EVIDENCE
Any sort of proof submitted to the court for the purpose of influencing the court's decision. Some special kinds of evidence are:

Circumstantial
Proof of circumstances which may imply another fact. For example, proof that a parent kept a broken appliance cord may connect the parent to infliction of unique marks on a child's body.

Direct
Generally consisting of testimony of the type such as a neighbor stating that he/she saw the parent strike the child with an appliance cord.

Hearsay
Second-hand evidence, generally consisting of testimony of the type such as, "I heard him say. . . ." Except in certain cases, such evidence is usually excluded because it is considered unreliable and because the person making the original statement cannot be cross-examined.

Opinion
Although witnesses are ordinarily not permitted to testify to their beliefs or opinions, being restricted instead to reporting what they actually saw or heard, when a witness can be qualified as an expert on a given subject, he/she can report his/her conclusions, for example, "Based upon these marks, it is my opinion as a doctor that the child must have been struck with a flexible instrument very much like this appliance cord." Lawyers are sometimes allowed to ask qualified experts "hypothetical questions," in which the witness is asked to assume the truth of certain facts and to express an opinion based on those "facts." (See also EXPERT TESTIMONY)

Physical
Any tangible piece of proof such as a document, X-ray, photograph, or weapon used to inflict an injury. Physical evidence must usually be authenticated by a witness who testifies to the connection of the evidence (also called an exhibit) with other facts in the case.

Evidentiary Standards
State laws differ in the quantum of evidence which is considered necessary to prove a case of child maltreatment. Three of the most commonly used standards are:

Beyond a Reasonable Doubt (the standard required in all criminal court proceedings). Evidence which is entirely convincing or satisfying to a moral certainty. This is the strictest standard of all.

Clear and Convincing Evidence. Less evidence than is required to prove a case beyond a reasonable doubt, but still an amount which would make one confident of the truth of the allegations.

Preponderance of the Evident (the standard in most civil court proceedings). Merely presenting a greater weight of credible evidence than that presented by the opposing party. This is the easiest standard of proof of all.

EXHIBIT
Physical evidence used in court. In a child abuse case, an exhibit may consist of X-rays, photographs of the child's injuries, or the actual materials presumably used to inflict the injuries. (See also EVIDENCE)

EXPERT TESTIMONY
Witnesses with various types of expertise may testify in child abuse or neglect cases; usually these expert witnesses are physicians or radiologists. Experts are usually questioned in court about their education or experience which qualifies them to give professional opinions about the matter in question. Only after the hearing officer determines that the witness is, in fact, sufficiently expert in the subject matter may that witness proceed to state his/her opinions. (See also EVIDENCE)

EXPERT WITNESS (See EXPERT TESTIMONY)

EXPLOITATION OF CHILDREN
1) Involving a child in illegal or immoral activities for the benefit of a parent or caretaker. This could include child pornography, child prostitution, sexual abuse, or forcing a child to steal.
2) Forcing workloads on a child in or outside the home so as to interfere with the health, education, and well-being of the child.

EXPUNGEMENT

Destruction of records. Expungement may be ordered by the court after a specified number of years or when the juvenile, parent, or defendant applies for expungement and shows that his/her conduct has improved. Expungement also applies to the removal of an unverified report of abuse or neglect that has been made to a central registry. (See also CENTRAL REGISTRY)

EXTRAVASATED BLOOD
Discharge or escape of blood into tissue.

FAILURE TO THRIVE SYNDROME (FTT)
A serious medical condition most often seen in children under one year of age. An FTT child's height, weight, and motor development fall significantly short of the average growth rates of normal children. In about 10% of FTT cases, there is an organic cause such as serious heart, kidney, or intestinal disease, a genetic error of metabolisin, or brain damage. All other cases are a result of a disturbed parent-child relationship manifested in severe physical and emotional neglect of the child. In diagnosing FTT as child neglect, certain criteria should be considered:
1) The child's weight is below the third percentile, but substantial weight gain occurs when the child is properly nurtured, such as when hospitalized.
2) The child exhibits developmental retardation which decreases when there is adequate feeding and appropriate stimulation.
3) Medical investigation provides no evidence that disease or medical abnormality is causing the symptoms.
4) The child exhibits clinical signs of deprivation which decrease in a more nurturing environment.
5) There appears to be a significant environmental psychosocial disruption in the child's family.

FAMILIES ANONYMOUS
1) Name used by the National Center for the Prevention and Treatment of Child Abuse and Neglect at Denver for self-help groups for abusive parents. These groups operate in much the same way as the more widely-known Parents Anonymous. (See also PARENTS ANONYMOUS)
2) Self-help groups for families of drug abusers.

FAMILIES-AT-RISK
May refer to families evidencing high potential for child abuse or neglect because of a conspicuous, severe parental problem, such as criminal behavior, substance abuse, mental retardation, or psychosis. More often refers to families evidencing high potential for abuse or neglect because of risk factors which may be less conspicuous but multiple. These include: 1) environmental stress such as unemployment or work dissatisfaction; social isolation; anomie; lack of child care resources; I and/or 2) family stress such as marital discord; chronically and/or emotionally immature parent with a history of abuse or neglect as a child; unwanted pregnancy; colicky, hyperactive, or handicapped baby or child; siblings a year or less apart; sudden changes in family due to illness, separation, or death; parentla ignorance of child care and child development. Increasingly, the maternal-infant bonding process at childbirth is evaluated and used as one means to identify families-at-risk. Families thus identified should be offered immediate and periodic assistance.

FAMILY
Two or more persons related by blood, marriage, or mutual agreement who interact and provide one another with mutual physical, emotional, social, and/or economic care. Families can be described as "extended," with more than one generation in a household; or "nuclear," with only parent(s) and child(ren). Families can also be described as "mixed" or "multiracial"; "multi-parent," as in a commune or collective; or "single-parent." These types are not mutually exclusive.

FAMILY COURT (See COURTS)

FAMILY DYNAMICS
Interrelationships between and among individual family members. The evaluation of family dynamics is an important factor in the

identification, diagnosis, and treatment of child abuse and neglect.

FAMILY DYSFUNCTION
Ineffective functioning of the family as a unit or of individual family members in their family role because of physical, mental, or situational problems of one or more family members. A family which does not have or use internal or external resources to cope with its problems or fulfill its responsibilities to children may be described as dysfunctional. Child abuse and neglect is evidence of family dysfunction.

FAMILY IMPACT STATEMENT
Report which assesses the effect of existing and proposed legislation, policies, regulations, and practices on family life. The purpose is to promote legislation and policies which work for, not against, healthy family life. At the federal level, this activity is being developed by the Family Impact Seminar, George Washington University Institute for Educational Leadership (1001 Connecticut Ave., N.W., Suite 732, Washington, D.C. 20036).

FAMILY LIFE EDUCATION
Programs focusing on educating, enlightening, and supporting individuals and families regarding aspects of family life; for example, child development classes, communication skills workshops, sex education courses, or money management courses. Family life education might well be part of every child abuse and neglect prevention program, and may be part of the treatment program for abusive or neglectful parents who lack this information.

FAMILY PLANNING
Information and counseling provided to assist in controlling family size and spacing of children, including referrals to various agencies such as Planned Parenthood.

As a condition of receiving federal funding for AFDC (see SOCIAL SECURITY ACT), states are required to offer family planning services to applicants designated as "appropriate."

Family planning should be part of a child abuse and neglect prevention program.

FAMILY POLICY
Generally refers to public social and economic policies that centrally affect families. There is considerable confusion about the term, with some persons believing that family policy should mean more direct policies affecting families, such as family planning policies. There is much more agreement that we should look at the impact of numerous policies on families, and that these should include a wide range of governmental policies. (See also FAMILY IMPACT STATEMENT)

FAMILY SHELTER
A 24-hour residential care facility for entire families. The setting offers around-the-clock care, and often provides diagnosis and comprehensive treatment on a short-term basis. In child abuse and neglect, a family shelter is used primarily for crisis intervention.

FAMILY SYSTEM
The concept that families operate as an interacting whole and are an open system, so that many factors in the environment affect the functioning of family members and the interaction among members. It is also conceptualized that the behavior of the family as an interacting unit has an effect on a number of factors in the outer environment.

FAMILY VIOLENCE
Abusive or aggressive behavior between parents, known as wife battering or spouse abuse; between children, known as sibling abuse; and/or between parents and children within a family, usually child abuse. This behavior is related to factors within the structure of a family system and/or society; for example, poverty, models of violent behavior displayed via mass media, stress due to excessive numbers of children, values of dominance and submissiveness, and attitudes toward discipline and punishment. It may also occur as a result of alcoholism or other substance abuse.

The terms family violence and domestic violence are sometimes used interchangeably but some persons exclude child abuse from the definition of domestic violence and limit it to violence between adult mates or spouses.

FEDERAL REGULATIONS
Guidelines and regulations developed by departments or agencies of the federal government to govern programs administered or funded by those agencies. Regulations specify policies and procedures outlined in a more general way in public laws or acts. Proposed federal regulations, or changes in existing regulations, are usually published in the *Federal Register* for public review and comment. They are subsequently published in the final form adopted by the governing agency.

FEDERAL STANDARDS (See STANDARDS)

FELONY
A serious crime for which the punishment may be imprisonment for longer than a year and/or a fine greater than $1,000. Distinguished from misdemeanor or infraction, both of lesser degree.

FIFTH AMENDMENT
The Fifth Amendment to the U.S. Constitution guarantees a defendant that he/she cannot be compelled to present self-incriminating testimony.

FONTANEL
The soft spots on a baby's skull where the bones of the skull have not yet grown together.

FORENSIC MEDICINE
That branch of the medical profession concerned withestablishing evidence for legal proceedings.

FOSTER CARE
A form of substitute care for children who need to be removed from their own homes. Usually this is a temporary placement in which a child lives with a licensed foster family or caretaker until he/she can return to his/her own home or until reaching the age of majority. Foster care all too often becomes a permanent method of treatment for abused or neglected children. Effective foster care ideally includes service to the child, service to the natural parents, service to the foster parents, and periodic review of the placement.

FOSTER GRANDPARENTS
Retired persons or senior citizens who provide nurturance and support for children to whom they are not related, including abused and neglected children, by babysitting or taking them for recreational outings. This enables parents to have some respite and allows retired or older persons an opportunity to become involved in community activities. Sometimes foster grandparents are volunteers and sometimes they are paid by an agency program.

FOUNDED REPORT
Any report of suspected child abuse or neglect made to the mandated agency which is confirmed or verified. Founded reports outnumber unfounded reports.

FRACTURE
A broken bone, which is one of the most common injuries found among battered children. The fracture may occur in several ways:

Chip Fracture
A small piece of bone is flaked from the major part of the bone.

Comminuted Fracture
Bone is crushed or broken into a number of pieces.

Compound Fracture
Fragment(s) of broken bone protrudes through the skin, causing a wound.

Simple Fracture
Bone breaks without wounding the surrounding tissue.

Spiral Fracture

Twisting causes the line of the fracture to encircle the bone like a spiral staircase.

Torus Fracture
A folding, bulging, or buckling fracture. See diagram on next page for names and locations of the major bones of the human skeleton.

FRONTAL
Referring to the front of the head; the forehead.

FUNDASCOPIC EXAM
Opthalmic examination to determine if irregularities or internal injuries to the eye exist.

GATEKEEPERS
Professionals and the agencies which employ them who are in frequent or periodic contact with families or children and who are therefore in an advantageous position to spot individual and family problems, including child abuse and neglect, and make appropriate referrals for early intervention or treatment.

GLUTEAL
Related to the buttocks, which are made up of the large gluteus maximus muscles.

GONORRHEA (See VENEREAL DISEASE)

GRAND ROUNDS
Hospital staff meetings for presentation and discussion of a particular case or medical problem.

GUARDIAN
Adult charged lawfully with the responsibility for a child. A guardian has almost all the rights and powers of a natural parent, but the relationship is subject to termination or change. A guardian may or may not also have custody and therefore actual care and supervision of the child.

GUARDIAN AD LITEM (GAL)
Adult appointed by the court to represent the child in a judicial proceeding. The *guardian ad litem* may be, but is not necessarily, an attorney. Under the Child Abuse Prevention and Treatment Act, a state cannot qualify for federal assistance unless it provides by statute "that in every case involving an abused or neglected child which results in a judicial proceeding a *guardian ad litem* shall be appointed to represent the child in such proceedings." Some states have begun to allow a GAL for children in divorce cases.

HEAD START
A nationwide comprehensive program for disadvantaged preschool children, funded by the HEW Administration for Children, Youth and Families to meet the educational, nutritional, and health needs of the children and to encourage parent participation in their children's development.

Through federal policy instructions (see *Federal Register,* January 26, 1977), all Head Start staff are mandated to report suspected cases of child abuse and neglect. These policy instructions supersede individual child abuse and neglect reporting laws in states which do not include Head Start staff as mandated reporters.

HEARING
Judicial proceeding where issues of fact or law are tried and in which both parties have a right to be heard. A hearing is synonymous with a trial.

HEARING OFFICER
A judge or other individual who presides at a judicial proceeding. The role of judge is performed in some juvenile court hearings by referees or commissioners, whose orders are issued in the name of the supervising judge. Acts of a referee or commissioner may be undone after the supervising judge has conducted a rehearing in the case.

HELPLINE
Usually a telephone counseling, information, and referral service characterized by caller anonymity, late hour availability, and the use

of trained volunteers as staff. The goal is usually early intervention in any kind of family stress, as well as crisis intervention in child abuse and neglect. Helplines relieve social isolation and offer ways of ventilating stress which are not destructive. Unlike hotlines, helplines generally cannot report cases of child abuse and neglect since they do not know the caller's name. Instead, the helpline attempts to have the caller himself/herself seek professional assistance and/or maintain a regular calling relationship for support and as an alternative to violent behavior. Helplines appear to be very cost effective in the preventive of child abuse and neglect. Major disadvantages are lack of visual cues to problems and limited opportunity for follow-up services. (See also HOTLINE)

HEMATEMESIS
Vomiting of blood from the stomach, often resulting from internal injuries.

HEMATOMA
A swelling caused by a collection of blood in an enclosed space, such as under the skin or the skull.

HEMATUREA
Blood in the urine.

HEMOPHILIA
Hereditary blood clotting disorder characterized by spontaneous or traumatic internal and external bleeding and bruising.

HEMOPTYSIS
Spitting or coughing blood from the windpipe or lungs.

HEMORRHAGE
The escape of blood from the vessels; bleeding.

HOME HEALTH VISITOR (See CHILD HEALTH VISITOR)

HOME START
A nationwide home-based program funded by the HEW Administration for Children, Youth and Families to strengthen parents as educators of their own children.

HOMEMAKER SERVICES
Provision of assistance, support, and relief for parents who may be unable or unwilling to fulfill parenting functions because of illness or being overwhelmed with parenting responsibilities. A homemaker is placed in a home on an hourly or weekly basis and assists with housekeeping and child care while demonstrating parenting skills and providing some degree of nurturance for parents and children.

HOSPITAL HOLD
Hospitalization for further observation and protection of a child suspected of being abused or neglected. This usually occurs when a suspected case is discovered in an emergency room. In most cases, holding the child is against the wishes of the parent or caretaker. (See also CUSTODY)

HOTLINE
Twenty-four hour statewide or local answering service for reporting child abuse or neglect and initiating investigation by a local agency. This is often confused with a helpline. (See also HELPLINE)

HYPERACTIVE
More active than is considered normal.

HYPERTHERMIA
Condition of high body temperature.

HYPHEMA
Hemorrhage within the anterior chamber of the eye, often appearing as a bloodshot eye. The cause could be a blow to the head or violent shaking.

HYPOACTIVE
Less active than is considered normal.

HYPOTHERMIA
Condition of low body temperature.

HYPOVITAMINOSIS

Condition due to the deficiency of one or more essential vitamins. (See also AVITAMINOSIS)

IDENTIFICATION OF CHILD ABUSE AND NEGLECT
Diagnosis or verification of child abuse and neglect cases by mandated agency workers or a diagnostic team following investigation of suspected child abuse and neglect (see INDICATORS OF CHILD ABUSE AND NEGLECT). Identification of child abuse and neglect therefore depends not only on professional diagnostic skill but also on the extent to which the public and professionals report suspected cases. Public awareness campaigns are important to effect identification, but at the same time it is important to have sufficient staff in the mandated agency to handle all the reports a public awareness campaign may generate (see COMMUNITY AWARENESS and COMMUNITY EDUCATION). More reporting and therefore identification will also occur as states strengthen their reporting laws so as to extend the number of persons who must report and penalize them more heavily if they don't. It is generally agreed that to date the identification of child abuse and neglect represents only a small proportion of the actual incidence of the problem. It is also generally agreed that a greater degree of identification occurs in minority and low income groups because these persons are more visible to agencies and professionals required to report. The incidence is probably as high in upper socio-economic groups, but identification is more difficult, particularly because private physicians generally dislike to report.

ILEUM
Final portion of the small intestine which connects with the colon.

IMMUNITY, LEGAL
Legal protection from civil or criminal liability.
1) Child abuse and neglect reporting statutes often confer immunity upon persons mandated to report, giving them an absolute defense to libel, slander, invasion of privacy, false arrest, and other lawsuits which the person accused of the act might file. Some grants of immunity are limited only to those persons who report in good faith and without malicious intent.
2) Immunity from criminal liability is sometimes conferred upon a witness in order to obtain vital testimony. Thereafter, the witness cannot be prosecuted with the use of information he/she disclosed in his/her testimony. If an immunized witness refuses to testify, he/she can be imprisoned for contempt of court.

IMPETIGO
A highly contagious, rapidly spreading skin disorder which occurs principally in infants and young children. The disease, characterized by red blisters, may be an indicator of neglect and poor living conditions.

IMPULSE-RIDDEN MOTHER
Term often used to describe one kind of neglectful parent who demonstrates restlessness, aggressiveness, inability to tolerate stress, manipulativeness, and craving for excitement or change. This parent may have a lesser degree of early deprivation than the apathetic-futile parent, but lacks self-control over strong impulses and/or has not learned limit-setting.

IN CAMERA
Any closed hearing before a judge in his chambers is said to be *in camera*.

IN LOCO PARENTIS
"In the place of a parent." Refers to actions of a guardian or other non-parental custodian.

INCEST
Sexual intercourse between persons who are closely related. Some state laws recognize incest only as sexual intercourse among consaguineous, or blood, relations; other states recognize incest as sexual relations between a variety of family members related by blood and/or law. In the U.S., the prohibition against incest is specified by many states' laws as well as by cultural tradition, with state laws

usually defining incest as marriage or sexual relationships between relatives who are closer than second, or sometimes even more distant, cousins. While incest and sexual abuse are sometimes thought to be synonymous, it should be realized that incest is only one aspect of sexual abuse. Incest can occur within families between members of the same sex, but the most common form of incest is between father and daughters. It is generally agreed that incest is much more common than the number of reported cases indicates. Also, because society has not until the present done much about this problem, professionals have generally not had adequate training to deal with it, and the way the problem is handled may prove more traumatic for a child victim of incest than the incest experience itself. It should be noted that sexual relations between relatives may be defined as incest, but that incest is not considered child sexual abuse unless a minor is involved. (See also CHILD ABUSE AND NEGLECT, SEXUAL ABUSE, SEXUAL MISUSE)

INCIDENCE
The extent to which a problem occurs in a given population. No accurate or complete data is available on the actual incidence of child abuse and neglect in the U.S. because major studies have not been able to obtain data from some states or have found the data not to be comparable. For continuing efforts to solve this problem, see NATIONAL STUDY ON CHILD ABUSE AND NEGLECT REPORTING. Informed estimates of incidence range from 600,000 to one million cases of child abuse and neglect per year in this country. It is generally agreed that child neglect is four to five or more times more common than child abuse. Incidence of actual child abuse and neglect should not be confused with the number of reported cases in a central registry, since the latter include reports of suspected but unconfirmed cases. On the other hand, it is generally agreed that because of insufficient reporting, the number of actual cases coming to the attention of local agencies is but a small proportion of the actual number of cases in the population. (See also CENTRAL REGISTRY and IDENTIFICATION OF CHILD ABUSE AND NEGLECT)

INDICATED CHILD ABUSE AND NEGLECT
1) In some state statutes, "indicated" child abuse and neglect means a confirmed or verified case.
2) Medically, "indicated" means a probable case.

INDICATORS OF CHILD ABUSE AND NEGLECT
Signs or symptoms which, when found in various combinations, point to possible abuse or neglect. See chart on next page for common indicators of child abuse and neglect.

INDICTMENT
The report of a grand jury charging an adult with criminal conduct. The process of indictment by secret grand jury proceedings bypasses the filing of a criminal complaint and the holding of a preliminary hearing in municipal court, so that prosecution begins immediately in superior court.

INFANTICIDE
The killing of an infant or many infants. Until modern times, infanticide was an accepted method of population control. It often took the form of abandonment. A few primitive cultures still practice infanticide.

Indicators of Child Abuse and Neglect

CATEGORY	CHILD'S APPEARANCE	CHILD'S BEHAVIOR	CARETAKER'S BEHAVIOR
Physical Abuse	—Bruises and welts (on the face, lips, or mouth; in various stages of healing; on large areas of the torso, back, buttocks, or thighs; in unusual patterns, clustered, or reflective of the instrument used to inflict them; on several different surface areas). —Burns (cigar or cigarette burns; glove or sock-like burns or doughnut shaped burns on the buttocks or genitalia indicative of immersion in hot liquid; rope burns on the arms, legs, neck or torso; patterned burns that show the shape of the item (iron, grill, etc.) used to inflict them). —Fractures (skull, jaw, or nasal fractures; spiral fractures of the long (arm and leg) bones; fractures in various states of healing; multiple fractures; any fracture in a child under the age of two). —Lacerations and abrasions (to the mouth, lip, gums, or eye; to the external genitalia). —Human bite marks.	—Wary of physical contact with adults. —Apprehensive when other children cry. —Demonstrates extremes in behavior (e.g., extreme aggressiveness or withdrawal). —Seems frightened of parents. —Reports injury by parents.	—Has history of abuse as a child. —Uses harsh discipline inappropriate to child's age, transgression, and condition. —Offers illogical, unconvincing, contradictory, or no explanation of child's injury. —Seems unconcerned about child. —Significantly misperceives child (e.g., sees him as bad, evil, a monster, etc.). —Psychotic or psychopathic. —Misuses alcohol or other drugs. —Attempts to conceal child's injury or to protect identity of person responsible.
Neglect	—Consistently dirty, unwashed, hungry, or inappropriately dressed. —Without supervision for extended periods of time or when engaged in dangerous activities. —Constantly tired or listless. —Has unattended physical problems or lacks routine medical care. —Is exploited, overworked, or kept from attending school. —Has been abandoned.	—Is engaging in delinquent acts (e.g., vandalism, drinking, prostitution, drug use, etc.) —Is begging or stealing food. —Rarely attends school.	—Misuses alcohol or other drugs. —Maintains chaotic home life. —Shows evidence of apathy or futility. —Is mentally ill or of diminished intelligence. —Has long-term chronic illnesses. —Has history of neglect as a child.
Sexual Abuse	—Has torn, stained, or bloody underclothing. —Experience pain or itching in the genital area. —Has bruises or bleeding in external genitalia, vagina, or anal regions. —Has venereal disease. —Has swollen or red cervix, vulva, or perineum. —Has semen around mouth or genitalia or on clothing. —Is pregnant.	—Appears withdrawn or engages in fantasy or infantile behavior. —Has poor peer relationships. —Is unwilling to participate in physical activities. —Is engaging in delinquent acts or runs away. —States he/she has been sexually assaulted by parent/caretaker.	—Extremely protective or jealous of child. —Encourages child to engage in prostitution or sexual acts in the presence of caretaker. —Has been sexually abused as a child. —Is experiencing marital difficulties. —Misuses alcohol or other drugs. —Is frequently absent from the home.
Emotional Maltreatment	—Emotional maltreatment, often less tangible than other forms of child abuse and neglect, can be indicated by behaviors of the child and the caretaker.	—Appears overly compliant, passive, undemanding. —Is extremely aggressive, demanding, or rageful. —Shows overly adaptive behaviors, either inappropriately adult (e.g., parents other children) or inappropriately infantile (e.g., rocks constantly, sucks thumb, is enuretic). —Lags in physical, emotional, and intellectual development. Attempts suicide.	—Blames or belittles child. —Is cold and rejecting. —Withholds love. —Treats siblings unequally. —Seems unconcerned about child's problem.

INSTITUTIONAL CHILD ABUSE AND NEGLECT

1) Abuse and neglect as a result of social or institutional policies, practices, or conditions. The rather widespread practice of detaining children in adult jails is one example. Usually refers to specific institutions or populations, but may also be used to mean societal abuse or neglect. (See also SOCIETAL ABUSE AND NEGLECT)
2) Child abuse and neglect committed by an employee of a public or private institution or group home against a child in the institution or group home.

INTAKE

Process by which cases are introduced into an agency. Workers are usually assigned to interview persons seeking help in order to determine the nature and extent of the problem(s). However, in child abuse and neglect, intake of reports of suspected cases is usually by telephone and an interview with the reporting person is not required. Child abuse and neglect workers who do intake must be skilled in getting as much information as possible from the reporter in order to determine whether the situation is an emergency requiring instant attention.

INTERDISCIPLINARY TEAM (See COMMUNITY TEAM)

INTRADERMAL HEMORRHAGE

Bleeding within the skin; bruise. Bruises are common injuries exhibited by battered children, and are usually classified by size:

Petechiae
Very small bruise caused by broken capillaries. Petechiae may be traumatic in nature or may be caused by clotting disorders.

Purpura
Petechiae occurring in groups, or a small bruise (up to 1 cm. in diameter).

Ecchymosis
Larger bruise.

INVOLUNTARY CLIENT

Person who has been referred or court-ordered for services but who has not asked for help. Most abusive and neglectful parents are initially involuntary clients and may not accept the need for services. They may deny that there is a problem and resist assistance. Motivation for change may be minimal or nonexistent; however, skillful workers have demonstrated that motivation can be developed and treatment can be effective.

INVOLUNTARY PLACEMENT

Court-ordered assignment of custody to an agency and placement of a child, often against the parents' wishes, after a formal court proceeding, or the taking of emergency or protective custody against the parents' wishes preceding a custody hearing. (See also CUSTODY)

JEJUNUM

Middle portion of the small intestine between the duodenum and the ileum.

JURISDICTION

The power of a particular court to hear cases involving certain categories of persons or allegations. Jurisdiction may also depend upon geographical factors such as the county of a person's residence. (See also COURTS)

JURY

Group of adults selected by lawyers who judge the truth of allegations made in a legal proceeding. Trial by jury is available in all criminal cases, including cases of suspected child abuse and neglect. Very few juvenile, probate, or domestic relations court cases can be tried before a jury and are instead decided by the presiding judge.

JUVENILE COURT (See COURTS)

JUVENILE JUDGE

Presiding officer of a juvenile court. Often in a juvenile court, there are several other hearing officers of lesser rank, usually called referees or commissioners. (See also HEARING OFFICER)

LABELING
The widespread public and professional practice of affixing terms which imply serious or consistent deviance to the perpetrators and/or victims of child abuse and neglect; for example, "child abuser." Since deviance may suggest that punishment is warranted, this kind of labeling decreases the possibility of treatment. This is unfortunate, because experts agree that 80% or 85% of all child abuse and neglect cases have the potential for successful treatment. Such labeling may also make parents see themselves in a negative, despairing way, and discourage them from seeking assistance.

LABORATORY TESTS
Routine medical tests used to aid diagnosis. Those particularly pertinent to child abuse are:

Partial Thromboplastin Time (PTT) Measures clotting factors in the blood.

Prothrombin Time (PT)
Measures clotting factors in the blood.

Urinalysis
Examination of urine for sugar, protein, blood, etc.

Complete Blood Count (CBC)
Measure and analysis of red and white blood cells.

Rumpel-Leede (Tourniquet) Test
Measures fragility of capillaries and/or bruisability.

LACERATION
A jagged cut or wound.

LATCH KEY CHILDREN
Working parents' children who return after school to a home where no parent or caretaker is present. This term was coined because these children often wear a house key on a chain around their necks.

LATERAL
Toward the side.

LAY THERAPIST (See PARENT AIDE)

LEAST DETRIMENTAL ALTERNATIVE
(See
BEST INTEREST OF THE CHILD)

LEGAL RIGHTS OF PERSONS IDENTIFIED IN REPORTS
Standards for legal rights stress the need for all persons concerned with child abuse and neglect to be aware of the legal rights of individuals identified in reports and to be committed to any action necessary to enforce these rights. According to the National Center on Child Abuse and Neglect *Revision to Federal Standards on the Prevention and Treatment of Child Abuse and Neglect (Draft)*, these rights include the following:

1. Any person identified in a report as being suspected of having abused or neglected a child should be informed of his/her legal rights.
2) The person responsible for the child's welfare should receive written notice and be advised of his her legal rights when protective custody authority is exercised.
3) A child who is alleged to be abused or neglected should have independent legal representation in a child protection proceeding.
4) The parent or other person responsible for a child's welfare who is alleged to have abused or neglected a child should be entitled to legal representation in a civil or criminal proceeding.
5) The local child protective services unit should have the assistance of legal counsel in all child protective proceedings.
6) Each party should have the right to appeal protective case determinations.
7) Any person identified in a child abuse or neglect report should be protected from unauthorized disclosure of personal information contained in the report.

LESION
Any injury to any part of the body from any cause that results in damage or loss of structure or function of the body tissue involved. A lesion may be caused by poison, infection, dysfunction, or violence, and may be either accidental or intentional.

LIABILITY FOR FAILURE TO REPORT
State statutes which require certain categories of persons to report cases of suspected child abuse and/or neglect are often enforced by the imposition of a penalty, fine and/or imprisonment, for those who fail to report. Recent lawsuits have provided what may become an even more significant penalty for failure to report: when a report should have been made and a child comes to serious harm in a subsequent incident of abuse or neglect, the person who failed to report the initial incident may be held civilly liable to the child for the damages suffered in the subsequent incident. Such damages could amount to many thousands of dollars. (See also MANDATED REPORTERS)

LICENSING PARENTHOOD
Proposed method of assuring adequate parenting skills. Various proposals have been developed, including mandatory parenthood education in high school, with a certificate upon completion. Serious advocates compare the process with certification of driving capability by driver's licenses. Many consider the proposal unworkable.

LOCAL AUTHORITY
Local authority refers to two groups: 1) the social service agency (local agency) designated by the state department of social services (state department) and authorized by state law to be responsible for local child abuse and neglect prevention, identification, and treatment efforts, and 2) the community child protection coordinating council (community council). The standards on local authority, as specified in the National Center on Child Abuse and Neglect *Revision to Federal Standards on the Prevention and Treatment of Child Abuse and Neglect* *(Draft)*, include:

Administration and Organization
1. The local agency should establish a distinct child protective services unit with sufficient and qualified staff.
2. The local agency in cooperation with the state department should allocate sufficient funds and provide adequate administrative support to the local unit.
3. The local agency should initiate the establishment of a community council which is to be representative of those persons providing or concerned with child abuse and neglect prevention, identification, and treatment services.

Primary Prevention
4. The local unit and the community council should work together to establish formalized needs assessment and planning processes.

Secondary and Tertiary Prevention
5. The local unit and the community council should work together to develop a comprehensive and coordinated service delivery system for children-at-risk and families-at-risk to be presented in an annual plan.
6. The local unit and the community council should develop standards on the care of children which represent the minimum expectations of the community and provide the basis for the local unit's operational definitions and referral guidelines.
7. The local unit and the community council should establish a multidisciplinary child abuse and neglect case consultation team.
8. The local unit should provide or arrange for services to assist families who request help for themselves in fulfilling their parenting responsibilities.
9. The local unit should ensure that reports of child abuse and neglect can be received on a twenty-four hour, seven days per week basis.

10 The intake services worker should intervene immediately if a report is considered an emergency; otherwise, intervention should take place within seventy-two hours.
11 The intake services worker should ensure the family's right to privacy by making the assessment process time-limited.
12 The treatment services worker should develop an individualized treatment plan for each family and each family member.
13 The treatment services worker should arrange for, coordinate, and monitor services provided to a family.

Resource Enhancement

14 The agency and the community council should assist in the training of the local unit and other community service systems.
15 The agency should promote internal agency coordination.
16 The local unit should implement community education and awareness.
17 The agency should participate in or initiate its own research, review, and evaluation studies.

(See also STATE AUTHORITY)

LONG BONE
General term applied to the bones of the leg or the arm.

LONG TERM TREATMENT
Supportive and therapeutic services over a period of time, usually at least a year, to restore the parent(s) of an abused or neglected child and/or the child himself/herself to adequate levels of functioning and to prevent recurrence of child abuse or neglect.

LUMBAR
Pertaining to the part of the back and sides between the lowest ribs and the pelvis.

MALNUTRITION
Failure to receive adequate nourishment. Often exhibited in a neglected child, malnutrition may be caused by inadequate diet (either lack of food or insufficient amounts of needed vitamins, etc.) or by a disease or other abnormal condition affecting the body's ability to properly process foods taken in.

MALTREATMENT
Actions that are abusive, neglectful, or otherwise threatening to a child's welfare. Frequently used as a general term for child abuse and neglect.

MANDATED AGENCY
Agency designated by state statutes as legally responsible for receiving and investigating reports of suspected child abuse and neglect. Usually, this agency is a county welfare department or a child protective services unit within that department. Police or sheriffs departments may also be mandated agencies. (See also STATE AUTHORITY and LOCAL AUTHORITY)

MANDATED REPORTERS or MANDATORY REPORTERS
Persons designated by state statutes who are legally liable for not reporting suspected cases of child abuse and neglect to the mandated agency. The persons so designated vary according to state law, but they are primarily professionals, such as pediatricians, nurses, school personnel, and social workers, who have frequent contact with children and families.

MARASMUS
A form of protein-calorie malnutrition occurring in infants and children. It is characterized by retarded growth and progressive wasting away of fat and muscle, but it is usually accompanied by the retention of appetite and mental alertness.

MATERNAL CHARACTERISTICS SCALE
Instrument designed to study personality characteristics of rural Appalachian mothers and the level of care they were providing their children. The purpose of this scale is to

sharpen caseworkers' perception of "apathetic-futile" or "impulse-ridden" mothers' personality characteristics for evaluation, diagnosis, and formulation of a treatment plan in cases of child neglect. Some authorities believe this scale has not been adequately validated.

MATERNAL-INFANT BONDING (See BONDING)

MEDIAL
Toward the middle or mid-line.

MEDICAID, TITLE 19 (See SOCIAL SECURITY ACT)

MEDICAL MODEL
Conceptualizing problems in terms of diagnosis and treatment of illness. With respect to child abuse and neglect, the medical model assumes an identifiable and therefore treatable cause of the abuse and/or neglect and focuses on identification and treatment in a medical or other health setting. For child abuse and neglect, some advantages of the medical model are financial support by the hospital, clinic, medical community; accessibility of medical services to the abused or neglected child; involvement of the physicians; and visibility and public acceptance. Possible disadvantages are overemphasis on physical abuse; overemphasis on physical diagnosis to the detriment of total treatment; and isolation from other professional and community resources. (Kempe)

MEDICAL NEGLECT (See CHILD ABUSE AND NEGLECT)

MENKES KINKY HAIR SYNDROME
Rare, inherited disease resulting in brittle bones and, eventually, death. It is found in infants and, because of the great number of fractures the child may exhibit, can be mistaken for child abuse.

MENTAL INJURY
Injury to the intellectual or psychological capacity of a child as evidenced by observable and substantial impairment in his/her ability to function within a normal range of performance and behavior, with due regard to his/her culture. The Child Abuse Prevention and Treatment Act and some state statutes include mental injury caused by a parent or caretaker as child abuse or neglect.

MESENTERY
Membrane attaching various organs to the body wall.

METABOLISM
The sum of all physical and chemical processes which maintain the life of an organism.

METAPHYSIS
Wider part of a long bone between the end and the shaft.

MINIMALLY ACCEPTABLE ENVIRONMENT
The emotional climate and physical surroundings necessary for children to grow physically, mentally, socially, and emotionally.

MINOR (See CHILD)

MIRANDA RULE
Legal provision that a confession is inadmissible in any court proceeding if the suspect was not forewarned of his/her right to remain silent before the confession was disclosed. (See also FIFTH AMENDMENT)

MISDEMEANOR
A crime for which the punishment can be no more than imprisonment for a year and/or a fine of $1,000. A misdemeanor is distinguished from a felony, which is more serious, and an infraction, which is less serious.

MODEL CHILD PROTECTION ACT
Guide for development of state legislation concerning child abuse and neglect and intended to enable legislators to provide a

comprehensive and workable law which will aid in resolving the problem. A draft *Model Child Protection Act* has been developed and is available from the National Center on Child Abuse and Neglect.

MONDALE ACT (See CHILD ABUSE PREVENTION AND TREATMENT ACT)

MONGOLIAN SPOTS
A type of birthmark that can appear anywhere on a child's body, most frequently on the lower back. These dark spots usually fade by age five. They can be mistaken for bruises.

MORAL NEGLECT (See CHILD ABUSE AND NEGLECT)

MORIBUND
Dying or near death.

MOTHERS ANONYMOUS
Original name of Parents Anonymous. (See PARENTS ANONYMOUS)

MULTIDISCIPLINARY TEAM
A group of professionals and possibly paraprofessionals representing a variety of disciplines who interact and coordinate their efforts to diagnose and treat specific cases of child abuse and neglect. A multidisciplinary group which also addresses the general problem of child abuse and neglect in a given community is usually described as a community team, and it will probably consist of several multidisciplinary teams with different functions (see COMMUNITY TEAM). Multidisciplinary teams may include, but are not limited to, medical, child care, and law enforcement personnel, social workers, psychiatrists and/or psychologists. Their goal is to pool their respective skills in order to formulate accurate diagnoses and to provide comprehensive coordinated treatment with continuity and follow-up for both parent(s) and child or children. Many multidisciplinary teams operate according to the Denver Model (see DENVER MODEL). Multidisciplinary teams may also be referred to as cross-disciplinary teams, interdisciplinary teams, or SCAN teams (see SCAN TEAM). However, the Child Abuse Prevention and Treatment Act uses the term "multidisciplinary team."

NATIONAL ASSOCIATION OF SOCIAL WORKERS (NASW)
1425 H St., N.W.
Washington, D.C. 20005
A national organization of professional social workers who are enrolled in or have completed baccalaureate, master's, or doctoral programs in social work education. Members must subscribe to the NASW Code of Ethics, and NASW provides a policy for adjudication of grievances in order to protect members and promote ethical practices.

NATIONAL CENTER FOR CHILD ADVOCACY (NCCA)
P.O. Box 1182
Washington, D.C. 20013
The National Center for Child Advocacy is part of the Children's Bureau of the Administration for Children, Youth and Families within the Office of Human Development Services of HEW. NCCA supports research, demonstration, and training programs and provides technical assistance to state and local agencies with the goal of increasing and improving child welfare services. These services include in-home support to families, such as parent education and homemaker services; foster care, adoption, and child protective services; and institutional care of children. A major project of NCCA is the Child Welfare Resource Information Exchange. (See also CHILD WELFARE RESOURCE INFORMATION EXCHANGE)

NATIONAL CENTER FOR THE PREVENTION AND TREATMENT OF CHILD ABUSE AND NEGLECT
1205 Oneida St.
Denver, Colorado 80220
This center, which is affiliated with the Department of Pediatrics of the University of Colorado Medical School, was established in

the fall of 1972 to provide more extensive and up-to-date education, research, and clinical material to professionals working in the area of child abuse and neglect. The center's multidisciplinary staff has provided leadership in formulating the views that child abuse and neglect is symptomatic of troubled family relationships; that treatment must consider the needs of all family members; and that outreach to isolated, non-trusting families and the multidisciplinary approach are necessary. Funded by the State of Colorado, the HEW Administration for Children, Youth and Families, and private foundations, the center's work includes education, consultation and technical assistance, demonstration programs for treatment, program evaluation, and research. This center also serves as the HEW Region VIII Resource Center.

NATIONAL CENTER ON CHILD ABUSE AND NEGLECT (NCCAN)
P.O. Box 1182
Washington, D.C. 20013
Office of the federal government located within the Children's Bureau of the Administration for Children, Youth and Families (formerly the Office of Child Development), which is part of the Office of Human Development Services of HEW. Established in 1974 by the Child Abuse Prevention and Treatment Act, the functions of NCCAN are to:
1) Compile, analyze, and publish an annual summary of recent and current research on child abuse and neglect.
2) Develop and maintain an information clearinghouse on all programs showing promise of success for the prevention, identification, and treatment of child abuse and neglect.
3) Compile and publish training materials for personnel who are engaged or intend to engage in the prevention, identification, and treatment of child abuse and neglect.
4) Provide technical assistance to public and nonprofit private agencies and organizations to assist them in planning, improving, developing, and carrying out programs and activities relating to the prevention, identification, and treatment of child abuse and neglect.
5) Conduct research into the causes of child abuse and neglect, and into the prevention, identification, and treatment thereof.
6) Make a complete and full study and investigation of the national incidence of child abuse and neglect, including a determination of the extent to which incidents of child abuse and neglect are increasing in number or severity.
7) Award grants to states whose child abuse and neglect legislation complies with federal legislation.

NCCAN is authorized to establish grants and contracts with public and private agencies and organizations to carry out the above activities. Grants and contracts may also be used to establish demonstration programs and projects which, through training, consultation, resource provision, or direct treatment, are designed to prevent, identify, and treat child abuse and neglect. (See also CHILD ABUSE PREVENTION AND TREATMENT ACT and REGIONAL RESOURCE CENTER)

NATIONAL CLEARINGHOUSE ON CHILD NEGLECT AND ABUSE (NCCNA) (See NATIONAL STUDY ON CHILD NEGLECT AND ABUSE REPORTING)

NATIONAL COMMITTEE FOR THE PREVENTION OF CHILD ABUSE
111 E. Wacker Drive
Suite 510
Chicago, Illinois 60601
The National Committee originated in Chicago in 1972 in response to increasing national incidence of deaths due to child abuse. It was formed to help prevent child abuse, which was defined as including non-accidental injury, emotional abuse, neglect, sexual abuse, and exploitation of children, at a time when most programs focused on identification and treatment. The commit-

tee's goals are to:
1) Stimulate greater public awareness of the problem.
2) Encourage public involvement in prevention and treatment.
3) Provide a national focal point for advocacy to prevent child abuse.
4) Facilitate communication about programs, policy, and research related to child abuse prevention.
5) Foster greater cooperation between existing and developing resources for child abuse prevention.

Activities of the committee include a national media campaign, publications, conference, research, and the establishment of state chapters of the committee.

NATIONAL REGISTER

Often confused with the National Study on Child Neglect and Abuse Reporting (National Clearinghouse), which compiles statistics on incidence of child abuse and neglect. A national register, which does not exist at this time, would operate in much the same way and with the same purposes as a state-level central register, but would collect reports of abuse and neglect nationwide. Collecting reports on a national scale would be highly problematic because of variance in state reporting laws and definitions of abuse and neglect. (See also CENTRAL REGISTER and NATIONAL STUDY ON CHILD NEGLECT AND ABUSE REPORTING)

NATIONAL STUDY ON CHILD NEGLECT AND ABUSE REPORTING

Formerly the National Clearinghouse on Child Neglect and Abuse, the National Study is funded by the National Center on Child Abuse and Neglect, Children's Bureau, HEW and is being conducted by the Children's Division of the American Humane Association. The study has been established to systematically collect data from official state sources on the nature, incidence, and characteristics of child abuse and neglect. Participating states receive reports generated from their own data on a quarterly basis so that they can monitor their own reporting mechanisms. At this time, about 40 states are submitting detailed incidence data to the study. It is hoped that the National Study will be able to produce accurate data on the national incidence of child abuse and neglect.

NEEDS ASSESSMENT

A formal or informal evaluation of what services are needed by abused and neglected children and their families within a specified geographical area or within another given population.

NEGLECT (See CHILD ABUSE AND NEGLECT)

NEGLECTED CHILD (See INDICATORS OF CHILD ABUSE AND NEGLECT)

NEGLIGENCE

Failure to act. May apply to a parent, as in child neglect, or to a person who by state statute is mandated to report child abuse and neglect but who fails to do so. Negligence lawsuits arising from failure to report are increasing, and any failure to obey the statutes proves negligence. Lawsuits claiming damages for negligence are civil proceedings.

NETWORKING

Formal or informal linkages of individuals, families, or other groups with similar social, education, medical, or other service needs with the public or private agencies, organizations, and/or individuals who can provide such services in their locale. Formal agreements are usually written and spell out under what circumstances a particular agency, group, or individual will provide certain services. Informal agreements are apt to be verbal and relate to a particular family or case.

NURTURANCE

Affectionate care and attention provided by a parent, parent substitute, or caretaker to promote the well-being of a child and encourage healthy emotional and physical development. Nurturance may also be needed by adults with inadequate parenting skills, or who were themselves abused or neglected as children, as a model for developing more positive relationships with their own children and as a way of strengthening their own self-esteem.

OCCIPITAL
Referring to the back of the head.

OMISSION, ACTS OF
Failure of a parent or caretaker to provide for a child's physical and/or emotional well-being. (See also CHILD ABUSE AND NEGLECT)

OSSIFICATION
Formation of bone.

OSTEOGENESIS IMPERFECTA
An inherited condition in which the bones are abnormally brittle and subject to fractures, and which may be mistakenly diagnosed as the result of child abuse.

OUTREACH
The process in which professionals, paraprofessionals, and/or volunteers actively seek to identify cases of family strees and potential or actual child abuse and neglect by making services known, accessible, and unthreatening. Effective outreach providing early intervention is important for the prevention of child abuse and neglect.

PA BUDDY
Term used by Parents Anonymous for a person who functions like a parent aide in relation to a Parents Anonymous member. (See also PARENTS ANONYMOUS and PARENT AIDE)

PARAPROFESSIONAL
Volunteer or agency employee trained to a limited extent in a particular profession. Since paraprofessionals are usually close in age, race, nationality, religion, or lifestyle to the clientele, they often have a greater likelihood of developing a trusting relationship with a client than do some professionals. The role of the paraprofessional in protective service work is usually to provide outreach or nurturance and advocacy for the family, often as a case aide or parent aide. (See also PARENT AIDE)

PARENS PATRIAE
"The power of the sovereign." Refers to the state's power to act for or on behalf of persons who cannot act in their own behalf; such as, minors, incompetents, or some developmentally disabled.

PARENT
Person exercising the function of father and/or mother, including adoptive, foster, custodial, and surrogate parents as well as biological parents.

PARENT AIDE
A paraprofessional, either paid or voluntary, who functions primarily as an advocate and surrogate parent for a family in which child abuse or neglect is suspected or has been confirmed. The Parent Aide particularly serves the mother by providing positive reinforcement, emotional support, and nurturance, and by providing or arranging transportation, babysitting, etc., as necessary. Rather than serving as a homemaker, nutrition aide, or nurse, the parent aide's function is more like a friend to the family. Parent aides may also be referred to as case aides, lay therapists, or visiting friends.

PARENT EFFECTIVENESS TRAINING (PET)
An educational program developed by Dr. Thomas Gordon and presented in his book, *Parent Effectiveness Training* (New York, Peter H. Wyden, Inc., 1970). The program, taught by trained and certified PET instructors, focuses on improving communication between parents and children by teaching listening skills and verbal expression techniques to parents. The PET course has proven useful for parents who are motivated to change, who are able to give it a consider-

able amount of time, and who can afford the relatively high tuition. For these and other reasons, PET has not proven particularly useful in child abuse and neglect treatment, especially when used as the only mode of treatment.

PARENTAL STRESS SERVICES
Services aimed at relieving situational and/or psychological parental stress in order to relieve family dysfunction and to prevent parents from venting rage or frustration on their children. Service usually begins via a telephone helpline and may include home visits. Workers are usually trained volunteers or paraprofessionals who focus on providing warmth, nurturance, friendship, and resource referrals to the distressed parent. Some parental stress services promote development and use of Parents Anonymous chapters for their clients. Parental Stress Services may refer to specific programs such as in Chicago, Illinois, or Oakland, California, although there is no organizational linkage between them, or this may be a functional description of services provided within a larger agency program.

PARENTING SKILLS
A parent's competencies in providing physical care, protection, supervision, and psychological nurturance appropriate to a child's age and stage of development. Some parents, particularly those whose own parents demonstrated these skills, have these competencies without formal training, but adequacy of these skills may be improved through instruction.

PARENTS ANONYMOUS
22330 Hawthorne Blvd., #208
Torrance, California 90505
Self-help group for parents who want to stop physical, psychological, sexual, or verbal abuse of their children. Because members do not need to reveal their full names, they feel free to share concerns and provide mutual support. Members are accountable to the group for their behavior toward their children, and the group functions like a family in supporting members' efforts to change. With chapters in every state, over 800 in all, Parents Anonymous has been formally evaluated as an effective method for treating child abuse. Unlike most other self-help groups with anonymous members, Parents Anonymous requires that each chapter have an unpaid professional sponsor who attends all meetings to facilitate discussion, provide a role model, and suggest appropriate community resources for members' problems. The Child Abuse Prevention and Treatment Act provides for funding of self-help groups, and Parents Anonymous is one of the few self-help organizations which has received funding from the federal government.

PARENTS' RIGHTS
Besides the rights protected by the Constitution for all adults, society accords parents the right to custody and supervision of their own children, including, among others, parents' rights to make decisions about their children's health care. This plus parents' rights to privacy may complicate investigations of suspected child abuse and neglect and treatment of confirmed cases. Parents' rights may be cited in court in order to prevent the state from taking custody of a child who is in danger in his/her own home. (See also CHILDREN'S RIGHTS)

PARENTS UNITED
Organization name sometimes used for self-help groups of parents in families in which sexual abuse has occurred. Begun in 1972, Parents United is one component of a model Child Sexual Abuse Treatment Program in Santa Clara County, California. (See also DAUGHTERS UNITED)

PASSIVE ABUSER
Parent or caretaker who does not intervene to prevent abuse by another person in the home.

PATHOGNOMONIC
A sign or symptom specifically distinctive or characteristic of a disease or condition from which a diagnosis may be made.

PERINATAL
Around the time of birth, both immediately before and afterward.

PERIOSTEAL ELEVATION
The ripping or tearing of the surface layer of a bone (periosteum) and the resultant hemorrhage, occuring when a bone is broken.

PERITONITIS
Inflammation of the membrane lining the abdomen (peritoneum); caused by infection.

PERJURY
Intentionally inaccurate testimony. Perjury is usually punishable as a felony, but only if the inaccuracy of the testimony and the witness's knowledge of the inaccuracy can be proven.

PETECHIAE (See INTRADERMAL HEMORRHAGE)

PETITION
Document filed in juvenile or family court at the beginning of a neglect, abuse, and/or delinquency case. The petition states the allegations which, if true, form the basis for court intervention.

PETITIONER
Person who files a petition. In juvenile and family court practice, a petitioner may be a probation officer, social worker, or prosecutor, as variously defined by state laws.

PHYSICAL ABUSE (See CHILD ABUSE AND NEGLECT)

PHYSICAL NEGLECT (See CHILD ABUSE AND NEGLECT)

PLEA BARGAINING
Settlement of a criminal prosecution, usually by the reduction of the charge and/or the penalty, in return for a plea of guilty. Plea bargains are sometimes justified by congested court calendars. They are attacked as devices which weaken the intended effect of penal statutes and which reduce the dignity of the criminal justice system. Far more than half of all criminal prosecutions in this country are resolved by plea bargaining.

POLICE HOLD (See CUSTODY)

POLYPHAGIA
Excessive or voracious eating.

PREDICTION OF CHILD ABUSE AND NEGLECT
There are no evaluation instruments or criteria to predict absolutely that child abuse or neglect will occur in specific families. Recently, experts have developed instruments and methods of evaluating the bonding process at childbirth in order to identify families where because of incomplete or inadequate bonding, it can be expected that without further appropriate intervention, child abuse or neglect may occur. Besides bonding, many other indicators can be used to identify families-at-risk for child abuse and neglect, but these factors are rarely sufficiently conclusive to enable absolute prediction. (See also BONDING and FAMILIES-AT-RISK)

PREPONDERANCE OF EVIDENCE (See EVIDENTIARY STANDARDS)

PRESENTMENT
The notice taken or report made by a grand jury of an offense on the basis of the jury's knowledge and without a bill of indictment. (See also INDICTMENT)

PRE-TRIAL DIVERSION
Decision of the district attorney not to issue charges in a criminal case where those charges would be provable. The decision is usually made on the condition that the defendant agrees to participate in rehabilitative services. In child abuse cases, this usually involves cooperation with child protective services and/or voluntary treatment, such as Parents Anonymous.

PREVENTION OF CHILD ABUSE AND NEGLECT
Elimination of the individual and societal causes of child abuse and neglect.

Primary Prevention
Providing societal and community policies and programs which strengthen all family functioning so that child abuse and neglect is less likely to occur.

Secondary Prevention
Intervention in the early signs of child abuse and neglect for treatment of the presenting problem and to prevent further problems from developing.

Tertiary Prevention
Treatment after child abuse and neglect has been confirmed.

Primary, and to varying degrees secondary and tertiary, prevention requires:

1) Breaking the tendency in the generational cycle wherein the abused or neglected child is likely to become the abusive or neglectful parent.
2) Helping a parent cope with a child who has special problems or special meaning to a parent.
3) Helping families cope with long term and immediate situational or interpersonal stress.
4) Linking families to personal and community sources of help to break their social isolation.
5) Eliminating or alleviating violence in our society, particularly sanctioned violence such as corporal punishment in the schools.

A major problem in preventing child abuse and neglect is the stigma attached to the problem and to receiving services from a county protective service agency. Therefore, prevention programs must include community education and outreach. Another problem is that stress is pervasive in our society, and ways must be found both to reduce it and deal with it if child abuse and neglect is to be prevented. (See also EARLY INTERVENTION)

PRIMA FACIE
A latin term approximately meaning "at first sight," "on the first appearance," or "on the face of it." In law, this term is used in the context of a "prima facie case." That is, the presentation of evidence at a trial which has been sufficiently strong to prove the allegations unless contradicted and overcome by other evidence. In a child maltreatment case, the allegations of maltreatment will be considered as proven unless the parent presents rebutting evidence.

PRIVILEGED COMMUNICATIONS
Confidential communications which are protected by statutes and need not or cannot be disclosed in court over the objections of the holder of the privilege. Lawyers are almost always able to refuse to disclose what a client has told them in confidence. Priests are similarly covered. Doctors and psychotherapists have generally lesser privileges, and their testimony can be compelled in many cases involving child abuse or neglect. Some social workers are covered by such statutes, but the law and practice vary widely from state to state. (See also CONFIDENTIALITY)

PROBABLE CAUSE
A legal standard used in a number of contexts which indicates a reasonable ground for suspicion or belief in the existence of certain facts. Facts accepted as true after a reasonable inquiry which would induce a prudent and cautious person to believe them. Also-Please note that the definitions on page 28 of EVIDENTIARY STANDARDS are incorrect. A suggested alternative follows:

PROBATE COURT (See COURTS)

PROBATION
Allowing a convicted criminal defendant or a juvenile found to be delinquent to remain at liberty, under a suspended sentence of imprisonment, generally under the supervi-

sion of a probation officer and under certain conditions. Violation of a condition is grounds for revocation of the probation. In a case of child abuse or neglect, a parent or caretaker who is convicted of the offense may be required, as part of his/her probation, to make certain promises to undergo treatment and/or to improve the home situation. These promises are made as a condition of the probation in which the child is returned home and are enforced with the threat of revocation of parental rights.

PROGRAM COORDINATION

Interagency of intra-agency communication for policy, program, and resource development for an effective service delivery system in a given locality. Program coordination for child abuse and neglect is usually implemented through a community council or community task force or planning committee under the direction of a program coordinator. The functions of these groups are:
1) Comprehensive planning, including identifying gaps and duplication in service and funding policies.
2) Developing interagency referral policies.
3) Educating members to new and/or effective approaches to child abuse and neglect.
4) Problem sharing.
5) Facilitating resolution of interagency conflicts.
6) Providing a forum where differing professional and agency expertise can be pooled.
7) Generating and lobbying for needed legislation.

(See also COMMUNITY TEAM)

PROTECTIVE CUSTODY (See CUSTODY)

PROTOCOL

A set of rules or guidelines prescribing procedures and responsibilities. Originally used primarily in medical settings, establishment of protocols is an increasingly important goal of the child abuse and neglect community team.

PROXIMAL

Near; closer to any point of reference; opposed to distal.

PSYCHOLOGICAL ABUSE (See CHILD ABUSE AND NEGLECT)

PSYCHOLOGICAL NEGLECT (See CHILD ABUSE AND NEGLECT)

PSYCHOLOGICAL PARENT

Adult who, on a continuing day-to-day basis, fulfills a child's emotional needs for nurturance through interaction, companionship, and mutuality. May be the natural parent or another person who fulfills these functions.

PSYCHOLOGICAL TESTS

Instruments of various types used to measure emotional, intellectual, and personality characteristics. Psychological tests should always be administered and interpreted by qualified personnel. Such tests have been used to determine potential for abuse or neglect, effects of abuse or neglect, or psychological makeup of parent or children.

PSYCHOTIC PARENT

A parent who suffers a major mental disorder where the individual's ability to think, respond emotionally, remember, communicate, interpret reality, or behave appropriately is sufficiently impaired so as to interfere grossly with his/her capacity to meet the ordinary demands of life. The term "psychotic" is neither very precise nor definite. However, the parent who is periodically psychotic or psychotic for extended periods and who abuses his/her children has a poor prognosis; permanent removal of the children is often recommended in this situation. It is estimated that well under 10% of all abusive or neglectful parents are psychotic.

PUBLIC AWARENESS (See COMMUNITY AWARENESS)

PUBLIC DEFENDER

Person paid with public funds to plead the cause of an indigent defendant.

PUBLIC LAW 93-247 (See CHILD ABUSE PREVENTION AND TREATMENT ACT)

PUNISHMENT
Infliction of pain, loss, or suffering on a child because the child has disobeyed or otherwise antagonized a parent or caretaker. Abusive parents may inflict punishment without cause, or may inflict punishment, particularly corporal punishment, in the belief that it is the only way to discipline children. Many parents confuse the difference between discipline and punishment. These differences are delineated under DISCIPLINE. (See also CORPORAL PUNISHMENT)

PURCHASE OF SERVICE
Provision for diagnosis and/or treatment of child abuse and neglect by an agency other than the mandated agency using mandated agency funds. The mandated agency subcontracts with the provider agency for specific services with specific clients, but the mandated agency retains statutory responsibility for the case. (See also CASE MANAGEMENT)

PURPURA (See INTRADERMAL HEMORRHAGE)

RADIOLUCENT
Permitting the passage of X-rays without leaving a shadow on the film. Soft tissues are radiolucent; bones are not.

RAREFACTION
Loss of density. On an X-ray photograph, an area of bone which appears lighter than normal is in a state of rarefaction, indicating a loss of calcium.

RECEIVING HOME
A family or group home for temporary placement of a child pending more permanent plans such as return to his/her own home, foster care, or adoption.

RECIDIVISM
Recurrence of child abuse and neglect. This happens relatively frequently because child protective service agencies heretofore have been mandated and staffed only to investigate and provide crisis intervention and not to provide treatment. Most cases where child abuse or neglect results in a child's death have been previously known to a child protection agency.

REFEREE (See HEARING OFFICER)

REGIONAL RESOURCE CENTER
With respect to child abuse and neglect, a regional resource center was funded as a demonstration project in each of the ten HEW regions under the 1974 Child Abuse Prevention and Treatment Act. These resource centers vary in program emphasis, but they all function to some degree as extensions of the National Center on Child Abuse and Neglect in Washington to help NCCAN fulfill the aims of the Child Abuse Prevention and Treatment Act (see NATIONAL CENTER ON CHILD ABUSE AND NEGLECT and CHILD ABUSE PREVENTION AND TREATMENT ACT). Besides regional centers, there are also state resource centers in Arizona, Maryland, New York, and North Carolina; and two national resource centers, operated by the Education Commission of the States and the National Urban League. The regional resource centers are:

Region I (Connecticut, Maine, Massachusetts, New Hampshire, Rhode Island, Vermont)
Judge Baker Guidance Center
295 Longwood Ave.
Boston, Massachusetts 02115
Region II (New Jersey, Puerto Rico, Virgin Islands)
College of Human Ecology Cornell University
MVR Hall
Ithaca, New York 14853
Region III (Pennsylvania, Virginia, Delaware, West Virginia, District of Columbia)
Institute for Urban Affairs and Research
Howard University

2900 Van Ness St., N.W.
Washington, D.C. 20008
Region IV (Alabama, Florida, Georgia, Kentucky, Mississippi, South Carolina, Tennessee)
Regional Institute of Social Welfare Research
P.O. Box 152
Heritage Building
468 N. Milledge Ave.
Athens, Georgia 30601
Region V (Illinois, Indiana, Michigan, Minnesota, Ohio, Wisconsin)
Midwest Parent-Child Welfare Resource Center
Center for Advanced Studies in Human Services
School of Social Welfare
University of Wisconsin-Milwaukee
Milwaukee, Wisconsin 53201
Region VI (Arkansas, Louisiana, New Mexico, Oklahoma, Texas)
Center for Social Work Research
School of Social Work
University of Texas at Austin
Austin, Texas 78712
Region VII (Iowa, Kansas, Missouri, Nebraska)
Institute of Child Behavior and Development
University of Iowa
Oakdale, Iowa 53219
Region VIII (Colorado, Montana, North Dakota, South Dakota, Utah, Wyoming)
National Center for the Prevention and Treatment of Child Abuse and Neglect
University of Colorado Medical Center
1205 Oneida St.
Denver, Colorado 80220
Region IX (California, Hawaii, Nevada, Guam, Trust Territories of the Pacific, American Samoa)
Department of Special Education
California State University
5151 State University Dr.
Los Angeles, California 90033
Region X (Alaska, Idaho, Oregon, Washington)
Northwest Federation for Human Services
157 Yesler Way, #208
Seattle, Washington 98104

REGISTRY (See CENTRAL REGISTER and NATIONAL REGISTER)

REHEARING
After a juvenile court referee or commissioner has heard a case and made an order, some states permit a dissatisfied party to request another hearing before the supervising judge of juvenile court. This second hearing is called a rehearing. If the original hearing was not recorded by a court reporter, the rehearing may have to be granted. If a transcript exists, the judge may read it and either grant or deny the rehearing.

REPARENTING
Usually describes a nurturing process whereby parents who have not received adequate nurturance during their own childhoods are provided with emotional warmth and security through a surrogate parent such as a parent aide. Abusive and neglectful parents are thus given an opportunity to identify with more positive role models.

REPORTING LAWS
State laws which require specified categories of persons, such as professionals involved with children, and allow other persons, to notify public authorities of cases of suspected child abuse and, sometimes, neglect. All 50 states now have reporting statutes, but they differ widely with respect to types of instances which must be reported, persons who must report, time limits for reporting, manner of reporting (written, oral, or both), agencies to which reports must be made, and the degree of immunity conferred upon reporters.

RES IPSA LOQUITOR
Latin expression meaning "the thing speaks for itself." It is a doctrine of law which, when applied to criminal law, means that evidence can be admitted which is acceptable despite the fact that no one actually saw what occurred, only the results. An example in

criminal law would be admitting into evidence in a child abuse case the medical reports of the injured child victim which reflect multiple broken bones and the doctor's opinion that said injuries could not have been caused by an accident. The court using the *res ipsa loquitor* doctrine can convict the person having had exclusive custody of the child without any direct testimony as to how, when, where, or why the injuries were inflicted.

RETINA
Inside lining of the eye. Injury to the head can cause bleeding or detachment of the retina, possible causing blindness.

RICKETS
Condition caused by a deficiency of vitamin D, which disturbs the normal development of bones.

ROLE REVERSAL
The process whereby a parent or caretaker seeks nurturance and/or protection from a child rather than providing this for the child, who frequently complies with this reversal. Usually this process develops as a result of unfulfilled needs of the parent or caretaker.

SACRAL AREA
Lower part of the back.

SCAN TEAM
Suspected Child Abuse and Neglect team which has as its objective the assessment of a child and his/her family to determine if abuse and/or neglect has occurred and what treatment is indicated. The team usually includes a pediatrician, a social worker, and a psychiatrist or psychologist, but other professionals are often involved as well. A SCAN team or unit is generally located in a hospital or outpatient facility. (See also MULTIDISCIPLINARY TEAM and DENVER MODEL)

SCAPEGOATING
Casting blame for a problem on one who is innocent or only partially responsible; for example, a parent or caretaker abusing or neglecting a child as punishment for family problems unrelated to the child.

SCURVY
Condition caused by a deficiency of vitamin C (ascorbic acid) and characterized by weakness, anemia, spongy gums, and other symptoms.

SEALING
In juvenile court or criminal court practice, the closing of records to inspection by all but the defendant or minor involved. Sealing is provided by statute in some states and may be done after proof is made that the defendant or minor has behaved lawfully for a specified period of years. Note that juvenile court records are never public, as are the records of most other courts; access to juvenile court records is theoretically very restricted, even before sealing. (See also EXPUNGEMENT)

SEIZURES
Uncontrollable muscular contractions, usually alternating with muscular relaxation and generally accompanied by unconsciousness. Seizures, which vary in intensity and length of occurrence, are the result of some brain irritation which has been caused by disease, inherited condition, fever, tumor, vitamin deficiency, or injury to the head.

SELF-HELP GROUP
Groups of persons with similar, often stigmatized, problems who share concerns and experiences in an effort to provide mutual help to one another. Usually these groups are self-directed. (See also PARENTS ANONYMOUS)

SELF-INCRIMINATION
The giving of a statement, in court or during an investigation, which subjects the person giving the statement to criminal liability. (See also DUE PROCESS, FIFTH AMENDMENT, IMMUNITY, and MIRANDA RULE)

SENTENCING
The last stage of criminal prosecution in which a convicted defendant is ordered imprisoned, fined, or granted probation. This is equivalent in a criminal case, to the disposition in a juvenile court case.

SEQUELAE
After-effects; usually medical events following an injury or disease. In child abuse and neglect, sequelae is used to refer to psychological consequences of abusive acts and also the perpetuation of maltreatment behavior across generations, as well as specific aftereffects such as brain damage, speech impairment, and impaired physical and/or psychological growth.

SERVICES
(See EARLY INTERVENTION, EMERGENCY SERVICES, PREVENTION OF CHILD ABUSE AND NEGLECT, SUPPORTIVE SERVICES, TREATMENT OF CHILD ABUSE AND NEGLECT)

SEXUAL ABUSE
In order to encompass all forms of child sexual abuse and exploitation within its mandate, the National Center on Child Abuse and Neglect has adopted the following tentative definition of child sexual abuse: contacts or interactions between a child and an adult when the child is being used for the sexual stimulation of the perpetrator or another person. Sexual abuse may also be committed by a person under the age of 18 when that person is either significantly older than the victim or when the perpetrator is in a position of power or control over another child. (See also CHILD ABUSE AND NEGLECT)

SEXUAL ASSAULT
Unlawful actions of a sexual nature committed against a person forcibly and against his/her own will. Various degrees of sexual assault are established by state law and are distinguished by the sex of the perpetrator and/or victim, the amount of force used, the amount and type of sexual contact, etc. Sexual abuse is one form of sexual assault wherein the perpetrator is known by the victim and is usually a member of the family. (See also CHILD ABUSE AND NEGLECT)

SEXUAL EXPLOITATION
A term usually used in reference to sexual abuse of children for commercial purposes; such as child prostitution, sexual exhibition, or the production of pornographic materials. (See also CHILD PORNOGRAPHY, CHILD PROSTITUTION)

SEXUAL MISUSE
Alternative term for sexual abuse, but particularly reflects the point of view that sexual encounters with children, if properly handled, need not be as harmful as is usually assumed. Its implication is that children are not necessarily harmed by so-called sexually abusive acts themselves, but rather the abuse results from damage generated by negative social and cultural reactions to such acts. (See also CHILD MISUSE AND NEGLECT, INCEST, SEXUAL ABUSE)

SEXUALLY TRANSMISSIBLE DISEASE (STD) (See VENEREAL DISEASE)

SIMPLE FRACTURE (See FRACTURE)

SITUATIONAL CHILD ABUSE AND NEGLECT
Refers to cases of child abuse and particularly child neglect where the major causative factors cannot be readily eliminated because they relate to problems over which the parents have little control. (See also APATHY-FUTILITY SYNDROME)

SKELETAL SURVEY
A series of X-rays that studies all bones of the body. Such a survey should be done in all cases of suspected abuse to locate any old, as well as new, fractures which may exist.

SOCIAL ASSESSMENT (See ASSESSMENT)

SOCIAL HISTORY
1) Information compiled by a social worker about factors affecting a family's past and present level of functioning for use in diagnosing child abuse and neglect and developing a treatment plan.
2) Document prepared by a probation officer or social worker for the juvenile or family court hearing officer's consideration at the time of disposition of a case. This report addresses the minor's history and environment. Social histories often contain material which would clearly be inadmissible in most judicial proceedings, either because of hearsay or lack of verification or reliability. The informal use of such reports has often been attacked as in violation of due process rights of minors and parents.

SOCIAL REPORT (See SOCIAL HISTORY)

SOCIAL ISOLATION
The limited interaction and contact of many abusive and/or neglectful parents with relatives, neighbors, friends, or community resources. Social isolation can perpetuate a basic lack of trust which hinders both identification and treatment of child abuse and neglect.

SOCIAL SECURITY ACT
Established in 1935 as a national social insurance program, this federal legislation includes several sections particularly applicable to child and family welfare:

Title IV-Parts A, B, C, D (Aid to Families with Dependent Children, Child Welfare Services, Work Incentive Program, Child Support and Establishment of Paternity)
Part A, now included under Title XX as services for children, was designed to encourage families to care for dependent children in their own or relatives' homes by providing services to families below a specified income level. As a condition of receiving federal funding for this program, states must provide family planning services. Part B authorizes support to states for child welfare services developed in coordination with the AFDC program to supplement or substitute for parental care and supervision. These services include day care, foster care, and other preventive or protective programs promoting child and family welfare. Part C offers job training and placement for AFDC parents in an effort to assist them in becoming self-supporting. Part D enforces the support obligations owed by absent parents to their children by locating absent parents, establishing paternity, and obtaining child support.

Title V-Maternal and Child Health and Applied Children's Services
Provides a broad range of health care services for mothers and children from low-income families in order to reduce maternal and infant mortality and to prevent illness.

Title XIX-Grants to States for Medical Assistance Programs (Medicaid or Title 19)
Designed to help families with dependent children and other low-income persons by providing financial assistance for necessary medical services. This act is additionally designed to provide rehabilitation and other psychotherapy services to help families and individuals retain or regain independence and self-sufficiency.

Title XX-Grants to States for Services
Provides grants to states for developing programs and services designed to achieve the following goals for families and/or children: economic self-support; self-sufficiency; prevention of abuse and neglect; preserving; rehabilitating, reuniting families; referring for institutional care when other services are not appropriate.

Mandated child protective service agency programs are primarily funded through Title IV-B and Title XX of the Social Security Act.

SOCIETAL CHILD ABUSE AND NEGLECT
Failure of society to provide social policies and/or funding to support the well-being of all families and children or to provide sufficient resources to prevent and treat child

abuse and neglect, particularly for minority populations such as migrant workers and Native Americans.

SPECIAL CHILD
A child who is abused or neglected or at risk of abuse or neglect because he/she has a special problem with which the parent(s) have difficulty coping or because the child has some psychologically negative meaning for the parent. Also referred to as "target child." If this child is abused, the cause may be referred to as "victim" precipitated abuse."

SPIRAL FRACTURE (See FRACTURE)

SPOUSE ABUSE
Non-accidental physical or psychological injury inflicted on either husband or wife by his/her marital partner. Some experts conjecture that husbands as well as wives are frequently abused, particularly psychologically, but the subject of husband abuse has not gained public or professional recognition to the extent that battered wives has. Domestic violence is the term used when referring to abuse between adult mates who may not be married. (See also BATTERED WOMEN)

STAFF BURNOUT
Apathy and frustration felt by protective service workers who are overworked, undertrained, and lacking agency or supervisory support. This is a common problem, and workers who do not leave protective services (see STAFF FLIGHT) or who do not have supervisory support often lose sensitivity to client needs. (Also referred to as Worker Burnout)

STAFF FLIGHT
Continous change of child protective services staff due to staff burnout (see STAFF BURNOUT). This creates the need to provide frequent training for new workers. Informed estimates place the overall national turnover rate of protective service workers at 85% annually.

STAFF SATISFACTION
Structuring a supportive and encouraging environment for protective service workers with regular periods when no new cases are assigned, thereby decreasing staff burnout and staff flight. Supervisors and administrators need to develop programs including the following elements: manageable caseloads, in-service training, participation in and responsibility for agency decision-making.

STANDARD OF PROOF (See EVIDENTIARY STANDARDS)

STANDARDS
Guides developed to ensure comprehensiveness and adequacy of programs or services. Issued by relevant agencies, such as the National Center on Child Abuse and Neglect for state and local level programs and the Child Welfare League of America for member agencies, standards have various levels of authority.

STATE AUTHORITY
State authority refers to the state department of social services (state department) and a state child protection coordinating committee (state committee). As designated in state law, these structures are to accept responsibility for child abuse and neglect prevention, identification, and treatment efforts. The standards on state authority, as specified in the National Center on Child Abuse and Neglect *Revision to Federal Standards on the Prevention and Treatment of Child Abuse and Neglect (Draft),* include:
Administration and Organization
1. The state department should establish child abuse and neglect policies that are consistent with the state law and conducive to state-wide delivery of uniform and coordinated services.
2. The state department should establish a distinct child protection division (state division) to facilitate the implementation of departmental policies.
3. The state department should designate child protective services units

(local units) within each regional and/or local social services agency.

4   The state committee, as required by state law, should be representative of those persons and agencies concerned with child abuse and neglect prevention, identification, and treatment.

Primary Prevention

5   The state division and the state committee should work together towards primary prevention of child abuse and neglect through formalized needs assessment and planning processes.

Secondary and Tertiary Prevention

6   The state division and the state committee should jointly develop a comprehensive and coordinated plan for delivery of services to high-risk children and families.

7   The state division should ensure that those persons who have reason to suspect child abuse or neglect can make a report at any time, twenty-four hours a day, seven days a week.

8   The state division should transmit reports to appropriate authority for assessment of the degree of risk to the child.

9   The state division should operate a central registry that facilitates state and local planning.

10   The state division's operation of the central registry should ensure that children and families' rights to prompt and effective services are protected.

Resource Enhancement

11   The state division should develop and provide public and professional education.

12   The state division should ensure that training is provided to all divisional, regional, and local staff.

13   The state division should conduct and/or sponsor research, demonstration, and evaluation projects.

(See also LOCAL AUTHORITY)

STATUS OFFENSE

An act which is considered criminal only because it is committed by a person of a particular status, such as a minor. If an adult did the same thing, it would not be an offense. For example, a minor staying out after curfew.

STIPULATION

A statement, either oral or written, between lawyers on both sides of a particular court case which establishes certain facts about the case that are agreed upon by both sides. The facts delineated usually involve such issues as the addresses of the persons involved in the case, their relationships to one another, etc.

STRESS FACTORS

Environmental and/or psychological pressures over a prolonged period which are associated with child abuse and neglect or which, without being prolonged, may be the precipitant event. While a certain amount of stress can be useful in motivating people to change, it is generally agreed that there is an overload of stress in our present society, perhaps because people feel decreasingly in control of the forces affecting their lives. Prevention of child abuse and neglect requires both reducing stress in society and helping people cope with it. Environmental stress which may influence child abuse and neglect includes, but is not limited to, unemployment, poverty, poor and overcrowded housing, competition for success, and "keeping up with the Joneses." Psychological stress besides that caused by environmental factors which may influence child abuse and neglect could include such problems as marital discord, in-law problems, unwanted pregnancy, role confusion resulting from the Women's Movement, and unresolved psychodynamic conflicts from childhood.

SUBDURAL HEMATOMA

A common symptom of abused children, consisting of a collection of blood beneath the outermost membrane covering the brain and spinal cord. The hematoma may be caused by a blow to the head or from shaking a baby or small child. (See also WHIP-

LASH-SHAKEN INFANT SYNDROME)

SUBPOENA
A document issued by a court clerk, usually delivered by a process server or police officer to the person subpoenaed, requiring that person to appear at a certain court at a certain day and time to give testimony in a specified case. Failure to obey a subpoena is punishable as contempt of court.

SUBPOENA DUCES TECUM
A subpoena requiring the person subpoenaed to bring specified records to court.

SUDDEN INFANT DEATH SYNDROME (SIDS)
A condition which can be confused with child abuse, SIDS affects infants from two weeks to two years old, but usually occurs in a child less than six months of age. In SIDS, a child who has been healthy except for a minor respiratory infection is found dead, often with bloody frothy material in his/her mouth. The cause of SIDS is not fully understood. The confusion with child abuse results from the bloody sputum and occasional facial bruises that accompany the syndrome. However, SIDS parents rarely display the guarded or defensive behavior that many abusive parents do.

SUMMONS
A document issued by a court clerk, usually delivered by a process server or police officer to the person summoned, notifying that person of the filing of a lawsuit against him/her and notifying that person of the deadline for answering the suit. A summons does not require the attendance at court of any person.

SUPERVISION
1) Provision of age-appropriate protection and guidance for a child by a parent or caretaker. This is a parental responsibility, but in some cases of child abuse and neglect or for other reasons, the state may have to assume responsibility for supervision. (See also CHILD IN NEED OF SUPERVISION)
2) Process in social work practice whereby workers review cases with supervisors to assure case progress, to sharpen the workers' knowledge and skill, and to assure maintenance of agency policies and procedures. Unlike many practitioners in law and medicine, social workers do not generally practice independently or make totally independent judgments. In general, social work supervisors hold Master's degrees, but in some local public agencies these supervisors may be just out of graduate school and have little experience. Since good supervision is a critical factor in reducing the problem of staff burnout and staff flight, it is important for child protective service agencies to provide training and continuing education opportunities for supervisors.

SUPPORTIVE SERVICES
Supportive services are a wide range of human services which provide assistance to families or individuals so that they are more nearly able to fulfill their potential for positive growth and behavior. The concept implies that individuals have basic strengths which need to be recognized, encouraged, and aided. Thus, a wide range of financial, educational, vocational, child care, counseling, recreational, and other services might be seen as supportive if they do indeed emphasize the strengths of people and de-emphasize their occasional needs for help in overcoming destructive and debilitating factors which may affect their lives.

SURROGATE PARENT
A person other than a biological parent who, living within or outside the target home, provides nurturance. This person may be self-selected or assigned to fulfill parental functions. A surrogate parent may nurture children or abusive or neglectful parents who were themselves abused as children and therefore are in need of a nurturing parental model. (See also PARENT AIDE)

SUSPECTED CHILD ABUSE AND NEGLECT
Reason to believe that child abuse or neglect has or is occurring in a given family. Anyone can in good faith report this to the local mandated agency, which will investigate and protect the child as necessary. However, all states have statutes which provide that members of certain professions must report and that failure to do so is punishable by fine or imprisonment. For specific criteria for suspecting child abuse or neglect, see INDICATORS OF CHILD ABUSE AND NEGLECT and FAMILIES-AT-RISK.

SUTURE
1) A type of immovable joint in which the connecting surfaces of the bones are closely united, as in the skull.
2) The stitches made by a physician that close a wound.

SYPHILIS (See VENEREAL DISEASE)

TARGET CHILD (See SPECIAL CHILD)

TEMPORAL
Referring to the side of the head.

TEMPORARY CUSTODY (See CUSTODY)

TEMPORARY PLACEMENT
Voluntary or involuntary short term removal of a child from his/her own home, primarily when a child's safety or well-being is threatened or endangered, or when a family crisis can be averted by such action. Temporary placement may be in a relative's home, receiving home or shelter, foster home, or institution. Temporary placement should be considered only if service to the child and family within the home, such as use of a homemaker or day care, is determined to be insufficient to protect or provide for the child or if it is unavailable. If the home situation does not improve while the child is in temporary placement, long term placement may be warranted. However, authorities agree that too many temporary placements unnecessarily become permanent placements. (See also CUSTODY)

TERMINATION OF PARENTAL RIGHTS (TPR)
A legal proceeding freeing a child from his/her parents' claims so that the child can be adopted by others without the parents' written consent. The legal bases for termination differ from state to state, but most statutes include abandonment as a ground for TPR. (See also ABANDONMENT)

TESTIMONY
A declaration or statement made to establish a fact, especially one made under oath in court.

THREATENED HARM
Substantial risk of harm to a child, including physical or mental injury, sexual assault, neglect of physical and/or educational needs, inadequate supervision, or abandonment.

TITLE IV (See SOCIAL SECURITY ACT)

TITLE V (See SOCIAL SECURITY ACT)

TITLE XIX (TITLE 19, MEDICAID) (See SOCIAL SECURITY ACT)

TITLE XX (See SOCIAL SECURITY ACT)

TORUS FRACTURE (See FRACTURE)

TRABECULA
A general term for a supporting or anchoring strand of tissue.

TRAUMA
An internal or external injury or wound brought about by an outside force. Usually trauma means injury by violence, but it may also apply to the wound caused by any surgical procedure. Trauma may be caused accidentally or, as in a ease of physical abuse, non-acciden-tally. Trauma is also a term applied to psychological discomfort or symptoms resulting from an emotional shock or painful experience.

TRAUMA X
Designation used by some hospitals for a child abuse and neglect program.

TREATMENT FOSTER CARE
Foster care for children with diagnosed emotional and/or behavioral problems in which foster parents with special training and experience become part of a treatment team working with a particular child. Treatment foster care may be indicated for abused or severely neglected children.

TREATMENT OF CHILD ABUSE AND NEGLECT
1) Helping parents or caretakers stop child abuse and neglect and assisting them and their children to function adequately as a family unit. 2) Providing temporary placement and services as necessary for abused or neglected children until their parents can assume their parental responsibilities without threat to the children's welfare. 3) Terminating parental rights and placing the children in an adoptive home if the parents abandon the children or absolutely cannot be helped. Experts believe that 80% to 85% of abusive and neglectful parents can be helped to function without threat to their children's welfare and, more often than not, without temporary placement of the children if sufficient supportive services are available.

Treatment for child abuse and neglect should include treatment for the abused and neglected children as well as for the parents.

Treatment for child abuse and neglect includes both crisis intervention and long term treatment. The mandated agency may provide services directly or by purchase of service from other agencies. Since a multiplicity of services is often necessary, a case management approach to treatment is usually most effective (see CASE MANAGEMENT). Because mandated agencies necessarily focus on investigation of suspected cases and crisis intervention, long term treatment is best assured through use of a community team (see COMMUNITY TEAM).

Both crisis intervention and long term treatment will usually require a mix of supportive and therapeutic services. Supportive services could include homemakers, day care, foster grandparents, parent education, health care, family planning, recreational activities, housing assistance, transportation, legal services, employment training and placement, financial counseling and assistance. Therapeutic services could include psychotherapy, casework, lay therapy from parent aides, group therapy, family or couple therapy, and self-help such as Parents Anonymous.

TURGOR
Condition of being swollen and congested. This can refer to normal or other fullness.

TWENTY-FOUR HOUR EMERGENCY SERVICES
Local services available at all times to receive reports and make immediate investigations of suspected cases of child abuse and severe neglect and to perform crisis intervention if necessary. The mode of providing twenty-four hour emergency services varies in different localities. However, often mandated agency protective service workers are on call for specific evening and weekend assignments. Often the after-hours number rings the police or sheriffs department which then contacts the assigned worker. (See also COMPREHENSIVE EMERGENCY SERVICES)

UNFOUNDED REPORT
Any report of suspected child abuse or neglect made to the mandated agency for which it is determined that there is no probable cause to believe that abuse or neglect has occurred. Mandated agencies may or may not remove unfounded reports from their records after a period of time. (See also EXPUNGEMENT)

VASCULAR
Of the blood vessels.

VENEREAL DISEASE
Any disease transmitted by sexual contact. The two most common forms of venereal disease are gonorrhea and syphilis. Presence of a venereal disease in a child may indicate that the mother was infected with the disease during the pregnancy, or it may be evidence of sexual abuse.

VERBAL ABUSE (See CHILD ABUSE AND NEGLECT)

VERIFICATION OF CHILD ABUSE AND NEGLECT
Substantiation of child abuse or neglect following investigation of suspected cases by mandated agency workers and/or assessment by a diagnostic team. Also referred to as a founded report.

VICTIM-PRECIPITATED ABUSE (See SPECIAL CHILD)

VISITING FRIEND (See PARENT AIDE)

VITAL SIGNS
Signs manifesting life, such as respiratory rate, heartbeat, pulse, blood pressure, and eye responses.

VOIR DIRE
1. Procedure during which lawyers question prospective jurors to determine their biases, if any.
2. Procedure in which lawyers question expert witnesses regarding their qualifications before the experts are permitted to give opinion testimony.

VOLUNTARY PLACEMENT
Act of a parent in which custody of his/her child is relinquished without a formal court proceeding. Sometimes called voluntary relinquishment.

VOLUNTEER ROLES
1) Extension and enrichment of direct services to families by unpaid, screened, trained, and supervised persons who generally lack professional training. Common roles are parent aides, child care workers, outreach workers, or staff for helplines. 2) Development and advocacy of child abuse and neglect programs by unpaid persons through participation on community councils, agency boards, or community committees. Scarce resources in relation to the magnitude of the problem of child abuse and neglect demands that volunteers be used increasingly.

WANTON
Extremely reckless or malicious. Often used in court proceedings in conjunction with "willful" to establish certain kinds of unlawful behavior only vaguely distinguished from careless but lawful conduct.

WARRANT
Document issued by a judge, authorizing the arrest or detention of a person or the search of a place and seizure of specified items in that place. Although a judge need not hold a hearing before issuing a warrant and although the party to be arrested or whose property will be seized need not be notified, the judge must still be given "reasonable cause to believe" that a crime has occurred and that the warrant is necessary in the apprehension and conviction of the criminal.

WHIPLASH-SHAKEN INFANT SYNDROME
Injury to an infant or child that results from that child having been shaken, usually as a misguided means of discipline. The most common symptoms, which can be inflicted by seemingly harmless shakings, are bleeding and/or detached retinas and other bleeding inside the head. Repeated instances of shaking and resultant injuries may eventually cause mental and developmental disabilities. (See also SUBDURAL HEMATOMA)

WILLFUL
Done with understanding of the act and the intention that the act and its natural consequences should occur. Some conduct

becomes unlawful or negligent only when it is done willfully.

WITNESS
1. A person who has seen or heard something.
2. A person who is called upon to testify in a court hearing.

WORKER BURNOUT (See Staff Burnout)

WORK-UP
Study of a patient, often in a hospital, in order to provide information for diagnosis. A full work-up includes past medical and family histories, present condition and symptoms, laboratory, and, possibly, X-ray studies.

WORLD OF ABNORMAL REARING (WAR)
A generational cycle of development in which abused or neglected children tend to grow up to be abusive or neglectful parents unless intervention occurs to break the cycle. The diagram which follows outlines the WAR cycle. (Heifer)

X-RAYS
Photographs made by means of X-rays. X-rays are one of the most important tools available to physicians in the diagnosis of physical child abuse or battering. With X-rays, or radiologic examinations, physicians can observe not only the current bone injuries of a child, but also any past injuries that may exist in various stages of healing. This historical information contributes significantly to the assessment of a suspected case of child abuse. Radiologic examination is also essential to distinguish organic diseases that may cause bone breakage from physical child abuse.

Acronyms

AAP	American Academy of Pediatrics	**PET**	Parent Effectiveness Training
ACSW	Academy of Certified Social Workers	**PINS**	Person in Need of Supervision
		CPS	Child Protective Services
ACYF	Administration for Children, Youth and Families (formerly Office of Child Development), U.S. Department of Health, Education and Welfare	**CWLA**	Child Welfare League of America
		DART	Detection, Admission, Reporting, and Treatment (multidisciplinary team)
		DD	Developmental Disability
ADC	Aid to Dependent Children (Title IV-A of the Social Security Act) (also referred to as AFDC)	**DHEW**	U.S. Department of Health, Education and Welfare (also referred to as HEW)
AF	Alleged Father	**DPW**	Department of Public Welfare
AFDC	Aid to Families with Dependent Children (Title IV-A of the Social Security Act) (also referred to as ADC)	**DSS**	Department of Social Services
		EPSDT	Early and Periodic Screening, Diagnosis, and Treatment
		ER	Emergency Room
AHA	American Humane Association	**FTT**	Failure to Thrive
AMA	Against Medical Advice; American Medical Association	**GAL**	*Guardian ad l item*
		HEW	U.S. Department of Health, Education and Welfare (also referred to as DHEW)
APA	American Psychiatric Association; American Psychological Association		
		IP	Identified Patient
APWA	American Public Welfare Association	**LD**	Learning Disability
		MINS	Minor in Need of Supervision
CALM	Child Abuse Listening Mediation	**NASW**	National Association of Social Workers
CAN	Child Abuse and Neglect		
CAP	Community Action Program	**NCCA**	National Center for Child Advocacy
CDAHA	Children's Division of the American Humane Association		
		NCCAN	National Center on Child Abuse and Neglect
CDF	Children's Defense Fund		
CES	Comprehensive Emergency Services	**NIH**	National Institutes of Health
		NIMH	National Institute of Mental Health
CHIPS	Child in Need of Protection and Supervision	**OCD**	Office of Child Development (now Adminstration for Children, Youth and Families). U.S. Department of Health, Education and Welfare
CLL	Childhood Level of Living Scale		
CNS	Central Nervous System		
	Office of Human Development Services), U.S. Department of Health, Education and Welfare	**OHD**	Office of Human Development (now
OHDS	Office of Human Development Services (formerly Office of Human Development), U.S. Department of Health, Education and Welfare	**PL 93-247**	Child Abuse Prevention and Treatment Act
		SCAN	Suspected Child Abuse and Neglect
PA	Parents Anonymous		

SIDS	Sudden Infant Death Syndrome	**VD**	Venereal Disease
STD	Sexually Transmissible Disease	**WAR**	World of Abnormal Rearing
TPR	Termination of Parental Rights	**WIN**	Work Incentive Program
UM	Unmarried Mother		